CULTURE*Shift*

A LEADER'S GUIDE TO MANAGING CHANGE IN HEALTH CARE

JOAN E. LOWERY
EDITOR

American Hospital Publishing, Inc.
An American Hospital Association company
Chicago

Cover designed by Jeanne Calabrese

Library of Congress Cataloging-in-Publication Data

CultureShift : a leader's guide to managing change in health care / Joan E. Lowery, editor.
     p.   cm.
    Includes bibliographical references and index.
    1. Health services administration. 2. Organizational change. I. Lowery, Joan E.
    [DNLM: 1. Health Services—organization and administration—United States. 2.
Health Personnel—organization and administration—United States. 3.
Organizational Culture. 4. Social Change. 5. Health Care Reform—United States.
WA 540 AA1 C96   1997]
RA971.C775 1997
362.1'068—dc21
DNLM/DLC
for Library of Congress
                                        97-25187
ISBN: 1-55648-208-6   Item Number: 088125

Dedication

This book is dedicated to two wonderful and loving people—my mother and father.

To the memory of my father, Harry Lefkowitz, who, in the last years of his life, courageously and lovingly experienced firsthand the dramatic shifts taking place in how health care is practiced in this country. His journey reflected the best and the worst of what the current system has to offer. It most certainly inspired me with the commitment to orchestrate this book.

And to my mother, Roslyn Lefkowitz, whose courage, loyalty, and love of life have always inspired me to "go for it!"

Contents

CHAPTER 13

About the Editor

Joan E. Lowery, M.Ed., is owner and president of Lowery Communications, a communications consulting firm with offices in Sarasota, Florida and Alameda, California. A trainer, speaker, and writer, Ms. Lowery specializes in several areas of communications skills. She facilitates seminars on culture shift issues, high-impact communications skills, media training, management coaching and team building, and individual coaching for managers in transition. She consults extensively in the health care field and serves on the faculty of the American College of Physician Executives. Ms. Lowery's background as a broadcast journalist includes reporting for the Associated Press Radio Network, CNN, and numerous local radio and television news programs. As a print journalist, she has published stories nationally and internationally.

Contributors

Cliff Bolster, Ph.D., is a senior consultant with Innovation Associates. His professional experience spans 30 years and covers all human resources disciplines. In 15 years of consulting and training, Dr. Bolster has worked with client firms of all sizes and in many industries, including pharmaceuticals, consumer products, petrochemicals, high-technology manufacturing, and consulting services. He has designed and led training programs in personal and organizational change, interpersonal skills, negotiations, and analytical skills. Bolster recently completed his Ph.D. at Case Western Reserve University.

Gita B. Budd is regional vice president for strategic planning and marketing of the St. Louis Health Care Network. She was formerly the managing director of the Borgess Institute for Health Care Leadership in southwestern Michigan. Ms. Budd's primary focus is strategic, business, and organizational planning. Ms. Budd is a frequent speaker for local, regional, and national health care organizations on topics related to planning, finance, and operations. She holds a master's degree in hospital and health services management, accounting, and organizational behavior from the J. L. Kellogg Graduate School of Management, Northwestern University. In 1995, Ms. Budd was selected as an Emerging Leader in Healthcare by the Healthcare Forum and Korn/Ferry International.

Jimmy Carter is a consultant and internationally known speaker on the subject of leading organizations that learn. As a senior manager of Innovation Associates, he has extensive background in implementing the concepts of "The Fifth Discipline" to build organizations that sustain inspired performance. With nearly a decade in the business, he has worked with clients in communications, manufacturing, and financial services, as well as health care, helping them achieve ongoing success by reducing product development time, enhancing team performance, and executing change strategies. Carter holds engineering and business degrees from Lehigh University.

Kenneth C. Cummings, M.D., F.A.C.P.E., is executive vice president for physician integration and services at Carondelet Health, an integrated delivery network in Kansas City, Missouri. A physician for 29 years, Dr. Cummings is a frequent national speaker and author of numerous technical and management articles and book chapters. He has held positions in several academic medical centers and a health system as clinical department chairman, researcher, medical director, and vice president for medical affairs. He currently chairs the editorial advisory board for the journal *Physician Executive*, is a director of the American College of Physician Executives, and is a member of the Healthcare Roundtable for Physician Executives.

C. Marlena Fiol, Ph.D., is a principal with the Implementation Institute, a Denver-based consulting and training firm. She is also a management professor at the University of Colorado at Denver. As a transition specialist with over 15 years' experience in strategic management and organization design, Dr. Fiol has worked with hospital administrators, physician leaders, and health care organizations to design the organizational structures and reporting relations needed to effectively implement integrated delivery systems and other quality initiatives. Dr. Fiol has authored numerous research articles, book chapters, and papers on topics related to strategic thinking, organizational learning, and change management, and is a frequent speaker at international, national, and regional meetings. She holds an M.B.A. in international business and a Ph.D. in strategic management from the University of Illinois.

Richard H. Gregg is director of the health care practice of Innovation Associates and a member of the leadership board of Arthur D. Little's Global Health Care Practice. He has been a management consultant to health care organizations for more than 21 years and has worked with trustees, executives, managers, and medical staff members of integrated health systems, hospitals, ambulatory care organizations, and physician group practices. Mr. Gregg specializes in strategy creation and organization development, especially designing and managing the process of change. He has given presentations at seminars sponsored by the American Hospital Association, VHA, the Institute for Healthcare Improvement, the New England Healthcare Assembly, and the Healthcare Financial Management Association. Mr. Gregg earned B.A. and M.A. degrees at Rutgers University, where he was a Graduate Fellow at the Eagleton Institute of Politics. He has an M.B.A. from New York University.

Michael B. Green is president and CEO of Capital Region Health Care and Concord Hospital, both located in Concord, New Hampshire. In his current position, Mr. Green has led his hospital to be one of the first to institute patient-focused work transformation, and has completed affiliations with several regional health care organizations, now subsidiaries of Capital Region Health Care. Prior to his current appointment, Mr. Green served as chief operation officer at Lawrence and Memorial Hospital in Connecticut and chief financial officer and interim president at Nashua Memorial Hospital in New Hampshire. He received a master's degree from the Sloan School of Management at the Massachusetts Institute of Technology.

Matthew J. Lambert III, M.D., M.B.A., F.A.C.S., is senior vice president for medical affairs at Catholic Health Partners in Chicago. Previously he served as medical director at Martha Jefferson Hospital in Charlottesville, Virginia, and was an associate professor of surgery at the University of Virginia Health Sciences Center, also located in Charlottesville. Dr. Lambert is currently a Pew Fellow in the doctoral program in health policy at the University of Michigan School of public health.

John C. Lewin, M.D., is currently executive vice president and CEO of the 35,000-member California Medical Association. As Director of Health for the state of Hawaii from 1986–1994, Dr. Lewin was a principal architect of many of Hawaii's recent public health accomplishments, and additionally served as CEO of Hawaii's public hospital system. Dr. Lewin, a family practice physician, has been a health care advisor to the White House, a clinical professor of international health at the University of Hawaii, and a recent recipient of the AHA's Justin Ford Kimball Award for advancing access to health care for the uninsured in the private sector.

Edward J. O'Connor, M.B.A., Ph.D., is a principal with the Implementation Institute, a Denver-based consulting and training firm specializing in helping organizations clarify strategic directions and remove the barriers to their successful accomplishment. In addition, he is a professor of management at the University of Colorado at Denver and a member of the faculty of the American College of Physician Executives. Formerly, he held several managerial positions with General Electric and served as President of WPRC, Inc., a financial services firm. He is the author of over 100 research articles, book chapters, papers, and technical documents, and has conducted research on such topics as the identification of success factors critical to the introduction of quality initiatives in hospitals. Dr. O'Connor recieved an M.B.A. from the Harvard Business

School and a Ph.D. in Industrial/Organizational Psychology from the University of Akron.

Marilyn Paul, Ph.D., is an adjunct consultant with Innovation Associates. Dr. Paul has more than 20 years of experience in strategic planning, organizational assessment and design, team building, and leadership development for health care, education, government, and business organizations. She also served as coordinator of the management development program for the Public Health System in the Gaza Strip. Her academic affiliations include the Institute for Health Professions at Massachusetts General Hospital, Hebrew University School of Public Health, and Yale School of Medicine.

Lawrence A. Pfaff, M.A., Ed.D., is owner and president of Lawrence A. Pfaff and Associates, a human resources consulting firm. Dr. Pfaff specializes in multi-rater assessment and is the author of *The Management-Leadership Practices Inventory* and *The Professional Communication Inventory*, both of which are used in health care settings. Dr. Pfaff has been a consultant to more than 200 organizations, and his research has been cited in *Inc.*, *Business Week*, *Working Woman*, *Incentive*, *Executive Female*, *Healthcare Forum*, *HR Magazine*, *Across the Board*, and the Associated Press Radio Network.

Patricia Chehy Pilette, Ed.D, C.N.S., is principal of EOD, Inc., a health care consulting firm based in Framingham, Massachusetts, which specializes in executive and organizational development. Dr. Pilette speaks and publishes frequently on such topics as management development, executive coaching, organizational adaptation to change, and leveraging team roles for success.

Scott W. Spreier is a national practice leader, based in Dallas, for the Hay Group's Healthcare Consulting Practice. A writer and consultant, Mr. Sprier helps organizations effectively communicate change, and writes frequently about health care and organizational change. Before joining Hay he was a journalist and editor and ran his own communications consulting firm.

R. Timothy Stack is president and chief executive officer of Borgess Health Alliance, an integrated delivery system based in Kalamazoo, Michigan. He is also the chairman of the Michigan Health and Hospital Association. Stack held the position of president and CEO of South Side Healthcare System in Pittsburgh from 1981 to 1987, the year the American College of Hospital Executives named him Young Administrator of the Year. His academic appointments include service on the adjunct faculty of the Office of Medical Education Research and Development of Michigan State University's College of Human Medicine. He holds a master's degree in hospital administration from the Medical College of Virginia.

Carolyn J. C. Thompson, M.Ed., is director of organizational learning at Presbyterian Healthcare Services in Albuquerque, New Mexico. She is formerly a partner in Higher Ground, Inc., a leadership development firm based in Maryland. Ms. Thompson is a frequent speaker at organizational development meetings, and she consults with organizations to help them apply systems dynamics to decision making.

Katherine W. Vestal, Ph.D., is vice president and managing director of the Hay Group's Healthcare Consulting Practice. In this position, Dr. Vestal leads a national health care practice that assists clients with a wide range of organizational and management issues, including change management and measurement, physician services, leadership development, organizational effectiveness and integration, and strategic human resources. With more than 20 years' experience as a consultant, educator, and health care professional, Dr. Vestal speaks and writes frequently about changing health care issues.

Thomas B. Wilson, M.B.A., Ph.D., is president of the Wilson Group, Inc., located in Concord, Massachusetts. He has 25 years of business and management consulting, having previously served as vice president and general manager of the Hay Group and vice president of Aubrey Daniels and Associates. He is the author of *Innovative Revised Systems for the Changing Workplace* and has lectured nationally and internationally for the American Society of Human Resources in Health Care, the HMO Group, the American Compensation Association, and the Conference Board.

Ellen Wingard, M.Ed., is a senior consultant with Linkage, Inc., an international corporate education and organizational development company based in Lexington, Massachusetts. She provides consultative services in executive coaching, leadership development, team learning, and collaborative change initiatives in health care settings throughout the United States.

Foreword

T hroughout the first half of the 20th century, health care employees
created respected institutions, earned well-deserved reputations as
community leaders, and produced modern-day miracles. They
bonded together—these physicians, caregivers, housekeepers, hospital
administrators, and a host of others—forming unique cultures and
close-knit work environments. And then the world changed. Powerful
forces, ranging from technological advancements to economic and
social pressures began to dramatically change the delivery of health
care. In a stampede of acquisitions, mergers, and closures, long-standing
institutions began to disappear and then resurface with new identities,
new missions, new expectations.

Call it culture shift ... culture clash ... culture shock. Whatever
you call it, each time it happens, it causes a painful wrenching apart of
a community of colleagues and their culture.

The health care field has struggled with its new collaborations, and
new identities. In the past, we have been a very fragmented system, and,
as we merge organizations, one of our greatest challenges is to transform our diverse cultures—integrating all the fragmented parts. If we
are successful, and I believe we can be, we have an unprecedented
opportunity to create new cultures for the new visions of the new organizations that are emerging.

*CultureShift: A Leader's Guide to Managing Change in Health
Care* does an excellent job of addressing the journey leaders face when
they embark on a change process. Its focus on the people-related issues
encountered during culture change are especially relevant for us in
health care. How to work through cultural differences and how to modify or create new cultures are challenges that most organizations underestimate. This book provides practical guidance in how to meet the
challenges. It is a helpful tool for all of the change agents in health care
who work together to transform their organizations. Whether you are a
manager, physician, nurse, trustee, or community partner, this book

offers important perspectives on how to lead and implement cultural change.

Over the past 20 years, I have personally been involved in six mergers. Some were horizontal and some were vertical, but in every instance, each organization's culture reflected "its way" of doing business, ingrained in the behaviors, management style, governance, and deeply held convictions of its employees. Once the ink dries on the merger papers, the hard work begins. There's no magic pill, no pat answers. And it can't be done alone. Nobody can develop the right vision and communicate it to all the stakeholders single-handedly. This book recognizes the range of issues that must be dealt with, from the establishment of a shared vision to the engagement of the entire workforce in cultural change so that every employee embraces the new organization.

The Spanish philosopher José Ortega y Gasset said, "Culture is not life in its entirety, but just the moment of security, strength and clarity." I believe culture is the conscience of an organization. It's the way you do business and the environment you create—reflected in the shared vision and values, ethics, communications, and organizational goals, strategies, and tactics. Culture is the sometimes elusive spirit that binds an organization and its people together.

Merging organizations and creating new cultures is a lot like moving into a new home. As you sort through your belongings before the move, decisions are made. You want to take what's best and most useful with you to your new home. The rest of your things, while still in working condition and certainly steeped in sentimental value, are relegated to the garage sale.

We in health care have moved a great deal in the past several decades. We've packed, unpacked, formed new relationships, settled in—and moved out again. We've become considerably more adept at dealing with the shift in culture each organizational change triggers. But because change is so difficult, visionary leadership is required to sustain the change process. We need, first and foremost, clear-thinking leaders, those who can toss out what's not needed, retain the best of what exists, reconfigure those elements, and create a new and better culture for their organization. Learning and applying the ideas and concepts presented in this book will help you do just that.

Gordon Sprenger
CEO
Allina Health System

Preface

As I travel around the country conducting communications-related seminars for health care professionals, I frequently ask the following question: "By a show of hands, how many of you are in the midst of unprecedented change in your organizations and in your sense of professional identity?" Invariably, the hands shoot up in a nearly unanimous "Yes." And with this answer, something in the room changes.

The fear, the hurt, the confusion, and even the excitement behind that simple "Yes" is reflected in their faces. It can be heard in what they say and do not say about the changes they are experiencing as they fulfill their roles as providers of health care to the American public.

For the most part, they are extremely dedicated men and women. They have chosen to care for the sick and dying from a true sense of calling. To them, health care is more than a job; it is a way of life. They love their professions, and they are committed to helping people.

As members of the health care industry, they have embarked on a long and challenging journey of change. It is a journey that has been gathering momentum for some time. Most will admit that change needed to happen. Yet change is difficult, because there are few markers to follow on the journey. The old maps no longer guide them to the desired destination. They are in the midst of an upheaval that will change the way health care is practiced in this country, and this upheaval can be frightening.

So when American Hospital Publishing's Audrey Kaufman asked me to put together a book that addresses the culture change issues that health care professionals are experiencing and to attempt to find some markers and new maps to help provide some direction, I, too, raised my hand and issued a resounding "Yes."

About This Book

This book addresses the people-related issues encountered during changes in health care. Although many business and management books address the subject of culture change, there is a dearth of literature on culture change as it relates specifically to the very complex and unique characteristics of the health care industry. Moreover, few books address the leader's role in managing the people side of change. This book is intended to provide practical information, direction, and inspiration for those faced with the challenge of spearheading a culture change effort.

Our intention was to be practical and to provide useful tools that readers can apply to their own situations. Thus, each chapter describes change-related issues in the context of real-world challenges faced by health care professionals every day. Each author analyzes how one factor influences clinical, economic, productivity, and job satisfaction outcomes. Each presents examples, scenarios, and cases to illustrate how to positively manage the people-related issues being discussed. And each presents how-to guidelines to help readers apply this material to their own health care settings.

The process of writing this book was analogous to the process many leaders undergo when building a shared vision among stakeholders: Each author adds his or her own unique perspective. Taken together, these perspectives provide a road map for planning and leading the culture change effort. I am certain you will find the writers' ideas to be informative, creative, stimulating, and refreshing, because they offer an unexpected and valuable slant on their topics.

OVERVIEW OF THE CONTENTS

In chapter 1, I set the stage for understanding the critical factors that have led to today's climate of uncertainty and fear about the future of health care. I define culture and the critical role it plays in helping organizations navigate through the waters of change. I address the key people-related issues that must be addressed in order to avoid the consequences of a culture clash. Cultural assessment is introduced as a tool for managing cultural change. The dominant themes involved in leading a culture change are explored, and the culture shift model is presented as a way of conceptualizing the strategies and processes that underlie culture change efforts.

In chapter 2, Katherine Vestal and Scott Spreier provide an in-depth explanation of what is meant by the term "organizational culture." They examine the role that culture plays in organizational change and detail how to accurately assess an organization's cultures so that it can better chart its future course, build consensus around that course, and ultimately reach its destination with fewer detours and roadblocks.

Edward O'Connor and Marlena Fiol provide a road map for understanding and managing the change process in chapter 3. They describe the characteristics of change and define what separates the winners from the losers in the change management arena. They present a model that addresses how to build energized support for change initiatives, how to identify and remove barriers to successful change, and how to carry out a timely and effective change process.

In chapter 4, Jack Lewin explores the critical role that leaders play in generating the support, understanding, and commitment so necessary to creating a shared vision that can move beyond words into action. He discusses the nature of vision and describes the processes and behaviors that lead to establishing a critical mass of people (at all levels of the organization) who can spearhead the process of making the vision a reality. He describes how, by starting with a shared vision, the state of Hawaii transformed its health care delivery system. He also explores the role that shared vision is playing in bringing about the transformation of the California Medical Association.

In chapter 5, Michael Green focuses on perhaps the most critical and all-encompassing skill required of today's leaders—communicating clearly and effectively. He describes how cognitive dissonance can give rise to culture clash and the "tyranny of the or." He identifies methods and communication strategies that can help leaders reach out to the various health care stakeholder groups. And he provides tools for listening and speaking more effectively.

Matthew Lambert, in chapter 6, reflects on the necessity of developing a team-based environment in order to achieve the goals of high-quality, cost-effective patient care. He explores methods that can be used to overcome barriers and improve collaboration between the members of what he calls the "three-legged stool" (physicians, administrators, and hospital trustees). He describes the cultural differences between these groups and provides suggestions for increasing understanding and improving communication among them. He also explores how payers and patients can be included as partners in a team effort to improve the future of health care.

Kenneth Cummings, in chapter 7, focuses on the importance of building trust in these turbulent times so that health care professionals will continue to give their best efforts to their work. He reflects on his own experiences as a physician executive and provides insights into how to replace fear and suspicion with trust. He describes the characteristics that make for trusting relationships and provides suggestions for removing the barriers and prejudices that are so common among diverse stakeholder groups.

In chapter 8, Gita Budd and Timothy Stack discuss the importance of creating an educational strategy that can build support for achieving the goals of the business strategy. They describe how the educational efforts of an organization can be dedicated to helping all constituents understand, explore, and ultimately embrace change. They describe how educational programs were designed to meet the specific concerns and needs of each stakeholder group during a medical center's change initiative, and they underscore the importance of providing just-in-time learning opportunities.

In chapter 9, Carolyn Thompson addresses the critical importance of stepping outside the "vortex" of change in order to reflect and examine difficult or complex situations from a systemic, or holistic, perspective. She distinguishes between crisis, or events-based thinking, and systems thinking. This chapter explores the physiology of the brain in relation to different types of stressful situations and provides a tool for managing change while thinking clearly, coherently, and holistically.

In chapter 10, Lawrence Pfaff discusses the value of using 360-degree feedback (one-on-one) in the context of an overall management and leadership development process. He presents a change readiness model and describes how best to position 360-degree feedback so that the experience is not just regarded as an isolated incident, but rather as part of a long-range developmental plan to prepare health care leaders to serve as change agents. He discusses the various phases of the 360-degree feedback process and provides guidelines for successfully implementing each step.

In chapter 11, Patricia Chehy Pilette and Ellen Wingard describe the coaching relationship and the profound impact it can have on preparing executives to manage the complexities and challenges of culture change. They describe how the coaching relationship provides a safe and much-needed "space" where leaders can step out of the everyday chaos and reflect on how to best lead their organizations forward. They describe the three-part coaching process and give examples of how coaching has affected not only individuals but also the organizations in which they work.

In chapter 12, Thomas Wilson elaborates on the importance of utilizing reward systems to help facilitate culture change. He describes the forces that drive human behavior and the various reward systems that can be implemented to encourage the desired behaviors and discourage the undesirable ones. He elaborates on how to create a reward strategy that can help an organization achieve its strategic goals.

In chapter 13, authors Marilyn Paul, Rick Gregg, Cliff Bolster, and Jimmy Carter describe the powerful role that practice fields—training settings in which individuals and groups can try out and practice new roles, tasks, and behaviors without risk—can play in helping individuals adapt to change. Practice fields are used to enhance participants' ability to think, interact, and perform. This chapter focuses on several types of practice fields and describes why they are important and for what purposes they can be best used.

THE AUDIENCE

The target audience for this book is senior and mid-level managers and directors who are engaged in planning and carrying out culture change initiatives. It will be of particular interest to chief executive officers, physician and nurse executives, department managers, human resources executives, marketing and communications directors, hospital trustees, training directors, and organizational consultants. Others who will find it useful are physicians, nurses, medical students, and undergraduate and graduate students who are preparing to enter the health care field.

Acknowledgments

I n attempting to describe what the experience of being managing editor of this book was like, two words come immediately to mind: wrestling and dancing. Many times over the course of working on the various phases of bringing it to publication, I have wrestled to put meaning to the flood of ideas; I have wrestled with finding the right words to express these ideas; and I have wrestled with the part of myself that didn't believe that I was up to the task of tackling such a challenging, far-reaching subject.

And then there was the dancing. These were the times when the struggle ceased, and the words flowed, and there was a wonderful sense of calm and surety. It was then that I knew that I was in the right place, at the right time, and doing the right thing. I wouldn't trade that awareness for anything.

It is safe to say that this particular book never would have happened without the foresight, talent, guidance, and inspiration of Audrey Kaufman at American Hospital Publishing. While I have often read writers' accounts of the pivotal role that their editors played in bringing their books to life, I now fully understand their meaning. Audrey is an incredible support and a wonderful teacher. Her gentle, yet laser-beam-like feedback was a source of constant wonder to me. I shall always be grateful for the experience of working with her.

I am indebted to each and every contributor to this book. They have been dedicated, cooperative and absolutely a joy to work with on the project. Their intelligence, their level of professionalism, and their commitment to the future of health care have been very inspiring to me and bode well for the future of the industry.

I want to thank Pat Fiene at American Hospital Publishing for her encouragement, professionalism, and fine editing talent. Also, thanks to Elizabeth Kennedy for being so helpful in bringing the "nuts and bolts" of this project together. And I am grateful to all the dedicated people behind the scenes at American Hospital Publishing who make things happen. Special thanks to Howard Horowitz at the American College of Physician Executives for first hiring me to develop the Culture Clash Seminar. I wish to thank my colleagues Ellen Messer of the Samson Group, Santalynda Marrero of Stanford Health Services, and Peter Stroh of Innovation Associates, who helped me to "wrestle" with ideas. I want to offer my heartfelt gratitude to Jan Kirchner, who listened to endless conversations about the book, made astute suggestions, nurtured me in so many ways, and who even "made" me eat when I was too involved in pulling the book together to think about practical matters. Thanks to family, friends and colleagues who had patience with me during this project. And finally I want to thank Adriaan Chipley-Kirchner who put up with all of this and who was so sweet about playing the piano softly!

Thank you, one and all.

1

Understanding the Culture Shift in Health Care

Joan E. Lowery, Ph.D.

You better start swimming or you'll sink like a stone
For the times they are a-changin'.

—*Bob Dylan, "The Times They Are A-Changin'"*

Although it was written more than 35 years ago, Bob Dylan's land-mark song captures the turbulent climate of today's health care industry. In an effort to survive daunting economic and compet-itive challenges, health care organizations and physician groups are engaging in a flurry of mergers, acquisitions, and affiliations; reengi-neering, downsizing, and reorganization. As the song cautions us, there is danger in the waters of change; if we do not swim with them, we risk sinking like a stone.

Swimming through the waters of change is not easy. As health care organizations undergo rapid change, they are faced with a number of dif-ficult *tangible* issues, including how best to merge assets, structure debt, reconfigure jobs, and obtain government approval for mergers. Given the complexity of these issues and the speed with which they must often be resolved, it is not surprising that *intangible* issues, such as governance and organizational culture, may be overlooked. Yet to ignore relationships and the cultural assumptions that underpin them is risky. It is, after all, people—individuals at all levels of the organiza-tion—who must carry out change. If the purpose of change is unclear to them, if the risks involved in change seem too great and the benefits too small, if they lack the requisite knowledge and skills to handle new responsibilities, then they will resist change and lessen its chance of suc-cess. No shift in strategy can succeed unless the culture shifts with it.

This chapter lays the groundwork for the cultural change manage-ment strategies and processes described throughout this book. The chap-ter begins by highlighting key people-related issues facing health care organizations and professionals today. It then defines culture, discusses culture clash and its potential consequences, and looks at cultural assessment as a tool for managing change. The chapter closes with an examination of the dominant themes inherent in leading cultural change, including a model for conceptualizing cultural change strategies and processes.

TODAY'S TURBULENT HEALTH CARE ENVIRONMENT

As a result of external forces, including the drive to contain costs, the U.S. health care system is experiencing a major remodeling. From structure to function to delivery, health care organizations are in the throes of change. Roles, goals, strategies, directions, and—perhaps most significantly—the manner in which people work together are all being reevaluated and reconfigured in an attempt to survive in the new health care milieu.

Changing Organizational Structures

The trend to merge, affiliate, acquire, form a variety of partnerships and networks, and ultimately to integrate is proceeding at a feverish pace. The impetus for these organizational changes is the need to remain competitive by reducing costs and taking advantage of the econonomies of scale offered by the consolidation of information systems, implementation of best-practice models, and sharing of medical technology and resources. The cost-containment movement, initiated in the early 1980s by diagnosis-related groups (DRGs), and the resulting changes in reimbursement were fueled by pressure from payers. Employer and patient purchaser populations, alarmed by the upwardly spiraling cost of health care and fed up with paying for it, used their purchasing clout to exert economic pressure on the medical community.[1]

Today a climate of tightening reimbursements prevails, resulting in a host of changes all geared toward achieving economies of scale. Medicare and Medicaid reimbursements are being squeezed. Managed care, shared risk, and capitated payment structures are on the rise, while the fee-for-service structure is declining. Hospital-centered care is transitioning into networks of outpatient and primary care. The dominant clinical role once played by the specialist is now played by the primary care physician, the "gatekeeper" of care. The emphasis has shifted from treating the sick to keeping people well. The resulting efforts to prevent illness and provide wellness education have given rise to a whole spectrum of new jobs and treatment modalities. At the same time, the advent of new information technology is promising to contribute to improved medical outcomes, better market positioning, greater efficiency, and reduced administrative costs. The stage has been set for a new era in health care delivery. There is no turning back on the march to provide high-quality, cost-effective medical care by exercising greater efficiency and appropriateness of service.

To accommodate new business arrangements while, at the same time, meeting the needs of the patient population, health care leaders are implementing a variety of internal organizational changes. These changes include reengineering, staff restructuring and streamlining, cross-training, removing layers of management, establishing clinical pathways, and instituting the team-oriented, patient-focused care model. Wherever these changes are introduced, they will have a profound impact, for better or for worse, upon the existing organizational culture.

Changing Professional Roles

With the dramatic restructuring of the health care industry has come an equally dramatic shift in professional roles. Physicians, nurses, administrators, and other health care professionals are being asked to take on new duties, set new priorities, and view clinical practices from a new perspective. These changes represent a radical shift in culture: in flux are the values, mores, and practices that help define professionals' sense of identity. This transition from one culture to another is a difficult one from which no one is immune. Whether it is surgical subspecialists who hear themselves being referred to as the "high cost" element of health care or RNs who are told that their patient care activities must be curtailed so that they can administer the nursing process, the changes can be rough, tough, and frightening.

Perhaps nowhere is the culture shift felt more acutely than among physicians. Trained to be independent and autonomous in their thinking and behavior, physicians are now being challenged to change many of the beliefs, attitudes, and behaviors that, in the past, made them successful. As members of networks and group practices, physicians are being called upon to work collaboratively, to help groups reach and support consensus on important issues, and to build new administrative, management, peer profiling, and other organizational skills. In addition, physicians must adapt to a variety of new and different incentive systems. Once "lone rangers," physicians are now part of health care teams, which may include nurses, nurse practitioners, physician assistants, psychologists, counselors, and community health workers.

With the advent of patient-focused care, the nursing profession is also undergoing major change. The RN now serves in an administrative, case-management capacity, heading up the care team that shares responsibility for patients. The members of the team are cross-trained to carry out each other's functions, and less-credentialed staff are trained to take over many of the nursing functions formerly filled by RNs, LPNs, and other professionally certified health care workers such as respiratory therapists and certified nursing assistants. The role of the nurse executive (NE) has dramatically expanded, with NEs now expected to play an active role in everything from fiscal management, marketing activities, and the development of clinical integration models to negotiations of mergers and other strategic alliances.

Changing Relationships

The relationships between health care administrators and physicians are also undergoing a significant change. Prior to the 1980s, these two groups of professionals operated separately and autonomously. Hospitals provided technology, personnel, and space, and physicians provided patients and clinical expertise. Incentives were aligned, job functions were clear, and there was no reason for collaboration.

With the advent of prospective payment, a conflict of interest began to grow between the two professional groups. While hospitals concentrated on shorter patient stays and resource conservation, physicians were still being rewarded for intensive care and prolonged hospitalizations. As administrators intervened, physicians came to view them as usurping their clinical authority and trying to dictate medical care. Administrators, in turn, suspected doctors of only being interested in filling their own coffers by prolonging patient stays and ordering unnecessary tests and procedures.[2] A climate of distrust and even antagonism arose between the two groups.

Today's climate of cost containment, coupled with the rise of managed care, fierce competition, and a business community that is hostile to the "old days" of health care delivery, has led to a reconciliation between physicians and administrators. Together, they have joined forces as "allies against a common enemy"—the "enemy" being those entities that advocate a DRG approach to reimbursement, including payers, managed care plans, and the business community.[3] However, long-held attitudes of distrust, along with different ways of viewing the business and practice of health care, have made it challenging for both physicians and administrators to move together toward integration.

The rise of the physician executive—a full-time, salaried position—has gone a long way toward building a bridge between an institution's administration and its physician body. But physician executives have also faced cultural challenges as a result of their shift in roles. While managers view them as valued members of the management team, they are frequently viewed with suspicion by fellow physicians, who perceive the transition from clinician to administrator as a move from one "camp" to another.

CULTURE: THE PEOPLE SIDE OF CHANGE

For the reasons just described, the atmosphere in the health care industry is currently one of uncertainty and fear. Major changes in organizational structure, roles, and relationships have shaken people's conceptions of who they are, how they fit in, and what is important— in short, their conceptions of health care culture.

Simply defined, culture is "the way things are done around here," the body of learned practices that members of an organization share and transmit to new members. More specifically, organizational culture is made up of beliefs and values; customs, rituals and mores; learned practices; and rewards.

Beliefs and Values

These elements encompass how people perceive the organization and their role within it. For example, is there value placed on professionals growing to their full potential as health care practitioners? Or do they view themselves and their organization as just doing a job or, ultimately, as making as much money as they can? Is there alignment between the organization's mission statement and the reality of how health care is practiced on a daily basis? Do they perceive the work setting as one that encourages and rewards creativity, innovation, and risk taking? Or do they view their organization as cautious, autocratic, and discouraging of new ideas and innovation?

Customs, Rituals, and Mores

These elements give a "folkloric" quality to the organization and involve behaviors such as dress, the occasions chosen to celebrate, and the ways in which people interact formally and informally. In some organizations clear lines divide peers, superiors, and subordinates. In others there is more a sense of family.

In an organization that celebrates achievements, people look forward to gathering together to recognize the accomplishment of goals. In one that feels like a family, the loss of a member (whether or not through personal choice) does not go unnoticed. Events such as the annual picnic or the holiday party are ways for people to bond and build a sense of community. In organizations where people face the insecurity of undergoing major change, the preservations of key customs, rituals and mores can become a critical factor in helping to maintain morale and gather support for the desired change.

Learned Practices

This element includes the behaviors that people engage in to carry out their work. It refers to how things are done. It involves how decisions are made and how tasks are carried out. That includes whether a democratic, participatory climate is encouraged or hierarchy and limited input are emphasized. In some environments, team-based behavior is encouraged; in others, autonomy is embedded into the system. The trend toward cross-functional work teams represents a major culture shift for many health care professionals and requires retraining in how the different disciplines must now work together simultaneously.

Rewards

Rewards are the mechanism through which an organization encourages or discourages certain attitudes and behaviors. It involves the subtle and not-so-subtle ways people are treated for acting in certain ways. Rewards can be monetary or nonmonetary, formal or informal. For example, if an organization chooses to place a high priority on teamwork, then its reward systems must be designed to reinforce team-based behaviors. Financial and nonfinancial rewards must be structured to reward those attitudes and behaviors that are considered desirable to the organization's success. "Team of the month" awards will replace "employee of the month" awards.

An organization that regards patient satisfaction as its number 1 priority will develop very different rewards than an organization that regards revenue above patient care. During times of culture change, it is particularly imperative that reward systems support the desired changes and that those who are being asked to change perceive rewards to be congruent with the new desired behaviors.

Culture gives a department, a work group, or an entire organization its identity. It provides a sense of cohesion, unifying different groups through shared meaning and behavior. When trying to get a sense of an organization's culture, it can be helpful to find answers to the following questions:

- What is and is not valued?
- How do people get ahead?
- What does the informal power structure look like?
- How do people stay out of trouble?
- What can and cannot be said?
- How are decisions made?
- How is conflict handled or not handled?
- What are the rituals concerning change, successes, and recognition?

- What stories about the organization do people tell?
- What kinds of socializing do or do not take place?
- How do people dress?

Note that an organization's culture may or may not be accurately reflected in the organization's mission, vision, and values statements. Cultural norms are implicit to an organization—taught through example and learned through observation—rather than explicitly stated in handbooks, manuals, or strategic plans. For this reason, leaders would be wise to get a picture of the culture as it actually is rather than as they assume or wish it to be.

CULTURE CLASH AND ITS CONSEQUENCES

Because culture is handed down from one "generation" of organizational members to the next and is based on fundamental beliefs and values, it tends to be firmly entrenched in an organization and resistant to change. It is not uncommon, then, for new strategic plans and goals to clash with the existing culture. The resulting conflicts lead to a workplace in "limbo"—one in which the old values and ways of doing things are no longer acceptable and yet the new prescribed ways are resisted.

Underlying Causes of Culture Clash in Health Care

Culture clash is felt particularly strongly in health care because it is an industry in which people typically identify more closely with their professional group than with the institutions where they work. Today's health care climate requires health care professionals to put their organizations—particularly the financial needs of their organizations—ahead of their professional identities, reversing a long-held cultural norm. As a result, some who went into the field out of a sincere commitment to helping others now derogatorily refer to their chosen profession as "just a job." They openly express dismay, anger, disappointment, and hurt over the new culture of health care delivery, with its emphasis on the bottom line. And they readily admit that they resent the changes they are required to make.

In some cases, culture clash has led to frustration on the part of an entire segment of the health care industry. For example, in the state of California, the California Nurses Association is waging a seemingly unending battle against what it perceives to be the untenable changes taking place in the delivery of nursing care in hospitals and HMOs throughout the state.[4]

Culture clashes resulting from poorly planned mergers, affiliations, and acquisitions have also damaged morale. Faced with the looming threat of losing market share, all too many health care leaders have rushed to create new strategic alliances without entering a "courtship" phase, in which they might explore the compatibility of the cultures involved. Consider, for example, the culture clash that occurs when a medical staff with a participatory, informal culture is asked to merge with a hierarchical, autocratic staff. Failure to anticipate and manage potential culture clashes like this virtually ensures that the alliance will not meet strategic goals. Poorly planned restructuring is likely to meet a similar fate. When leaders forge ahead without analyzing whether the existing culture supports the desired change, the resulting clash puts the success of the entire effort in jeopardy.

In short, the consequences of ignoring cultural change and its impact on people can be devastating: reduced morale; lowered productivity; resistance to initiatives; absenteeism; accidents; staff turnover; sabotage; and competitive, uncooperative, and adversarial relationships. Whatever the particular culture clash, ultimately customers—the patient population—bear the brunt of conflicts, as their care is delivered in an atmosphere of high stress, conflict, and fear.

Using Assessments to Plan for Cultural Change

On closer examination, the seemingly unavoidable resistance to change and the problems it causes are not unavoidable at all. They are, perhaps, consequences of organizations' failure to plan for and effectively manage cultural change. The importance of managing cultural change cannot be overstated. Research conducted by the Hay Management Group indicates that an organization's strategic plans are unlikely to be implemented, much less sustained, unless there is an appropriate organizational culture in place to support the strategy.[5] In the words of Michael Cooper and James Williams, "managing culture for competitive advantage is the key to successful implementation of strategy. The role of the CEO and the Executive Management team can no longer be limited to formulating strategy. They must ask probing questions about the culture of the organization and determine whether it's suitable in light of strategic business objectives. They must ask, how can the culture be managed to gain competitive advantage?"[6]

Clearly, it is critical that the characteristics of a culture are understood *before* change is introduced, as part of the overall business strategy. The question is, how can leaders get an accurate picture of their organization's culture?

A number of excellent health care–specific cultural assessment tools are available to leaders seeking to define current and desired cultures.

(See chapter 2.) Through the use of these tools, leaders who are considering making a change can find answers to the following questions:

- What is the current cultural reality in the organization?
- What is the desired reality?
- What gaps exist between the current and desired realities?
- Can the gaps be bridged?
- If so, what are the best ways to bridge them?

By answering these questions honestly, leaders can anticipate culture clashes and plan ways to manage them effectively. The process of assessing organizational culture can also open the door to better communication, better decision making, and improved performance.

In the Hay Management Survey, a research study conducted by the Hay Management Group, it was found that "there is a clear, strong correlation between hospital culture and performance."[7] The primary *performance* criterion was found to be return on equity. Other measures were return on assets, return on revenues, return plus charitable contributions divided by revenues, number of full-time employees per occupied bed, and three-year average revenue growth.[8] Managers in the higher-performing organizations rated their organizations higher on decision making, communications, internal cooperation, and strategic long-term planning than did the managers in the lower-performing organizations.[9]

THE NEED FOR EFFECTIVE LEADERSHIP

Culture shift, if handled sensitively and intelligently, *can* be successful and culture clash effectively avoided. But it takes inspired, committed, and sensitive leadership to help organizations navigate the bumpy waters of cultural change.

Using the "Five C's" to Manage Change

To be effective, today's leaders must recognize that they are, indeed, change agents. They must appreciate the critical importance of communication and seek to understand, as well as to be understood. In the words of CEO Michael Green, "Leadership is about involving as many people as possible and listening intently to what they have to say and then being willing to learn from what you hear."[10] In addition, leaders must create clarity about the direction in which the organization has chosen to go, demonstrate courage in the face of change, show commitment to the organization and its success, and demonstrate genuine curiosity about others' points of view. These effective change agent behaviors are summarized in the "five C's" below:

1. *Clarity:* Have a keen understanding of where the organization is, where it needs to go, and how it can get there. To achieve clarity, leaders must
   - Create a clearly articulated shared vision
   - Design a road map for realizing the vision
   - Implement self-assessments and organizational assessments to help identify current and desired realities and the gaps between the two
   - Create reward systems to facilitate change
2. *Communication:* Create a climate that encourages two-way communication in which both parties seek "first to understand, then be understood." This requires that leaders
   - Share information openly with all constituents
   - Seek input from all constituents
   - Listen with the intent to understand
   - Deliver clear, unambiguous messages
   - Give constructive, honest feedback
   - Coach and support constituents through the emotional and cognitive challenges inherent in the change process
   - Demonstrate congruence in words and actions
3. *Courage:* Be willing to take risks and step out of your "comfort zone" in order to create a shared vision. To develop courage, leaders must
   - Examine assumptions
   - Be curious
   - Be willing *not* to have all the answers
   - Seek and learn from feedback
   - Work collaboratively
   - Try out new roles
   - Learn new behaviors and skills
   - Demonstrate the willingness to explore new relationships and organizational structures in an effort to meet the health care needs of the patient population
4. *Curiosity:* Adopt an attitude of inquiry and openness to learning from all people. Curious leaders
   - Continuously learn
   - Seek to understand the thinking and perspectives of others
   - Engage in open inquiries without preconceived ideas about outcomes
   - Are willing to suspend judgments about people and ideas
   - Solicit and entertain ideas from varied sources

5. *Commitment:* Exercise persistence, patience, and dedication to achieving the vision. To demonstrate commitment, leaders should
   - "Keep the end in mind" and give priority to what is best for the patient population
   - Exercise flexibility and ingenuity in the interests of achieving the shared vision
   - Create a climate in which mistakes are tolerated as part of the learning process
   - Provide learning opportunities for constituents to help them successfully create or adapt to the desired new culture
   - "Walk the talk" and demonstrate congruence between words and actions

Examining a Model for Managing Change

Out of the collective thinking of the authors, a culture shift model has emerged. (See figure 1-1.) It can be useful in planning and tracking your culture change strategy. It also serves as a means of conceptualizing the strategies and processes that form the content of the book.

The culture shift model is divided into two major elements: creating the foundation for change (*left*) and managing the process of change (*right*). In the illustration, the foundation loops represent those structural elements that help form the building blocks for the culture change effort. Typically, these strategies require detailed planning in order to be most effective. The process loops include the more behavioral, cognitive, and even spiritual aspects of the change journey.

Notice that the foundation and process loops are actually connected and do not start or stop at any point in time. We drew it this way to represent the interwoven, constantly changing, and transformational nature of the change process.

The order of the chapters corresponds to the model. Therefore, a foundation-oriented chapter is followed by a process-oriented one. The model (and the order of the readings) is not meant to suggest a linear, step-by-step approach to managing culture change. It is doubtful that any such approach would be effective, given that each culture change situation is unique and requires flexible, just-in-time interventions.

However, with a bit of imagination and poetic license, you'll find that the foundation and process loops *do* relate to one another, and we are suggesting that these culture change issues do, indeed, interweave and flow into one another in a fluid, nonlinear fashion. So it is with the ordering of the chapters—each topic adds and integrates the learnings of the previous ones, continually expanding the reader's thinking.

FIGURE 1-1.   Culture Shift Model

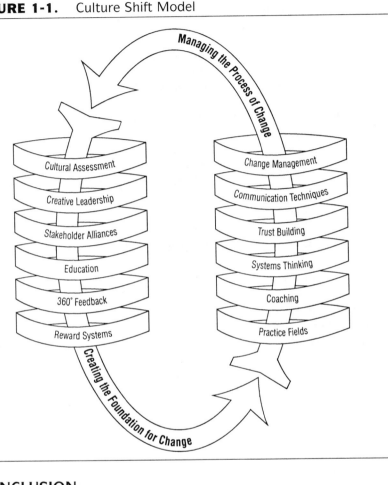

CONCLUSION

Over the past several years, traditional health care structures, roles, and relationships have undergone dramatic change, and forecasters predict that more are sure to come. To excel in a volatile environment, health care organizations must learn to embrace change rather than resist it. Given people's natural resistance to change, the shift from "conscientious objector" to change agent does not come easily. By making cultural change part of the overall strategic plan, however, leaders can avoid culture clash and its destructive consequences.

References and Notes

1.   J. Matthew Lambert III, M.D., "Strategies for Communicating with Physicians in the Era of Health Care Restructuring," in *Building*

and Managing Effective Physician Organizations under Capitation, ed. Douglas Goldstein (Gaithersburg, Md.: Aspen, 1996).

2. Ibid.

3. Ibid.

4. Jill L. Scherer, "Union Uprising," *Hospitals and Health Networks* (December 20, 1994): 36-38.

5. Michael R. Cooper and James B. Williams, "Managing Cultural Change to Achieve Competitive Advantage," *Handbook of Health Care Human Resources Management*, 2d ed. (Rockville: Aspen, 1990) p. 107.

6. Ibid., p. 107.

7. Carol Dubnicki, Ph.D., and Kristine McKean, "The Link between Management Culture and Organization Performance," *Health Care Productivity Report*. This is part of an ongoing series of research projects conducted by the Hay Group into culture, compensation, and human resource strategies.

8. Ibid.

9. Ibid.

10. Michael Green, personal communication, 1997.

Bibliography

Bracey, Hyler, Jack Rosenblum, Aubrey Sanford, and Roy Trueblood. *Managing from the Heart.* New York: Dell, 1990.

Bridges, William. *Managing Transitions: Making the Most of Change.* Reading, Mass.: Addison-Wesley, 1991.

Connor, Daryl R. *Managing at the Speed of Light.* New York: Villard, 1992.

Covey, Stephen R. *The Seven Habits of Highly Effective People.* New York: Simon and Schuster, 1990.

DePree, Max. *Leadership Is an Art.* New York: Dell, 1989.

Hurst, David K. *Crisis and Renewal: Meeting the Challenge of Organizational Change*. Cambridge, Mass.: Harvard Business School Press, 1995.

Shortell, Stephen, Robin R. Gillies, David A. Anderson, and John B. Mitchell. *Remaking Health Care in America: Building Organized Delivery Systems*. San Francisco: Jossey-Bass, 1996.

Shortell, Stephen, Ellen M. Morrison, and Bernard Friedman, *Strategic Choices for America's Hospitals: Managing Change in Turbulent Times*. San Francisco: Jossey-Bass, 1992.

Stevens, George H. *The Strategic Health Care Manager: Mastering Essential Leadership Skills*. San Francisco: Jossey-Bass, 1991.

2

Facilitating Change through Cultural Assessment

Katherine W. Vestal, Ph.D.

Scott W. Spreier

In today's competitive environment, it is essential that your health care organization create a culture that helps it achieve its desired business results. Whether your organization is a huge integrated system that wants to stay ahead of the competition, the progeny of a recent merger still seeking its identity, or a stand-alone hospital that wants to maintain its position of leadership in the local community, it is critical that your organization's culture supports its strategic goals. As John Kotter and James Heskett so accurately note in their book *Corporate Culture and Performance*, "corporate culture can have a significant impact on a firm's long-term economic performance [and] will probably be even more important in determining the success or failure of firms in the next decade."[1] Organizational culture is especially important in the health care industry, where rapid change is creating the need for new and varied cultures that not only enhance performance and efficiency, but also increase both employee and customer satisfaction.

As discussed in chapter 1, cultural assessment is a critical early step for any health care organization that wants to create rapid, sustainable change. A thorough assessment of culture helps an organization to determine its readiness for change, to evaluate the degree of change necessary to get from its current to its desired state, and to create consensus and ultimate buy-in for the desired changes. In addition to facilitating strategic change and cultural alignment before and after mergers and acquisitions, an assessment can be an effective tool for setting a new human resources agenda; for building teams; for defining mission, vision, and values; and for refining employee surveys.

A cultural assessment can be implemented only if there is clarity about the concept of culture itself—only if there is consensus among the organization's decision makers as to what "culture" really means. This chapter provides that clarity. More important, it will provide you with an overview of major steps in the cultural change process—from planning and implementing an assessment to using the results of the assessment to create and sustain change.

DEFINING CULTURE, THE DREADED "C-WORD"

The first step in managing the cultural change process is to establish a working definition of what culture really means. Unfortunately, every organizational expert seems to have a different definition of culture. A number of experts have even written books on the subject. For example, Kotter and Heskett view culture as a two-tiered concept that includes visible, malleable attributes as well as less visible, harder to change elements.[2] MIT's culture guru, Edgar Schein, defines culture as a "pattern of shared basic assumptions that the group learned as it solved its problems of external adaptation and internal integration, that has worked well enough to be considered valid and, therefore, to be taught to new members as the correct way to perceive, think, and feel in relation to those problems."[3]

If that definition gives you pause, try noted business author and philosopher Charles Handy's explanation. He defines various cultures through analogy to Greek mythological figures: Zeus, the autocratic organization; Apollo, the orderly and bureaucratic god of the task force and expertise; and Dionysus, the god of the professional.[4]

The truth is, organizational cultures can be described in a number of ways, many of which are perfectly valid. What is important when an organization begins to probe its cultures is not so much *which* definition is used, but that everyone within the organization uses the *same* definition. A common baseline not only helps create mutual understanding and consensus but also alignment. If, as research suggests, culture is the critical link between strategy and results, then everything from the selection, development, leadership, and rewarding of people to the organization of work and the design of roles must be aligned with that culture.

For the purposes of this chapter, culture is defined as an organizing concept that encompasses how work is done (work processes) and how people are selected, developed, managed, led, and rewarded (people processes).[5] The organization's culture and all the elements that it encompasses must be aligned with the organization's structure, work processes, and human resource strategies if the culture is to support the organization's business strategy and achieve the desired results.[6] As shown in figure 2-1, culture integrates the organization's core competencies, critical success factors, people competencies, and critical roles and processes. Culture is a critical driver in transforming strategic intent into real performance.

Take, for example, a rapidly growing health care system. Its strategic intent may be to become the community's number 1 provider of health care. Its critical success factors in achieving that goal may include not only financial performance and the quality of care, but also customer satisfaction and the creation of strategic alliances. The organization must have core competencies that support business development and growth, financial performance, and speed to market, as well as the more traditional skills in quality of care and customer service. To be successful in this new environment, it needs performance-focused people who are flexible, take the initiative, enjoy working as part of a team, and thrive on risk and change. To develop those competencies and achieve the desired performance, the organization must change roles and work processes and create new people strategies around selection, development, performance management, and rewards.

Four Primary Organizational Cultures in Health Care

Based on the above definition of culture, it is possible to create a model of the primary organizational cultures present in health care today. There are at least four cultures worth noting—functional, process, time-based, and network. (See figure 2-2.) It is likely that your organization's culture reflects one (or more) of these paradigms.

FIGURE 2-1. Culture and Performance

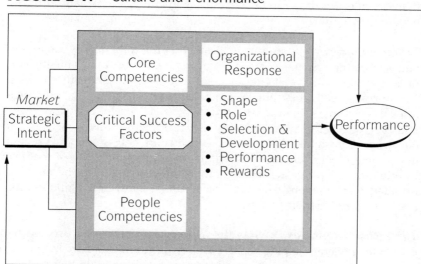

FIGURE 2-2.   Four Primary Cultures

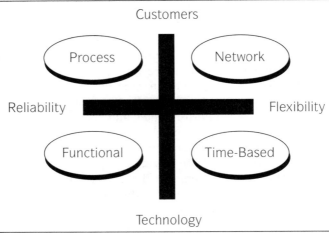

© HayGroup Healthcare. Used with permission

Functional Cultures   For decades the dominant culture in most large health care organizations has been functional, that is, focused on making the most reliable use of the best technology at hand. To achieve that steady performance over the long haul, the emphasis is on narrowly defined, usually individual functions and heavy command and control. Work is built around the specialization of individuals, be it the compensation specialist in human resources or the phlebotomist on the floor, and integrated through deep management hierarchies. Order and entitlement rule the day. Employees stay with the same organization for many years, slowly and steadily working their way up the ladder.

Process Cultures   With the emergence of the total quality movement and a growing emphasis on customer satisfaction, many health care organizations found that they needed to create a culture that emphasized processes for continually improving services and meeting obligations to customers. In process cultures, work is designed around teams, and planning, execution, and control are integrated as closely to the customer as possible. The new team-based care delivery models seen in many acute care facilities often incorporate this type of culture. Employees in process-focused environments need to be service-oriented team players who are not afraid to learn new skills or take responsibility for their actions.

Time-Based Cultures   While the increased emphasis on process has gone a long way in helping health care organizations improve the quality of care and patient satisfaction, it is not the magic solution that will give them a long-term competitive edge. If they are to remain contenders, they have to become faster, more flexible, and financially more agile. In short, they need to create time-based cultures that emphasize speed to market and rapid development of products and services. Time-based cultures—which have been successfully utilized by other industries, such as manufacturing (General Electric and Chrysler are two well-known examples)—are rapidly becoming key elements of large integrated health care systems. Such organizations require self-starting, inquisitive, confident people who thrive on risk and change.

Network Cultures While a new emphasis on speed and an increased focus on processes to improve quality and customer satisfaction have helped many organizations weather the storms of change, others are finding that speed and processes alone aren't enough. These organizations are discovering the need for outside technical expertise and strategic partnerships and alliances. As a result, many are developing complex and far-ranging networks. Indeed, in the era of managed care and the full integration of services, networks and alliances are becoming a mainstay of the health care industry. Successful employees in such organizations must be highly adaptable. They must relish taking on new, often temporary assignments, enjoy high-risk situations, and not be daunted by steep learning curves. Confidence, innovation, and the ability to quickly develop new relationships are critical competencies in network organizations.

Evolving Health Care Markets and Cultures

Cultures, like health care organizations, tend to evolve over time. Thus, the evolution of the four health care organizational cultures tracks very closely with the evolution of the industry itself. (See table 2-1) The traditional unstructured market of the past was served well by the functional culture. The emphasis on process—which was of some importance in this first stage—grew in the second stage of market evolution, when HMOs and preferred provider organizations (PPOs) began proliferating, and loose organizational frameworks, or federations, began developing.

As health care organizations have begun moving toward the later stages of market evolution—consolidation and integration—their cultures have continued shifting. Again, because of an increased focus on speed, flexibility, and the need for strategic alliances, many are becoming more time-based and network oriented.

It is important to note that the four-part model is just that—a model. In the real world, such "pure," clear-cut distinctions seldom exist. The truth is that most organizations contain a number of cultures. The accounting department, for example, probably continues to be very

TABLE 2-1.   The Evolution of Health Care Markets and Cultures

Stage of Market Evolution	Stage I:	Stage II:	Stage III:	Stage IV:
Stage of Cultural Evolution	Traditional Functional	Federations Process	Consolidation Time Based	Integration Network
Traits	• Dominated by major indemnity insurers • Few provider "systems" • Long-standing power of teaching/university hospital	• Proliferation of HMOs/PPOs • Beginning of formation of provider "networks" • Bed capacity declining uniformly across competitors	• Shakeout of marginal players • Emergence of a few dominant HMOs • Formalized "system" developing • Provider/payer alliances forming	• Fewer HMOs in each regional market • Fully integrated systems • Solidified provider/payer alliances • Direct employer/provider contracts
HMO Penetration	Less than 10%	10%–30%	30%–50%	More than 50%
Pricing	Fee for service	Discount, per diem	Per diem, per case, physician capitation	Cost per covered life per health system
Basis for Purchasing	Encounter, cost of claim	Encounter, cost of claim	Cost per covered life per health plan	Beneficiary health status, total health care cost
Basis of Competition	Service, technology	Service, technology, price	Price	Price, outcomes

© HayGroup Healthcare. Used with permission.

functional in its approach, while patient care delivery probably is—or should be—much more process focused. At the same time, the organization's overriding strategy and structure—especially if it is a system in the throes of a merger, acquisition, or integration initiative—is probably more time based and network oriented. To stay ahead of the competition, the organization moves with all the speed that it can muster to create the necessary business relationships with physicians, insurers, and other partners.

Given this complex hybridization of organizational cultures, it is important that organizations recognize the need for both overarching or "primary" cultures as well as "secondary," yet equally valid, subcultures. It is also important to remember that there are no inherently good or bad cultures—just appropriate and inappropriate ones.

PLANNING FOR A CULTURAL ASSESSMENT

Agreeing on a definition of culture is the first step toward managing the cultural change process. Once your health care organization has established a working definition, it can move to the next step—planning for the cultural assessment. As with the implementation of any initiative, certain management and logistical concerns need to be addressed. In addition, the organization must consider which assessment tool will best meet its needs.

Management and Logistical Concerns

Among the management and logistical questions to be answered during the planning stage include the following:

- When should assessment take place?
- What should the organization expect from the assessment?
- Who should participate in the assessment?
- How should the launch and results be communicated?

Answering these questions before implementing the assessment will help ensure that it achieves the desired results.

Timing Assessments   As has been previously stated, a cultural assessment should be one of the first steps your organization takes during any major change initiative. It should, for example, take place prior to any significant restructuring or reengineering efforts. It should also take place prior to any merger or the creation of new partnerships and alliances. That doesn't mean that once you've established your culture you need never examine it again. Indeed, with the rapid changes that continue to take place in our industry, some form of ongoing or regular assessment and measurement is critical. Another major assessment may not be required for some time, but there is certainly a need for ongoing "cultural navigation," using a variety of measures, such as periodic employee focus groups and surveys. And, as the industry and market evolve, no doubt new cultures will also emerge. So it is also critical to stay on top of the development of successful new cultures both in health care and other industries.

Understanding the Capabilities of Assessment For a cultural assessment to be truly useful, everyone concerned must understand what it can and cannot do. Unfortunately, many organizations launch major cultural assessments believing that they have finally discovered a crystal ball that will tell them—with a high degree of clarity and precision—just exactly what they are or should become. Most of these same organizations are sorely disappointed when they get the results. In frustration they protest, "Why is it that we've generated a lot of opinion, but very few hard answers?" The answer is that the results of most cultural assessments should be viewed as cultural compasses rather than cultural calipers. Assessments are wonderful tools for creating clarity and consensus around where your organization is as a culture and where it should be. They also provide an excellent measure of the distance that must be covered between the "as is" and "to be" states. But they will not tell you how to make the trip. For that reason, it is critical that the capabilities and limitations of any assessment process be addressed beforehand.

Selecting Participants To get a true picture of the organization's culture, your organization must give careful consideration to who should participate in the assessment. An assessment can be implemented at a variety of levels in an organization. Typically, it is first done at the executive team level in order to build consensus among the leaders, who, as a group, must drive the change efforts. By having the leadership team be the first in the organization to go through the assessment process, much of the dissension and many of the barriers that surround any major organizational change can be identified and eliminated early in the process, thereby avoiding costly and time-consuming delays further down the road.

But that doesn't mean that a cultural assessment must start and end at the top of the organization. Frequently, similar assessments are also carried out at a variety of levels throughout the organization. These lower-level assessments, which are usually limited to small groups of employees, help build credibility and consensus for coming changes. More importantly, they provide a more accurate "reading" of the organization's cultures and subcultures and help validate—or negate—leadership's "view of the world." After all, perceptions of an organization typically differ greatly from one level of the organization to another. Research has shown that the higher the level of the employee, the more likely that he or she will have a favorable perception of the organization. Top management, for example, has a more favorable view of the organization than do middle managers, professional and technical employees, and clerical and hourly ones.[7]

Nor do assessments have to be linked to major changes or organization-wide initiatives. Narrowly focused culture assessments can also be effectively used within departments or divisions, small work groups, and teams. Such exercises provide both participants and their leaders with excellent insight into group dynamics and are a quick way to identify cultural issues that affect performance. We offer as an example an assessment that involved the senior partners of a professional service organization. The results showed that as a group, they placed little value on "achieving budgeted objectives." Not surprisingly, the organization's nonplussed leaders quickly moved to shift the culture.

Communicating the Launch and Assessment Results Like many initiatives in health care organizations, cultural assessments typically follow one of two courses: (1) they are implemented with absolutely no warning, generating rumors and tremors of uncertainty throughout the organization, or (2) they are launched with great fanfare and never spoken of again—also generating rumors and tremors of uncertainty throughout the organization.

Both paths should, of course, be avoided. Cultural assessments, like any new initiative or process, will no doubt raise some eyebrows, trigger some dissension, and create a moderately high level of "organizational noise." That's exactly what they should do. To make effective changes, you have to build consensus, and to build consensus, you have to create a certain amount of discussion and dissension. The key is not to *avoid* discussion, but to manage it through effective communication. Employees should be told prior to an assessment what it is, why it is being carried out, what sort of outcomes they are likely to see, and when the results are likely to be disseminated. Such communication will go a long way not only toward building acceptance of and credibility around the assessment, but also toward establishing the trust needed to execute any needed changes that the assessment identifies.

Talking about the assessment prior to its implementation also provides some incentive for sharing the results once it is completed. As with the initial communication, the assessment and the results must be put in context of the organization's broader strategic intent and business goals. Both at the beginning and end of an assessment, open, proactive, clear communication is critical.

Selecting an Assessment Tool

Equally important to the success of the assessment is the selection of an appropriate assessment tool. A wide array of tools are available. Some are based on highly complex, well-researched methodologies. Others are relatively simple, informal tools that, although perhaps less accurate, can still provide valid results. Whatever tool you use, it should be

- *Framed in terminology that is universally understood by all participants.* It should not need to be "translated." We have found that the same language may carry a very different meaning for different audiences, even within the same organization.
- *Thoroughly tested so that its validity is ascertained before it is trotted out to the troops.* That way, the findings will be credible for both immediate and future purposes, by setting benchmarks for comparison. It is therefore wise to consider using a proven assessment tool rather than attempting to create your own.
- *Easy to administer and tally, with findings that are easily communicated to—and understood by—participants.* Remember, assessment is basically a consensus-building, gap-analyzing process. Its value does not necessarily rest in the complexity of the methodology, but in the accuracy and clarity of the results.

A Simple Tool: A Series of Questions   For the organization that has little time or budget or that wants to get a quick, albeit somewhat general, "cultural positioning report," the best approach may be simply to examine its key values. In their book *People, Performance, and Pay*, authors Tom Flannery, David Hofrichter, and Paul Platten list a series of basic questions that they believe address these values and provide a solid cultural snapshot of the organization.[8] These questions include

1. What is the overriding strategic intent of the organization?
2. How is the organization structured?
3. What are its values?
4. How is work organized?
5. How are decisions made?
6. How are resources allocated?
7. What behaviors are encouraged?
8. What behaviors are prohibited?
9. What kind of people work for the organization?
10. What are their values?
11. How do they think?
12. How do they act?
13. How much power do they have?
14. How much risk are they allowed?

15. How much risk do they want?
16. How are they selected?
17. How are they developed?
18. How are they rewarded? (Is pay viewed as an investment or a cost of doing business?)

While certainly not complex in its methodology or finely focused in the results it produces, this approach can work very well, especially among such small groups as executive teams. By answering questions about the current culture and comparing the answers to their conception of the ideal culture, executives can begin to build consensus around the cultural shift that must take place.

A Complex Approach: Targeted Culture Modeling   For the large health care organization that is doing an extensive assessment involving numerous participants or that wants more precise results, a more complex methodology may be valuable. One that has proven effective for a number of health care organizations is Targeted Culture Modeling. Using this methodology, cultural profiles are developed through the "ordering" of 56 attributes—that is, behaviors and activities that research has shown to define a culture.[9] (See chapter appendix.) Using a simple form and cards that are color coded to indicate current and target cultures, participants group the attributes into seven categories based on the extent to which they are rewarded, encouraged, and supported (ranging from "a great extent" to "a small extent"), which should follow a normal bell-shaped curve.

Once the participants—typically the executive team—define the current and desired culture, the results are analyzed and plotted on a graph to show which attributes need more emphasis, which should be de-emphasized, and which should remain the same. For example, the current culture of the organization in figure 2-3 is highly functional, has some process- and time-based elements, but has very little network orientation (see gray line). Its desired or target culture (represented by the solid line) de-emphasizes the traditional functional aspects. Instead, it is highly process and network oriented, and it requires an increased orientation toward speed.

The advantage of a more complex assessment of this nature is not only its accuracy, but also the speed and convenience with which it can be used. Rather than plodding through a list of open-ended questions—around which there is often debate because of ambiguity—participants can sort through a series of established responses validated through use in dozens of organizations across a wide variety of industries.

It is worth noting, however, that even a more finely focused and accurate assessment instrument like this cannot determine the right strategy or predict the best path to successful change. Like the simpler

FIGURE 2-3.   Graphing Results of Targeted Culture Modeling

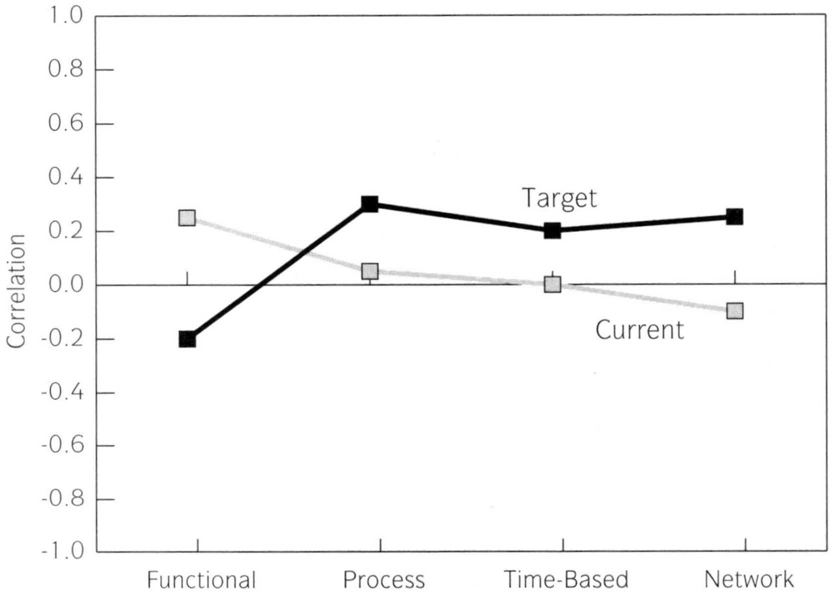

© HayGroup Healthcare. Used with permission.

process, it is primarily a tool for building consensus around current and desired cultures.

DESIGNING A CULTURAL SHIFT TO SPEED CHANGE

Once consensus has been created and your organization has determined the culture it needs to create to support its business strategy, it must begin making the necessary changes toward the desired new culture. Typically, a shift in cultures requires a shift in four areas: (1) values, (2) behaviors, (3) work processes, and (4) organizational structures. For example, the traditional health care organization moving toward integration (a shift in organizational structure) will probably need people—at all levels—who are not adverse to risk, who feel comfortable working in a team setting, and who are not afraid of learning new skills (a shift in values). It will require a new style of leadership that focuses on coaching and supporting rather than commanding and controlling (a shift in behaviors). And it will need new, more effective work processes that emphasize speed, flexibility, and the delivery of high-quality, cost-effective customer service (a shift in processes).

Such new behaviors, competencies, and processes do not just miraculously happen. They must be developed, nurtured, and rewarded. Indeed, effective cultural change is only one piece of an integrated change process that requires a variety of carefully aligned people and process interventions. (See figure 2-4.) For example, if a traditional, highly functional stand-alone hospital is moving toward becoming a fully integrated health system that calls for new emphasis on teamwork, speed, and the creation of networks or alliances, it will need to change not only work processes and roles, but also the behaviors needed in those new roles. Changes in behavior will, in turn, call for new selection, development, performance management, and reward strategies.

How important is this integrated approach to culture change? Based on our own work and research, we believe it is vital. Indeed, all those organizations that have changed most rapidly and then maintained gains over the long haul have embraced some form of integrated change.

Many are like the large, highly successful academic system we worked with that determined it had to become more flexible, efficient,

FIGURE 2-4.   An Integrated Approach to Change

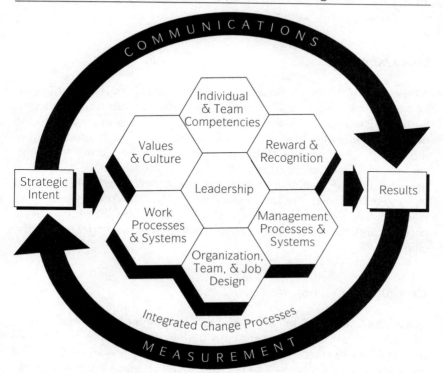

© HayGroup Healthcare. Used with permission.

and cost-effective if it was to maintain its long-held position of market leader. After an intense and thorough assessment, it quickly charged ahead, restructuring management, redesigning work, and creating new roles. At the same time, it developed a new human resources strategy, complete with new competency-based selection and compensation programs to reinforce the new behaviors and values that were needed. As one of its last steps in the integrated-change journey, the system also developed an organization-wide measurement model so that it could more accurately chart its progress.

INTEGRATING CULTURE IN THE CHANGE PROCESS: SIX KEY COMPONENTS

Just as there is a variety of culture models and assessment tools, there is a seemingly endless array of good integration strategies. Most, if not all of these, are built around the same basic elements: strong, flexible leaders; well-designed changes in organizational structure and work processes; effective training, measurement, and reward programs; and clear, open communication.

Leadership

As the title of this book suggests, leadership is one of the most important elements of successful change. Unless the organization's leaders— both the executive team and the managers—are in agreement as to the new direction and course, and unless they take collective ownership of the change process, the chances of successfully effecting long-term changes are marginal. As many of us have learned the hard way, effective leadership doesn't just happen. It must be developed, nurtured, and ultimately rewarded. For that reason, it is critical that the organization's leaders come to consensus on the change, accept responsibility for its success, and, when necessary, change their behavior in order to lead the change.

Organization, Team, and Job Design

Organizing and clarifying accountabilities throughout the organization also are critical to the success of any major change initiative. Certainly the right management structures—usually flatter, process-driven, and more team-oriented ones—are necessary. But redesign can't stop there. Structural changes typically are needed throughout the organization to support the new course and business strategies. What those changes are, of course, depends on the department or business unit and the specific focus and goals of each. Care delivery, for example, may be organized around cross-functional teams. At the same time, the human resources department may be transformed into a group of internal consultants who, instead of providing traditional, highly functional gatekeeping roles, now network with other departments and areas as needed, focusing on speed and internal customer service.

Work Processes and Systems

New structures alone can't support effective culture changes. As most health organizations have already discovered, processes have to be redesigned and new roles created. The reengineering boom of the past few years offers strong proof of this need. Unfortunately, much reengineering has been done in isolation rather than integrated with the other "levers" of change. As a result, much of it has either worked poorly or failed outright.

To be effective, the redesign of work processes must not only be preceded by a thorough assessment, but also be aligned with the other change initiatives and incorporate proven methodology. Current processes must be documented and analyzed, data and ideas must be collected for developing improvements, and new process models must be created and implemented.

Individual and Team Competence

New processes and roles almost always require new skills and competencies. For example, people frequently have to learn to work as individual specialists rather than as part of a cross-functional team. They frequently also have to accept more responsibility and take more risks. Beyond identifying these critical new competencies, organizations must also create new selection processes, new training and development programs, and new performance assessment processes that more accurately measure the progress of both individuals and teams.

Reward and Recognition Programs

The requisite new competencies and behaviors needed to support these changes will be slow in coming if they are not appropriately rewarded. Most health care organizations are discovering that they must also create new compensation programs that reinforce their new values and business strategies.

To that end, many are developing team reward strategies to support the efforts of work groups and teams, along with such variable, performance-based strategies as gain sharing. According to the 1996 Hay Hospital Survey, 59 percent of the health care organizations going though major change initiatives reported they were using or considering some form of individual incentives tied to performance to help support those changes. Nearly one-third reported using team or group incentives.[10]

Measurement of Progress

Another important element that should be integrated into any major change initiative is a measurement tool. Because of the massive changes taking place and the increased emphasis on performance, a growing number of organizations are reevaluating their results in terms of *what* is measured and *how* it is measured. Many are creating specific measurement models not only to better measure performance, but also to more accurately determine the progress and success of the changes they are making. These change measurement models are helpful in several ways: they force organizations to decide what's really important, help the organizations to communicate those priorities, and ultimately help to define the organization's critical success factors.

Measurement, like other elements of change, is not a one-time event. Performance—and progress—must be measured on a regular, ongoing basis.

Communication

Communication frequently determines whether a change initiative will succeed or fail. Unfortunately, this critical component is often overlooked in the rush to remake processes, structures, and strategies. Most organizations spend very little time or energy on the process. Preoccupied with the scope and complexity of the changes they are undertaking and the speed with which they must be addressed, they frequently wait until the last minute to begin communicating and then fall back on traditional, often reactive methods.

It is a common and understandable approach, but one that no longer works, given the uncertainty, ambiguity, and sometimes cynicism that permeate many health care organizations these days. To support effective change initiatives in such an environment, communication must be viewed as an ongoing process—not a product—that begins as the other change initiatives begin and is fully aligned and integrated with the organization's culture, work processes, and strategic intent.

As James Champy and Michael Hammer write in *Reengineering the Corporation*, "getting people to accept the idea that their work lives—their jobs—will undergo radical change is not a war won in a single battle. It is an educational and communications campaign that runs from reengineering's start to its finish."[11]

PUTTING ASSESSMENT THEORY INTO PRACTICE: TWO CASE EXAMPLES

Of course, the true test of a theory is how well it works in the real world. To that end, we offer two case examples that illustrate the major concepts described in this chapter. As you will see, the health care organizations in these two cases are very different as far as size, scope, and strategic intent. Yet, as you will also see, all found cultural assessment to be a foundation on which to build for the future.

Case 1: Clash of the Titans

It is a scenario that is being replayed with greater and greater frequency in the health care industry these days: the merger of two large, geographically diverse systems. Each was highly successful in its own right and could have continued to prosper on its own. But both organizations recognized that by coming together, they could cover a much larger area and grow much more rapidly.

Despite many similarities, the two organizations had radically different cultures. One was a highly flexible, fast-moving organization that valued the entrepreneurial spirit. It was an organization of risk takers, of forward-looking leaders who were continually seeking new ventures. The organization's culture could be described as time-based/network, in that it was continually seeking new market opportunities. The organization had its share of successes, and its leaders viewed themselves as having an almost aristocratic flair, despite the obvious downside—when they lost, they lost big.

The other half of the merger was much more of a "blocking and tackling" type of organization. It was conservative, functional, risk adverse, and control oriented. Its tendency was to process every decision to death.

The new organization's executive team had conducted extensive discussions about what their business strategy should look like. While members agreed in principle, they could not achieve consensus on specifics. Indeed, they had some lofty and rather esoteric discussions about their philosophy and culture. They agreed, for example, that they should organize regionally and focus the regions on their local markets. But they could not agree on how to carry out that strategy. Some wanted to create new service lines, while others clung to the old functional departments. The factions involved made consensus even more difficult. In addition to the opposing executive camps, physician leaders from both organizations saw the merger from yet a third perspective and believed that any change should come slowly, in small, incremental steps.

To overcome this impasse and get the leaders to agree on the tangible attributes underpinning their strategy, a cultural assessment was done, using the Targeted Culture Modeling tool. The results can be seen in figure 2-5.

The leaders saw the organization's current culture as highly functional, with little focus on processes, speed, or networking (gray line). But they saw an ideal culture as one that downplayed the functional aspect and focused instead on processes and networking, with a strong element of speed (solid line). Using the assessment results, the group began to build much-needed consensus around the future direction. It also began to understand that the new organization would be embedded with a variety of cultures—and that the variety was actually a good thing. Delivery of care, for example, probably needed to be much more process focused, while the corporate structure needed to emphasize

FIGURE 2-5.   An Increased Emphasis on Process

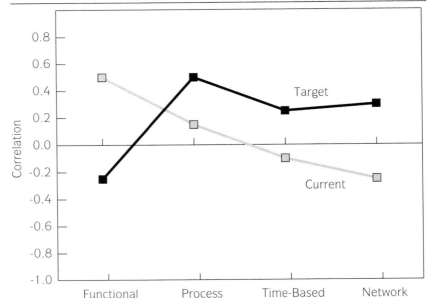

© HayGroup Healthcare. Used with permission.

speed and networking, with the ability to move quickly to build new alliances and innovative business ventures.

The leadership also determined that while each hospital in the system should maintain its own unique identity and remain closely tied to the community in which it was located, there were broader cultural issues—trust, for example, and risk taking—that had to be addressed organization wide.

The assessment led to more discussion, this time about those tangible attributes that were so critical to the merger's success. Rather than continuing to focus on "big picture" concepts, the group began looking at specific things that they needed to value and reward in the organization. They determined that they might need a new structure as well as new work processes if they really planned to change. And they came to the conclusion that the merged organization would need people with very different sets of competencies. Thus, new selection and reward strategies were established, which sent an important signal throughout the organization.

Within a few weeks, the "circling of the wagons" that had slowed progress of the merger was over. The executive team had nailed down many of the details that had eluded it and had begun to move forward.

While cultural assessment was an excellent intervention, the assessment should have been done sooner. Rather than waiting until after the merger, when the new system was being put into operation, the executive team should have implemented the assessment earlier, during the premerger due-diligence phase. Doing so would have provided much-needed focus earlier in the process.

Case 2: Staying ahead of the Curve

When it comes to changes in the health care industry, you can run, but you can't hide. Such was the case of a large, highly successful tertiary care hospital located in a somewhat isolated, primarily rural market. Although it could see, hear, and smell the industry chaos that swirled around it, this organization was largely untouched.

The CEO, a forward-looking executive, knew that such a seemingly carefree time was quickly coming to an end. At any moment, new competitors, sensing a lucrative market, might charge in. Sooner or later, something had to give. And if the hospital wanted to remain the leading player, then it had to proactively shift its strategy and transform itself into a fully integrated, outwardly focused regional health system.

The hospital's executive team understood, at least intellectually, that the hospital's business strategy had to shift. But the executives had a hard time translating these "pie-in-the-sky" concepts into reality. They didn't understand how and why that shift would affect their organizational culture. They were, after all, successful. So why should they have to change their values, work processes, or the way they measured and rewarded performance?

Although they had created a 40-plus-page strategic plan, they had no idea how to implement it. And with each executive interpreting the strategy in terms of his or her own "silo," there was certainly no consensus.

Not surprising, an assessment (again, the Targeted Culture Modeling was used with the CEO and executive team) revealed a current culture that was entrenched and highly functional (much like the organization in the first example) with little emphasis on processes, speed, and networking. (See figure 2-6.) Roles and processes were highly specialized and very individual: everyone was an expert in his or her own area. To successfully implement the new strategy, the team agreed, the organization had to create a culture that put much less emphasis on function and that was much more time based and network oriented, with some emphasis on process. Given that consensus on the broad vision and direction, the executive team finally began looking at how to begin putting it into practice.

The assessment created the momentum that had been desperately needed to begin moving the organization forward. It was the critical trigger that not only crystallized the vision, but also mobilized the leaders to work as a team to achieve the new business strategy.

CONCLUSION

Despite all the talk, research, and writing that has been focused on culture, it remains, for many organizations, an ambiguous, fuzzy concept. The concept of culture is frequently misunderstood and on occasion maligned, even though it is critical to the success of any organization, especially those in industries such as health care, which are experiencing substantial change.

The fact is, a thorough assessment of your culture can be an effective step in moving your organization forward if you follow a few basic guidelines: first, choose a common definition; second, pick a tool that is right for your organization; and, finally—perhaps most important—make the assessment an initial and integral part of the overall change process.

Naturally, cultural change doesn't end there. In fact, it never ends. As long as the health care industry continues to evolve, so, too, must health care organizations. To stay ahead of that evolutionary curve, they must continually measure their progress, reassess their cultures, and adapt as necessary.

FIGURE 2-6.   Moving from a Functional Culture to a Time-Based and Network Culture

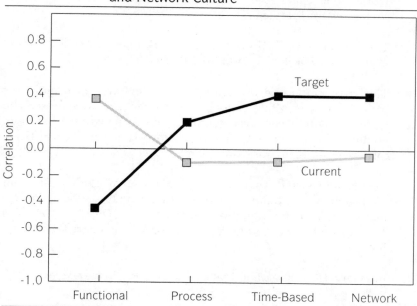

© HayGroup Healthcare. Used with permission.

In his book *Jamming: The Art and Discipline of Business Creativity*, author John Kao talks about the need to orchestrate the change process. "Change," he writes, "is the sum of a thousand acts of reperception and behavior change at every level of the organization. The leader must conduct the process as if he or she were Duke Ellington leading a large jazz orchestra."[12]

He's right, of course. But conducting an orchestra or changing an organization can be a disastrous process unless you know the score— unless you have a sense of where you're going. That is why a thorough culture assessment is critical to any successful change initiative.

References and Notes

1. John P. Kotter and James L. Heskett, *Corporate Culture and Performance* (New York: Free Press, 1992), p. 11.

2. Ibid., p. 4.

3. Edgar H. Schein, *Organizational Culture and Leadership* (San Francisco: Jossey-Bass, 1992), p. 12.

4. B. Ettorre, "A Conversation with Charles Handy on the Future of Work and an End to the 'Century of the Organization,'" *Organizational Dynamics* (summer 1996): 15

5. T. P. Flannery, D. A. Hofrichter, and P. E. Platten, *People, Performance, and Pay* (New York: Free Press, 1996), p. 24.

6. This description and evolution of work cultures in health care organizations was first reported in "Organizational Culture: The Critical Link between Strategy and Results," a paper by the authors commissioned for the April 1996 MDRC/AHSR conference: Leading Organizational Transformation.

7. "Are Employees 'Buying In'?: How American Workers Feel about Management's Attempts to Strengthen Quality, Boost Performance, and Foster Employee Involvement," *The 1995–96 Hay Employee Attitudes Study*, Research for Management, Hay Group, Inc.

8. Flannery, Hofrichter, and Platten, *People, Performance, and Pay*, p. 26.

9. The Targeted Culture Modeling process was developed by Hay's Research for Management group and has been used successfully with a variety of clients.

10. R. H. Sachs and S. W. Spreier, "Reward Ceremonies," *Hospitals and Health Networks* 70, no. 17 (Sept. 5, 1996): 27.

11. M. Hammer and J. Champy, *Reengineering the Corporation* (New York: Harper Business, 1993), p. 148.

12. J. Kao, *Jamming: The Art and Discipline of Business Creativity* (New York: Harper Business, 1996), 194.

Bibliography

Cartwright, Sue, and Cary L. Cooper. *Managing Mergers, Acquisitions, & Strategic Alliances: Integrating People and Cultures*, 2d ed. Newton, Mass.: Butterworth-Heinemann, 1996.

Collins James, and Jerry I. Porras. "Building Your Company's Vision." *Harvard Business Review* 74, no. 5 (September-October 1996): 65.

Kaplan, Robert S., and David P. Norton. *The Balanced Scorecard.* Cambridge, Mass.: Harvard Business Press, 1996.

Larkin, T. J., and Sandar Larkin. "Reaching and Changing Frontline Employees." *Harvard Business Review* 74, no. 3 (May–June 1996): 95.

Weiss, Tracey B., and Franklin Hartle. *Reengineering Performance Management: Breakthroughs in Achieving Strategy through People.* Boca Raton, Fla.: St. Lucie, 1997.

APPENDIX: FIFTY-SIX CULTURE ATTRIBUTES OF TARGETED CULTURE MODELING

1. Encouraging teamwork
2. Supporting the decisions of one's boss
3. Providing secure employment
4. Maximizing customer satisfaction
5. Experimenting with new management techniques
6. Demonstrating understanding of the customer's point of view
7. Being highly organized
8. Using proven methods to serve existing markets
9. Significantly decreasing cycle times
10. Providing employees with resources to satisfy customers
11. Maintaining existing customer accounts
12. Establishing new ventures or new lines of business
13. Delivering reliably on commitments to customers
14. Being flexible and adaptive in thinking and approach
15. Using limited resources effectively
16. Selling successfully
17. Promoting one's point of view strongly
18. Maintaining clear lines of authority and accountability
19. Establishing clear, well-documented work processes
20. Continuously improving operations
21. Attracting top talent
22. Treating employees fairly and consistently
23. Rewarding superior performance
24. Pioneering new ways of doing things
25. Maintaining a high sense of urgency
26. Establishing clear job descriptions and requirements
27. Capitalizing on windows of opportunity
28. Applying innovative technology to new situations
29. Tolerating well-meaning mistakes
30. Responding to customer feedback

31. Participating in training and continuing education
32. Limiting the downside of risks
33. Using resources outside the company to get things done
34. Capitalizing on creativity and innovation
35. Anticipating changes in the business environment
36. Taking initiative
37. Respecting the chain of command
38. Organizing jobs around the capabilities of individuals
39. Increasing decision-making speed
40. Encouraging innovation
41. Building strategic alliances with other organizations
42. Adapting quickly to changes in the business environment
43. Taking action despite uncertainty
44. Quality checking employees' work
45. Minimizing unpredictability of business results
46. Gaining the confidence of customers
47. Encouraging expression of diverse viewpoints
48. Being precise
49. Acquiring cross-functional knowledge and skills
50. Supporting top management decisions
51. Pushing decision making to the lowest levels
52. Minimizing human error
53. Finding novel ways to capitalize on employees' skills
54. Developing new products or services
55. Being loyal and committed to the company
56. Achieving budgeted objectives

3

Creating a Road Map to Lead People through Change

Edward J. O'Connor, Ph.D.

C. Marlena Fiol, Ph.D.

For many health care organizations, change has become a way of life. Care providers, administrators, and staff are bleary-eyed from responding to such external forces as payers and competitors; from redefining strategic goals and implementing organizational initiatives; and from redesigning structures, systems, processes, and operations. In the midst of such organizational upheaval, many managers neglect the human side of change. This neglect can be costly. Failure to build shared commitment to the success of an initiative often triggers a cycle of failure—lack of commitment leading to lack of teamwork, missed objectives, finger-pointing, and, ultimately, more change, as the organization strives to "get it right this time."

How can you, as a leader, manage the human side of change? Helping people "get from here to there" is difficult when your map is inadequate or outdated. The knowledge and experience that served you well under stable conditions are unlikely to help you reach your destination during turbulent times like these. You need a fresh, systematic approach—a road map, if you will—for the journeys that your organization is undertaking. (See figure 3-1.) In mapping out change, three major components of change management should be addressed:

1. *Energizers—motivators that compel people to take action.* Planes, trains, and ships at rest stay at rest unless a source of energy is provided to impel forward motion. The same is true of organizations.
2. *Barriers—impediments to change.* Just as water resistance increases as ships begin to move forward, so individual and organizational resistance become more evident as you begin to move toward your objectives.

FIGURE 3-1.   Road Map for Change

Energizers

Where   Where are you now and where do you intend to be?
             Define ultimately and incrementally what outcomes
             the initiative is intended to produce. What is the
             target you are aiming at? Do the people who must
             change have a common understanding of these
             pictures?

Why   Create the need, desire, and willingness to travel
             from the status quo toward the desired future state.
             How much do you want/need this? How can you
             reduce the risks? Will this change really make a
             difference?

Barriers

Who   Identify the resisters and potential leaders of this
             transition. What are the sources of concern and
             resistance? How can they best be understood and
             managed? Who will lead this change process, and do
             they have the required time, resources, and skills to
             achieve intended outcomes?

What   Understand the scope of the journey. What are the
             systems, styles of behavior, and structures that must
             change to support the new outcomes?

Action Steps

When   Determine the right timing and rate of change. Do
             available resources meet change requirements?
             When will you be ready to move forward and by
             when must you arrive if this venture is to be
             successful?

How   Determine the strategies and tactics needed for
             moving forward toward your objectives. What is the
             initial implementation plan? How will you translate it
             into concrete action steps? How will you obtain
             feedback and make adjustments to the plan to
             achieve success?

3. *Action steps—techniques for managing change.* As currents press against a moving ship, steering adjustments may be necessary to maintain course. Likewise, as organizational barriers become evident, periodic adjustments may be needed to meet objectives.

The value of this map is that it gives you a systematic approach to managing change. Under pressure, many managers make the mistake of focusing on barriers before energizers have been addressed. Using this map as a guide encourages you to "begin at the beginning" with energizers, thereby motivating people to move forward. Once movement has begun, barriers will become self-evident. At that point, appropriate action steps will also become more apparent and support for them more likely to emerge.

ENERGIZERS: THE "WHERES" AND "WHYS" OF CHANGE

There is little motivation for people to embark on a journey if they do not understand where they are going. For people to engage in a collaborative effort to produce successful change, they must see a worthwhile future to work toward. Help people envision a better future, and you make it easier for them to leave the past behind and to risk venturing into unfamiliar territory.

Equally important is a sense of why the journey will be worth the risk. What benefits will the change bring? What costs or other consequences will the organization suffer if it fails to go? Answers to questions like these provide people with a sense of purpose. People see where they fit in the larger picture—and how their own dreams and aspirations can be realized through change.

Beyond providing a shared perspective, a common understanding of where and why you are going focuses and coordinates people's energies. Communication is enhanced, innovation and creativity increased, and conflict and absenteeism reduced. Although moving beyond the status quo always creates some degree of disruption and dissent, clarity about where you as a group are going—and why the destination will be worth the trip—gives people good reason to change.

Objectives as Energizers

While a sense of direction and purpose helps people envision a better future, it takes specific, measurable objectives to make the vision a reality. Outside of work, people's imaginations and enthusiasm are captured by games in which outcomes are measured and teams compete to see who is the best. Surely few people would attend sporting events if there were no way to keep score. Similarly, at work, people need incremental and end objectives to measure their progress. Objectives provide focus, generate healthy competition and enthusiasm, and give people a means by which to obtain feedback about what is and is not working.

All people are not energized by the same objectives. What motivates one group to commit to change may not motivate another. For example, some people are motivated by the pursuit of improved clinical outcomes, such as a reduced medication error rate or reduction in unscheduled readmissions. Others are energized by the prospect of improved technical outcomes or efficiencies, such as fewer late starts in the operating room or a reduction in the length of the average emergency department visit from three hours to two. Still others may be moved to action by the prospect of enhanced human conditions, such as improved patient satisfaction, better communication among staff, or increased physician commitment to team objectives. For yet others, the prospect of improved financial outcomes, such as reduced costs or a more positive cash flow, is an effective stimulus to change.

Consider the example of a large acute care facility that planned to implement a new decision-support system. Senior management was quite enthusiastic about the system, viewing it as a way to standardize practices, streamline decision making, and thereby cut costs. Physicians, on the other hand, perceived the system quite differently. To them, it was an attempt to dictate clinical practices and undermine their autonomy. Physicians resisted the innovation until it became evident that the system would provide better information on risk factors, clinical treatments, and outcomes for each of a set of diagnostic categories. At this point, resistance gave way to support. Senior management proceeded to create widespread buy-in by pointing out other desirable outcomes that the system would provide—outcomes that appealed to groups other than physicians. For example, the managers pointed out that the system was likely to result in fewer treatment errors and unscheduled readmissions. They also noted that as severity of disease and length of stays were reduced, patient and employee satisfaction would grow. And they explained how the system could result in reduced treatment costs, improved access to health care, and more efficient utilization of resources. By providing a variety of desirable outcomes that appealed to different groups, leaders built shared commitment from individuals quite different in their orientations.

Two important principles can be drawn from the preceding example. First, engaging the committed support of dissimilar groups is critical to the success of your change initiative. Second, by defining changes in terms of their impact on diverse outcomes, you can build commitment from those whose support you need. Figure 3-2 lists a variety of outcomes that appeal to different groups. With some tailoring, these outcomes could be made to apply to virtually any initiative implemented in a health care organization.

Benefits as Energizers

Another powerful energizer is personal gain. When people see how change can benefit them—how it can help them realize their own dreams and aspirations—they develop a personal stake in the initiative's success and work harder to achieve it. As you have seen, one way to help people envision benefits is to point out a variety of desirable outcomes that might be realized. Another way is to ask people themselves to envision the personal benefits that they might realize from change. For example, you might ask:

- If you successfully complete this change, what will the benefits be?
- What will this achieve that you really want?
- What will you then be able to do that is really important?
- What will this get you that you really value?

FIGURE 3-2.   Change Outcomes

Clinical Outcomes

- Decreased mortality
- Reduced infection rates
- Fewer treatment errors
- Fewer unscheduled readmissions
- Improved patient outcomes

Financial Outcomes

- Reduced costs
- Improved cash flow
- Increased output
- Greater sales
- Enhanced market share
- Increased profitability
- Greater return on investment
- Reduced lawsuits

Human Outcomes

- Improved patient satisfaction
- Increased patient retention
- Improved employee satisfaction
- Enhanced communication
- Increased cooperation
- Increased motivation/commitment
- Expanded empowerment
- Improved growth and development
- Reduced absenteeism/turnover
- Improved safety
- Improved skills/performance
- Expanded community contribution

Technical Outcomes

- Improved efficiency/productivity
- Enhanced quality
- Increased capacity
- Improved continuity of care
- Increased innovation
- Improved management skills

Questions like these go beyond mere clarification of overall goals. Rather, they give people a new perspective, encouraging them to see change as an opportunity for personal gain.

Consider the case of a proposed merger between two group practices. Physicians could view this move as an attempt to control each group's practice patterns. However, by answering the questions above, they might gain a very different perspective of the merger. For example, they might see that a successful merger could enhance the group's ability to get and keep managed care contracts by providing a larger, more diverse group of physicians willing to assume risk. Maintaining more contracts might stabilize the group practice as a long-term, financially viable entity. This, in turn, might enhance the organization's ability to partner with other organizations, which would position the group to be the leading practice in its region. Ultimately, being the leader would give the physicians greater control over their own destinies—the very thing that the physicians feared losing. By envisioning benefits, the physicians might come to interpret the merger as a way to gain something they value.

Negative Consequences as Energizers

In some cases, desirable outcomes and personal gain may be insufficient to effect the buy-in you need. People may also need to anticipate pain—even experience pain itself—in order to let go of the past and move forward. Consider the behavior of people in a burning building: they do not hesitate to take action; they immediately search for a way out. Similarly, people in an organization can be motivated to take action when they see that failure to do so will harm the group in some tangible way. Crisis, dissatisfaction, tension, and stress energize people to search for improved conditions.

This is not to suggest that you should threaten people with dire consequences. Threats are likely to backfire, causing people to view *you* as the source of pain and to therefore reject what you have to say. Instead, provide your people with the information they need to recognize the consequences of inaction for themselves. Environmental data, information about competitors, data from other departments—any information that shows how current conditions are becoming untenable—can be powerful motivators.

Consider the case of a hospital administrator who realized the importance of encouraging changes in the practice patterns of a powerful and prestigious group of surgeons. He believed that these changes would both improve quality indicators and reduce costs. After all, other surgeons had tested the new approaches and were satisfied with the results. He first made what he considered persuasive arguments directly to those whose behavior departed from the newly developing norms. When that failed he encouraged other leaders who shared his views to try to convince their peers to alter their behavior. Little success was achieved until systematic data were collected linking practice patterns with clinical outcomes and costs. Shortly after these data were made publicly available, with each surgeon identified only by an anonymous personal code, practice patterns began to shift in the desired direction. Few of us think of ourselves as being in the lower half of our peer group in terms of professional competence. When confronted with legitimate and irrefutable data suggesting that their performance is below expectations, competent professionals will often feel sufficient discomfort to change their behavior.

Despite your best efforts, it is likely that you will still hear statements such as "We'll never pull this off, and even if we do, it won't make any difference." To continue to make progress, you must address common concerns like these. Left unaddressed, even minor concerns can grow to become major barriers on the road to change.

BARRIERS: THE "WHOS" AND "WHATS" THAT IMPEDE PROGRESS

The most common barrier to change is human resistance. And make no mistake about it—there will be resistance. In times of change, you may be confronted with such overt shows of resistance as public or private statements of opposition and demands that certain issues be immediately addressed. Also present may be covert resistance, manifested in such unproductive emotional responses as stubbornness, apathy, and anxiety, or such unproductive behaviors as increases in errors, accidents, absenteeism, and turnover. When it comes to managing resistance, you have many options. The one option that you do not have during change is to have no resistance. Confronting resistance is not easy. It requires you to listen to that which is unpleasant. However, the consequences of not listening—increasing frustration, isolation, anger, failure—are even more unpleasant.

During change, people are inevitably filled with questions and concerns. Encourage people to ask the tough questions and to voice their honest concerns. Take them for what they are: natural human responses indicating that you have people's attention. Once you have that attention, use it to identify the sources of resistance so that you can address them. Individuals, organizational structures, even your leadership style itself may act as barriers on the road to change.

Individuals as Barriers to Change

While some people are likely to view an initiative as an opportunity for much-needed improvements, others are likely to view the same initiative as a nuisance, an unnecessary disruption in systems and processes, or worse. People interpret the events that they experience—including change—differently. The meaning that they assign to a given event is shaped by a variety of factors: needs, interests, values, experiences, areas of expertise, and others. Together, these factors form frames of reference, or "mental maps," that provide

- A model for assessing progress toward our goals; for example, "We got a lot done at the medical staff meeting," or "We still have much to do."
- A perspective for assessing value; for example, "How much does an expensive ambulatory center cost?"
- A framework for making judgments; for example, basing decisions on principles of science rather than on principles of religion.

Because mental maps are developed over long periods of time and are based on very fundamental beliefs, they are resistant to change. Consider that when Johannes Kepler correctly solved the orbital problem of the planets by using ellipses rather than circles, he was denounced. A similar fate met Galileo when he demonstrated that the sun does not revolve around the Earth. It is a fact of human nature that people reject ideas that conflict with their view of the world.

To manage resistance, you must seek to understand why an initiative clashes with resisters' views of "the ways things should be." This requires that you attempt to view the initiative through their eyes, understanding their frames of reference, using their mental maps. Both the purpose of change and the process of changing can evoke confusion, uncertainty, and resistance. Certain conditions can increase the intensity of these responses. Some of the most common conditions that "set people off" are presented in figure 3-3. Recognizing, acknowledging, and minimizing these sources of resistance help smooth the path to change.

Altering the Initiative to Overcome Resistance   In addition to minimizing common sources of resistance, you might consider altering some aspect of the initiative to meet your people's needs. Do not make the mistake of believing that your conception of a change is the only "right" one. In other words, do not confuse your mental picture of change with the reality of the change itself. If it is widely felt that an initiative needs to be altered, consider adjusting it. For example, if your staff feel that change is occurring too quickly, consider adjusting the time frame in which the initiative is to be implemented. Or if change requires new skills or competencies that your staff feel they do not have, consider providing special training. You might also omit elements of a change that are not required in the short run if your staff find them objectionable, or you might refine the change by collecting pilot data.

FIGURE 3-3. Sources of Resistance

Where Are You Going?

- Lack of understanding
- Unclear expectations
- Too many risks
- Confusion and uncertainty

Why Are You Going There?

- Comfort with the present
- Lack of incentives
- No faith that it will matter
- Appropriate caution

Disruption of Lives

- Habits interrupted
- Self-confidence/competence threatened
- Fear of failure
- Implied poor past performance
- Relationships disturbed

Leadership Commitment/ Credibility Questioned

- Inconsistent behaviors
- Unsuccessful past initiatives
- Unresolved past grievances

What Is It That Must Change?

- Lost jobs, power, status, and money
- Inconsistent with values and identity
- Lost satisfaction

When Will This Change Occur?

- Current overloads
- Lack of readiness
- High stress

How Will This Change Be Implemented?

- Lack of involvement
- Loss of control
- Irreversibility
- Lack of resources and time

Any alteration that will align the initiative more closely with your people's conception of what it should be can help dispel resistance.

Tailoring the Presentation to Meet People's Needs As an alternative, you might alter the manner in which you present a proposed change, tailoring your presentation to meet the needs of a particular audience. Rather than presenting the same change benefits for all audiences, effective leaders often emphasize those consequences that are most likely to be important to the individual or group with whom they are speaking. For example, when addressing a health care organization's chief financial officer, you may be wise to focus on the positive financial implications of a proposed quality initiative. On the other hand, when addressing the medical staff, you might build your presentation around the clinical improvements that will result from altering laboratory processes. Adjustments like these can do much to elicit support from those who resist your change effort.

Identifying and Supporting Change Leaders   As an additional step, you might seek the support of those who have the potential to be change leaders. For example, successful professionals typically believe that they have something to contribute and should be listened to. Excluding them from the change process often results in increased resistance, longer transitions, and uncertain outcomes. Enlist the aid of those whom others view as natural leaders, and you increase your chances of successfully implementing change. Where natural leaders go, many others may follow.

Natural leaders, those who are most credible to the people who must change their behavior in order to ensure success, may not have the time, resources, or skills required to assume the needed leadership roles. Successfully enlisting their support may require making those resources available.

Consider, for example, the case of a primary care group practice–hospital alliance. The senior administrator of the practice realized that the alliance needed an integrated information system that would provide user-friendly access to both inpatient and ambulatory clinical data. While he might have investigated alternative systems, negotiated a potential contract, and tried to sell his choice to the physicians, he recognized that physician leadership throughout the project would improve the likelihood of building the strong support needed to ensure acceptance and success. In order to free the physician time required for developing technical skills, investigating needs and alternatives, gathering feedback, and finalizing decisions, physicians were compensated for the hours they devoted to this project. Their leadership and support did much to legitimize the need for the new information system as well as to smooth its successful implementation within the alliance.

Leadership Style as a Barrier to Change

Another barrier to change is one that many leaders overlook—their management style itself. In today's team-based environment, a dictatorial, top-down management style is likely to heighten, rather than reduce, resistance. To foster shared commitment and teamwork, managers must be team players themselves. This requires that they exhibit effective team-building behaviors.

Analyzing Effective Leadership Behaviors   In times of change, certain leadership behaviors can help unite people to work together in a common cause. These behaviors include

- *Seeking to relate:* Establish rapport with people by involving them in the change process, sharing information, acknowledging responsibility for contributions to problems, and looking for ways to meet people's needs.

- *Clarifying purpose and direction:* Present change in terms of its impact on people, creating clear expectations and using data to initiate, drive, and refocus the change.
- *Being understanding:* Continually seek to understand other people's views by being a good listener and minimizing disruptions caused by change.
- *Providing focus:* Clarify common desires and objectives, focusing on future solutions rather than past misunderstandings, keeping people informed about progress and challenges, and demonstrating commitment with action.

These behaviors not only build teamwork but also smooth the path to change. By striking a balance between the needs of the organization and the needs of individuals, leaders can do much to defuse the confusion, anxiety, and anger often elicited by change.

Evaluating and Changing Your Management Style   How closely does your management style mesh with the team-building behaviors just described? To uncover behaviors that may be impeding progress, try to see yourself as your staff see you. Identify an individual or group that is currently resisting your leadership. If they were describing your leadership style using criteria such as those presented in figure 3-4, which of these behaviors would they say are currently missing? Which of these would they see as justification for their resistance? (Remember to look from their perspective, not yours.) Would they indicate that your rapport with them is weak, that you haven't involved them in the change process, that you tend to blame them rather than acknowledge responsibility for your contribution to the problems, or that you rarely seek to understand their views?

To get a more complete picture of the resistance you face, repeat the above process for each additional individual or group that is currently resisting your leadership, or ask the group to complete the questionnaire. Then review each of the items on which ratings were low. For example, if your ratings were low on "involving change recipients in the process," identify the current behaviors (or lack thereof) that people would use to confirm their belief that they are not being involved. What behaviors will you have to change to alter this perception? When, specifically, could you exhibit these new behaviors? How frequently and under what circumstances would you exhibit these new behaviors if it was more important to you to minimize resistance than to defend your perspective of an initiative as the "right" one?

As you begin to think about new behaviors that you might exhibit or old ones you might give up, notice whether you are beginning to defend your position and view the other person or group as wrong. Remember that from their perspective, their interpretations make perfect sense. To build the rapport, trust, and communication necessary to gain feedback and minimize resistance, you must respect and work within their frames of reference.

It will take time for people to recognize any shifts you make in your behavior. While inevitably some people may not come along, it is impor-

FIGURE 3-4.   Analyzing Your Leadership Style: How Do People See You?

Relating by . . .	*Rarely*				*Always*
Establishing rapport?	1	2	3	4	5
Involving change recipients in the process?	1	2	3	4	5
Being vulnerable; sharing information?	1	2	3	4	5
Acknowledging responsibility for contribution to problems?	1	2	3	4	5
Looking for ways to meet their needs?	1	2	3	4	5
Clarifying by . . .					
Presenting the change in terms of its impact on them?	1	2	3	4	5
Creating clear expectations?	1	2	3	4	5
Using data to initiate, drive, and refocus the change?	1	2	3	4	5
Clarifying areas of current discretion?	1	2	3	4	5
Understanding by . . .					
Seeking to understand their views (over and over)?	1	2	3	4	5
Not asking them "Why?"	1	2	3	4	5
Listening! Listening! Listening! Listening?	1	2	3	4	5
Minimizing the disruptions in their lives?	1	2	3	4	5
Recognizing that some people are not coming along?	1	2	3	4	5
Focusing by . . .					
Clarifying common desires/objectives?	1	2	3	4	5
Focusing on future solutions, not prior misunderstandings?	1	2	3	4	5
Keeping them informed about progress and challenges?	1	2	3	4	5
Demonstrating your commitment with action?	1	2	3	4	5

tant to give them the opportunity to communicate, contribute, and participate in your change initiatives. Those who continue to resist (and who may be left behind) will have made their choice of this course of action clear to all. As a result, your relationship with those who remain and support the initiative will be both stronger and deeper, leaving you in a better position to effectively manage future changes.

Systems, Structures, and Cultures as Barriers to Change

Further barriers to change flow from organizational systems, structures, and cultures. If these elements of an organization are not aligned with the goals of an initiative—a likely prospect, since they are slow to change—progress will be limited. For example, if the information system in your organization is inadequate for providing the clinical and financial data needed to unify an integrated delivery system, few efficiencies will occur as a result of a merger. Or if your organization rewards people for "keeping their mouths shut and just doing their jobs," the organizational culture is likely to make people risk aversive behavior and increase their resistance to change. This reaction will be even stronger if the organization's hierarchical structure requires multiple levels of sign-offs on most new projects. The behaviors that leaders model, measure, and reward are the ones that will continue to occur.

Aligning the Organization and the Initiative   Figure 3-5 presents examples of systems, structures, and aspects of culture that must be aligned with an initiative in order for it to be successfully implemented. Do they point in directions congruent with changes you currently are attempting to implement in your organization? To the degree that they do not, a significant opportunity exists. For example, does the hospital's patient transportation system provide the resources needed to support your new customer-focused patient satisfaction initiative? If not, what actions are required to demonstrate your commitment to this initiative? Once you identify systemic, structural, and cultural barriers that block change, you know where to focus your attention in order to move forward. By removing these barriers, progress will naturally occur.

These barriers are equally applicable to the myriad problems that arise during mergers. The task of combining divergent cultures and management styles, systems, and structures into an effective partnership can be daunting. At the individual level, people often struggle with uncertainties regarding where they are going and why they are going there. Significant disruption to lives—for example, layoffs due to downsizing, new promotion criteria, or moves to new locations—and disagreements regarding what must change, when this will occur, and how to bring about these results can produce ever-increasing levels of stress.

FIGURE 3-5.   Systems, Structures, and Culture

Focusing

- Budgeting
- Feedback
- Goal Setting/Planning
- Performance Measurement/Appraisal
- Reward/Compensation

Preparing

- Continuous Improvement
- Maintenance
- Policy/Procedure
- Problem Solving
- Selection/Retention
- Training/Development/ Advancement
- Work Layout/Technology

Relating

- Conflict Resolution
- Communication
- Customer/Vendor Relation
- Information

Operating

- Billing/Payment
- Decision Making
- Documentation
- Leadership/Coordination
- Purchasing
- Transportation

The grief involved in loss, compounded with anger, stubbornness, and apathy as forms of self-protection, makes answering critical questions regarding the future difficult.

Building Systems and Support   People's perceptions of a merger determine their emotional response and the energy they are willing to invest. A leader's responsibility includes articulating the positive opportunities available to people if they embrace change as well as the consequences of nonsupport. By providing information that allows people to make informed, intelligent choices, you give them support in moving forward.

In addition, make every effort to gather accurate information about people's perceptions of the change so that you can address them. Provide opportunities for people to give you their honest feedback, such as anonymous surveys, meetings, and electronic mail. Elicit suggestions for improvement and, when appropriate, implement them.

While the flow of information will nourish people, minimize resistance, and generate support, your organization's systems, styles, and structures will also need to be altered in order to reach objectives. For example, creating a regional board or CEO (to replace the separate boards and CEOs) will provide a structural realignment necessary to support the success of the integration effort. Beyond uniting diverse factions, it may also provide a symbolic demonstration of the "new reality." Attacking many problems at once (cutting costs, improving operating room scheduling, building a new management team) will similarly provide potential solutions by removing barriers to a change initiative while also demonstrating leadership commitment to moving forward.

ACTION STEPS: THE "WHENS" AND "HOWS" OF CHANGE

Now that you have looked at various ways to motivate your staff, identify barriers, and overcome them, you are ready to begin making an action plan for managing a change initiative in your own organization. Having committed to start, you must choose where to concentrate your initial attention. Unfortunately, no right answer exists regarding where to begin. You can start with the whole organization, with pilot projects, or with temporary management structures. The following questions can guide you in making your decision:

- *What does the amount of time available, the magnitude of the change, or the level of support from participants and leaders suggest about where you should begin?* The more radical the change and the greater the time pressures, the more important it is to begin by developing top-level physician, administration, and board support.
- *Who will have to behave differently in order to effectively implement your change? What new behaviors will they have to exhibit?* Identify all individuals and groups that will have to behave differently for the change to be successful. Next, identify the formal or informal leaders who can authorize or legitimize these changes. Different leaders will be necessary, for example, to implement changes in nursing and medical staff groups.
- *With whom do you need to partner to increase your likelihood of success?* Begin in such a way that critical alliances are built early on. For example, if your change cannot be successful without support from primary care group practice leaders, begin by implementing a strategy to obtain that support.
- *What resources will be required to effectively implement your change? Do the resources currently available meet these requirements?* Start by identifying those resources (for example, equipment, training, budgets, information) required to implement your plan. Next, identify the degree to which these are currently available and develop a strategy for obtaining those elements that are missing.

When you launch the initiative, your goal is to build enthusiasm. Characterizing the initiative change in terms of stories and analogies that appeal to fundamental values can aid you in enlisting support. For example, simply arguing that adherence to traditional ways of delivering health care may lead to becoming noncompetitive often has little impact on those who see no reason to change. However, stories from physician groups that have lost their competitive position by ignoring change and additional stories from groups who control their own destinies because they have responded to the competitive conditions in their environment frequently have a greater effect.

Beyond generating enthusiasm and support, you must plan how you will help people make the transition into change. People making transitions pass through identifiable stages. While these stages take time, which can be frustrating, they also provide opportunities. As people move from the present into new beginnings and on to change, the opportunity exists to let go of the past, envision a new future, and become comfortable with the thinking and behaviors that lead to success.

Moving People through Transitions

As individuals struggle to adapt to change, they move through emotional phases. These phases include naive confidence or denial, hopelessness, hopefulness, and confident completion. (See figure 3-6.) It is important to expect, understand, and manage people's transitions through these phases. Completely avoiding the phases is unlikely. Even transitions one looks forward to—such as a new relationship, a new job, or a new information system—are initially disruptive, and the behavioral changes they require are often resisted. You can, however, influence the amount of time people spend in each phase and the intensity of their emotions. Your challenge is to diagnose current conditions and to move people creatively through each of these transition phases.

Managing the Initial Phases   People may begin a transition in a state of naive confidence and optimism or a state of denial and resistance. When people are optimistic, it is reflected in such statements as "Things are great. This will really work." If in denial, they are more likely to express it through withdrawal or such statements as "Things were great in the past," or "This doesn't really apply to me. Managed care will never come to this part of the world."

When people are in a state of naive confidence, it is important to get started, involve participants, develop realistic expectations about what you will face in the future, and begin to explore potential solutions. While it is not desirable to kill off the optimism, your later credibility as a leader will, to a degree, be dependent upon not having acted as a cheerleader during this time of natural enthusiasm.

FIGURE 3-6.   Emotional Reactions to Change

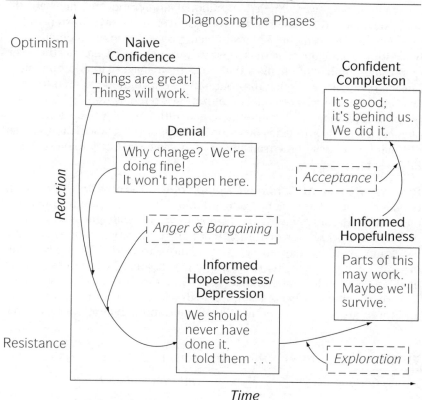

Diagnosing the Phases

Moving through the Middle Phases   As the reality of new information becomes available, the optimists often realize that things are not going to be quite as easy as they expected, and those in denial are forced to recognize that much work lies ahead of them. Reactions including anger, attempts to bargain, complaints, and informed hopelessness or depression replace the earlier emotional responses. People indicate their dissatisfaction through such statements as "I gave my all and now look what I get," or "We should have never done this. I told them this would never work."

As resistance intensifies and people perceive the situation to be hopeless, communication is critical to move forward effectively. During this stage, provide feedback on what is and is not going well. Acknowledge the reality of people's feelings, and make any needed adjustments to support progress and demonstrate commitment to the initiative.

Ineffective leaders believe in the ability to jump directly from wherever they are to the final phase of confident completion and commitment.

They often claim that people are being paid to put their feelings aside and do what is necessary. Such a traditional autocratic and mechanistic approach drives resistance underground and simply slows down people's psychological movement. While sufficient pressure can often obtain their behavioral compliance, it develops little readiness to handle the ever increasing number of changes that must be managed. In addition, such pressure is unlikely to elicit the committed contribution required for success in a complex professional organization. To the degree that you need people's confidence and commitment in addition to their behavioral compliance, using the strategies described to support psychological progress through the phases of the transition process is more likely to be successful. (See figure 3-7.)

Bringing People to Confident Completion   Eventually, when anger, bargaining, and depression produce limited sympathy and no improvement in conditions, pain drives people toward a willingness to explore new options. With the recognition that part of the situation may actually work and that they may survive, people move toward informed hopefulness, signifying both an improvement in psychological conditions and the likelihood of implementation success. While this is a time of confusion, new responsibilities become increasingly clear, initial successes occur, and there are periods of actual excitement and exhilaration. From this

FIGURE 3-7.   Psychological Reactions to Change

Naive Confidence

- Get started
- Involve participants/gather perspectives
- Develop realism
- Explore solutions/begin measurement of results

Denial

- Strengthen relationships
- Provide information from diverse sources
- Focus on first steps
- Avoid confrontation

Informed Hopelessness

- Acknowledge reality
- Obtain needed information
- Make adjustments
- Demonstrate commitment

Informed Hopefulness

- Continue the process
- Acknowledge/celebrate/ reward successes
- Build confidence
- Remove remaining barriers to success

Confident Completion

- Celebrate and reward successes
- Maintain the gains
- Identify next opportunities
- Apply learnings to other transitions

base, the opportunity exists to move toward confident completion, a time of high satisfaction, teamwork, and optimism.

Transitions do not always go this well. People get stuck in hopelessness and depression. Instead of supporting progress forward, people often try to go back to earlier stages they found more pleasant. For example, leaders sometimes move from one program to the next (from empowerment to quality initiatives to reengineering) rather than ever completing the cycle for any one of these initiatives. There is something enchanting about returning to the world of optimistic naive confidence by forgetting that which was difficult and trying something new. Unfortunately, each of these cycles will move to the difficult emotional states that must be managed if you are to achieve success.

Moving people through and beyond each phase of the emotional transition cycle requires different sets of leadership responses. Energy costs of the transition can be reduced by providing what is needed for people as they pass through these phases. All people will not pass through the phases simultaneously. Ideally, leaders will put the more difficult times behind themselves before moving masses of people into the discouraging realm of informed hopelessness. By doing so, they will be in a better position to acknowledge that they, too, faced similar concerns and to provide the support necessary to allow people to look beyond this phase.

Drafting Your Own Action Plan

Consider a particular change that you are currently attempting to implement in your organization. Revisit each component of the road map to determine your effectiveness in leading the way.

Revisiting the Energizers
1. Have you taken the actions necessary to develop a common understanding of where you are going?
2. Do people fully understand why the changes are necessary?
3. Have benefits flowed to those who supported the change and consequences to those who blocked or inhibited success?
4. Has success led to an increased confidence in leadership and commitment to future initiatives?

Revisiting the Barriers
1. Have people who are not willing to move been identified, listened to, and given numerous opportunities for involvement?
   - Have you identified sources of resistance stemming from both the content of the change and the process of changing?

- Have manifestations of resistance been observed, understood, and addressed through open and overt communication?
2. Have you identified what is not allowing the organization to move forward?
   - Have you reviewed your systems and structures to ensure that they provide messages consistent with desired change results?
   - Have leadership styles as well as cultural beliefs and assumptions been recognized and altered as necessary so that changes are supported within your organization?

Revisiting the Action Steps
1. Have your leadership actions demonstrated how to effectively begin a change initiative?
   - Have visions of future possibilities come alive through the use of stories and analogies?
   - Have you identified and taken concrete first steps so that feedback can be obtained and adjustments made?
2. Have your leadership acts been a demonstration of how to build momentum for a change initiative?
   - Have you taken steps to minimize individual resistance?
   - Have you taken steps to reduce organizational barriers?
3. Have the emotional reactions to change been dealt with on a timely basis?
   - Have you diagnosed how critical individuals or groups currently view the change initiative?
   - Are you providing them with the emotional support and resources needed to move successfully into the next phase of the emotional transition?
   - How will you know when you have succeeded?

CONCLUSION

To be an effective leader in today's turbulent environment, you must move people into and through continuous change. This requires you to identify early signs of the need for change, to move quickly, and to build the capacity for future changes. You cannot do it alone, however. Old cultural assumptions and beliefs, the foundation of past successes, must give way to new ones that will support the journey into the future.

To assist you in developing your ability to travel this journey successfully, we have described a model that can serve as a road map. The model rests on the premise that a sound foundation for change is built on a clear and common understanding of where and why you are going, how to energize your fellow travelers, and how to recognize and over-come the barriers you are likely to encounter along the way. Equipped with this knowledge, you can develop an action plan that specifies when and how you will reach your destination.

Bibliography

Beckhard, R., and W. Pritchard. *Changing the Essence.* San Francisco: Jossey-Bass, 1992.

Block, P. *Stewardship.* San Francisco: Berrett-Koehler, 1993.

Bridges, W. *Managing Transitions.* Reading, Mass.: Addison-Wesley, 1991.

Coddington, D. C., K. D. Moore, and E. A. Fischer. *Making Integrated Health Care Work.* Denver: Medical Group Management Association, 1996.

Covey, S. R., A. R. Merrill, and R. A. Merrill. *First Things First.* New York: Simon and Schuster, 1994.

Fisher, Anne B. "Making Change Stick," *Fortune* 131, no. 7 (April 17, 1995): pp. 121–28.

Galpin, T. J. *The Human Side of Change.* San Francisco: Jossey-Bass, 1996.

Jick, T. D. *Managing Change.* Boston: Irwin, 1993.

Kouzes, J. M., and B. Z. Posner. *The Leadership Challenge.* San Francisco: Jossey-Bass, 1995.

Nadler, D. A., and others. *Discontinuous Change.* San Francisco: Jossey-Bass, 1994.

Quinn, R. E. *Deep Change.* San Francisco: Jossey-Bass, 1996.

"Restructuring Isn't Always Effective," *Wall Street Journal* (June 6, 1991): B1.

Schaffer, R. H., and H. A. Thomson. "Successful Change Programs Begin with Results." *Harvard Business Review* (Jan.–Feb. 1992): 81–89.

Shortell, S. M., and others. *Remaking Health Care in America.* San Francisco: Jossey-Bass, 1996.

Thompson, R. *Winning Physician Support.* Tampa, Fla.: American College of Physician Executives, 1991.

Tichy, N., and S. Sherman. *Control Your Own Destiny or Someone Else Will.* New York: Currency Doubleday, 1993.

Watkins, K., and V. Marsick. *Sculpting the Learning Organization.* San Francisco: Jossey-Bass, 1993.

4

Building a Proactive Culture through Creative Leadership

John C. Lewin, M.D.

Health care organizations face many challenges. They must keep pace with developments in information systems and biomedical technology, demands from consumers and payers for new services and lower costs, and a rapidly changing—and sometimes overcrowded—market. To excel in this volatile environment, health care organizations must shift their cultures from slow-moving bureaucracies to proactive, team-based cultures. As Rosabeth Moss Kanter, consultant, author, and former editor of the *Harvard Business Review*, puts it, "Organizations which are winning the new game are more focused, fast, flexible, and friendly."[1]

This chapter provides leaders with practical insights and approaches to creating a shared vision of a team-oriented, change-friendly organizational culture. The chapter examines the type of leadership that fosters a proactive culture, looks at ways that leaders can prepare their organizations for this shift, and describes techniques for moving the organization toward a shared vision. The chapter then closes with a case study that illustrates how one organization revitalized itself through a shared vision and culture shift.

THE NEW VISIONARY LEADER

In times of great change, organizations must be future oriented. Success depends on envisioning what a better future might look like and being the first to reach it. This takes creative, visionary leadership. Even in these days of horizontal management structures and "intrapreneurship," health care still needs strong visionary leaders.

The assertion that organizations need visionary leaders may seem to depart from some of the excellent leading-edge theories of management consultant Peter Senge and others, who denounce the traditional concept of the "hero-leader" responsible for the vision, creativity, and management of the organization. According to this school of thought, the hero-leader absolves the organization from developing leadership skills among the staff and instills a feeling of powerlessness among the ranks. The hero takes care of everybody and everything, and if things go sour, it's presumably time for a new leader.[2]

Although the hero-leader is clearly *unlikely* to succeed in today's health care environment, the absence of leadership is equally ineffective. When an organization's direction and purpose need to undergo transformation, when consensus does not come easily and decisions must be made quickly, strong, focused leadership is critical to keep the organization on track. But instead of all-knowing heroes, today's visionary leaders must be team builders who base their vision on continuous input from the entire organization and on the feedback they receive from patients, partners, and other stakeholders. The health care environment is simply too swiftly changing and too competitive for leaders to work in isolation. To keep abreast of developments and stay ahead of the competition, leaders need timely information from all stakeholders, both those who work for the organization and those who depend on it for care.

Leaders also need to use the talents of everyone in the organization to the fullest. The profound influence of W. Edwards Deming on Japan and later on the United States attests to the value of an empowered workforce—one that takes responsibility for improving quality without waiting for management to direct such a change. A proactive workforce is especially critical in times of change, when failure to take action in a timely manner can quickly lead to obsolescence. Creating a culture that embraces change is an essential step toward long-term viability and success.

THE LEADER'S ROLE IN EFFECTING CULTURAL CHANGE

Changing a culture is not easy. As pointed out in chapter 1, culture tends to be firmly entrenched in an organization and resistant to change. The values, beliefs, and customs that make up a culture provide a comforting sense of order and predictability. When the world outside the organization is fast moving and unpredictable, organizational members tend to cling to "the way things have always been done" all the more tenaciously.

Leaders are not immune from this desire to cling to the past. Although health care leaders know that change is certain, many still act as though they might postpone it or avoid it altogether. To create a proactive culture that thrives on change, leaders must model the behavior they want to see in the workforce. This means that leaders themselves must embrace change and position the organization to benefit from it. In addition to being role models, leaders must be effective persuaders. They must overcome the organization's natural resistance to change by presenting compelling reasons for leaving the past behind. Finally, and perhaps most important, leaders must be inspirational. They must fire the imagination of the organization with a bold vision of a better future and the unshakable conviction that it can be attained. In word and deed, leaders must foster a culture that views change as an opportunity for the organization to reinvent itself for the better.

Modeling Desired Behavior by Embracing Change

The first step toward creating a proactive culture is for leaders themselves to become proactive. If the CEO and other key managers are unable to effect a radical change in their own thinking and behavior, they can hardly expect the workforce to alter theirs. Intellectualizing the decision to become a "change master" is, of course, quite different from becoming one. Because change is stressful and carries the risk of failure, even leaders committed to change can find themselves longing for the solace of "the good old daze." But in today's market, resisting change carries even greater risks.

Consider the example of a public "safety net" hospital that provided essential indigent inpatient service in a community with an excess number of hospital beds. When HMO reimbursements decreased and even more beds were left unfilled, private hospitals in the community actively went after Medicaid admissions. This move left the public hospital with a large base of uninsured, nonpaying patients. Leadership held numerous meetings condemning the profit motives of the market and discussing the need for change, but they took no further action. As a result, the public hospital's income dropped, its costs increased, layoffs occurred despite union threats, and the hospital eventually closed, leaving the uninsured with no recourse but to go to private hospital emergency departments for care. Failure to participate in change caused everyone to lose—the leaders of the public hospital, the staff, and the people in the community who depended on them.

Could this failure have been avoided? Absolutely—if the leaders had sought to embrace, rather than resist, change. For example, in response to the oversupply of inpatient services, the leaders might have met with representatives of the unions, community, and private hospitals to explain the hospital's need to close all or most of its inpatient care beds. As inpatient services were reduced, the workforce might have been retrained to provide outpatient and community care for the rising numbers of uninsured. After contracting with government, the hospital might have begun to attract private-paying and Medicaid outpatients to specialized outpatient care by offering multilingual services, multidisciplinary home care, and prevention and wellness services based on new models of chronic disease outpatient management. Efficient use of existing government subsidies and new revenues might have enabled the safety net facility to continue caring for the uninsured—a winning resolution for everybody.

For some readers, this example will sound familiar. It mirrors scenarios that have already occurred in many communities heavily penetrated by managed care. The lessons these hospitals learned should not be forgotten. Health care leaders can resist change and play the role of the victim—or position the organization to benefit from change and play the role of the participant. What leaders choose to do will serve as a model for the rest of the organization.

Persuading the Workforce of the Need for Change

Leaders' participation in change sets the tone for the rest of the organization. But the participation of leaders alone is not enough. A shift in culture requires the support and involvement of people at all levels of the organization. Such support is not likely to come easily. Leaders may have to jolt the organization out of a sense of complacency in order for people to address the need for change. There are many ways that leaders can persuade people to change; of all the motivational tools available to leaders, open and honest communication is likely to be the most productive.

Building Trust through Open Communication   As many of us in health care can testify, it is not uncommon for leaders to use fear as a catalyst for change. A surprise restructuring, downsizing, or merger is certain to open the eyes of the workforce and ensure that the survivors actively participate in the new strategic planning process. The problem is that the product of the planning is likely to be as flawed as the technique for generating interest in it. Fear simply is not a good way to begin envisioning a better future. Even among the relatively small numbers of staff who are informed in advance of an impending crisis and assured of job security, the fear that they will be the "next" often prevails. Thus, surprise announcements create an "us versus them" mentality that breeds suspicion, greed, and ultimate failure.

In contrast, honesty and openness breed trust. Involving the entire organization in an open discussion of the reasons for change shows respect for the workforce and demonstrates that leaders can be relied upon to tell the truth. Open and honest communication is also empowering. When people are given the information they need to understand the problems that the organization faces, they are equipped to propose creative solutions. Finally, open, honest communication can also inspire a tremendous sense of loyalty and dedication to building a better future before a crisis is reached. Even if the organization subsequently undergoes a significant downsizing or reorganization, open and honest communication leaves a legacy of trust to build upon.

Creating an Artificial Shock   All that said, honest and open communication is, in some cases, insufficient to move people out of their comfortable grooves. In such cases, the visionary leader may need to create an artificial shock to revitalize the stagnant organization. The leader's role is to make a future crisis feel present and real by providing early evidence of trends so that the workforce is willing to take the risks associated with leaving the past behind. The potential crisis should be far enough into the future in order for the entire organization to come together as a team to address the threat, but not so far away as to make the process seem abstract or able to be postponed.

Take, for example, the need for Medicare and social security reform to take place before the baby boomer generation reaches retirement age. Congress, the White House, and the public are aware of the impending threat, but because it is unpleasant and politically dangerous to address, each administration wants to pass the problem on to its successor. Waiting for a full-blown crisis will be catastrophic; therefore, a short-term "mini-crisis," or artificial shock, may need to be engineered—quite legitimately—to avert a long-term disaster.

That is certainly the approach taken by scientists who believe global warming represents an impending environmental and human catastrophe. This contention is being debated and downplayed by most industrial and political leaders. But whenever the average temperatures increase during a season, or the El Niño oceanic current weather conditions capture the public's attention, activist scientists use the media to create a shock, to attempt to awaken people from their complacency and to advocate the incredibly difficult process of planning for a world that depends on something other than fossil fuels and forest products for its energy needs. Leaders may need to do the same thing to awaken a sleeping organization.

Developing an Inspiring Vision

Once an organization has been awakened to the need for change, it needs a powerful vision to work toward. True vision is inspiring, ethical, and purposeful. Although ventures in other industries may thrive without an ethical foundation or purpose beyond making money, in health care, long-term success is linked with altruistic values. Greed and fear, while powerful motivators, are also relatively short-lived; long-term success is built by instilling employees at all levels with a sense of public service. A vision built on integrity, honor, and social benefit is key to inspiring the organization to risk change, face the unknown, and make the significant extra effort required to change the status quo.

Giving Permission to Dream   Note that it is important to "give permission" to project the vision at least slightly beyond that which is theoretically achievable. The most significant achievements and breakthroughs occur only when this kind of permission is present. It is tough enough to get people up and out of their habits, traditional belief systems, and comfortable old behaviors. Once people have been lured out of complacency for a few precious moments, it is vital to encourage them to take a good look around, ponder the vast expanse of the unknown, and reexamine their horizons. For people to be truly inspired, their reach must exceed their grasp.

People must also understand that visions are works in progress. Because the health care environment is constantly changing, visions must change along with it. When the workforce accepts the need to envision and continuously reenvision, the culture begins to shift. Even the most traditional and stagnant culture can become proactive, flexible, and future oriented when inspired to participate in a continuous reenvisioning of the future.

Understanding the Transforming Power of Vision: A Case Study
In the mid-1980s, Hawaii's Department of Health (DOH)—a comprehensive statewide public agency with over 6,500 employees and 80 major program areas—was experiencing a disheartening loss of public confidence. The department, which had responsibility for all Environmental Protection Agency (EPA) functions in the state, at first did not recognize and then tried to cover up the pesticide contamination of dairy products with the carcinogen heptachlor. Once the scandal was exposed, the public rightfully felt betrayed, and DOH employees were demoralized.

At about the same time, the public hospital system, which was administered by the DOH and was failing to keep pace with changes in the health care marketplace, was falling into deficit and disrepair. The public hospitals were the only options for inpatient health care on the islands of Maui, Hawaii, and Lanai, and they were major providers on Oahu and Kauai as well. The public began to doubt the competence of their heath care services on the neighbor islands.

Then the AIDS/HIV epidemic hit Hawaii and the public doubted the ability or commitment of the DOH (or the government leaders responsible for the DOH) to respond appropriately. This concern, combined with the others, fueled growing disillusionment with the DOH by its employees, the media, and the public. Fortunately, a new governor, John D. Waihee III, had a vision of a better future.

When I was appointed Director of Health for Hawaii in December 1986, I shared with the governor the idea that Hawaii ought to be known as the "Health State." The vision was that Hawaii, a nonmanufacturing state, would use the concept of health to promote and enhance its main business of tourism in such a way that its own citizens would be the primary beneficiaries. The idealistic and talented new governor understood and endorsed the vision.

After gathering considerable public and employee input, the new vision was crafted and launched. Hawaii was to be known as the Health State—not as a statement of previous accomplishment or boasting, but *as a goal of what could be*. A complete restructuring of the entire mega-agency was begun. The environmental programs were strengthened and redesigned. The media began to be cautiously encouraged, along with the DOH employees, from whom most of the new ideas came. The public hospital system was reconfigured to function like a private system, and a plan was created within the system to achieve financial solvency. The AIDS epidemic was attacked by establishing America's first statewide anonymous testing, school education, and needle exchange programs, along with strong protections of confidentiality and special health care services for infected persons. Many other preventive programs of national significance were developed. Hawaii experienced a rebirth of its public health traditions. It wasn't perfect; it wasn't easy; it wasn't even necessarily sustainable because, in government, as political administrations change, funding and priorities can change rapidly. However, it was as if the thousands of dedicated employees were suddenly freed to do the things they had been long ready to do once permission and flexibility were offered.

The idea of Hawaii as the Health State caught on in the media, and all across the state people began contributing to this vision and the values it evoked. Soon enough, the momentum called for Hawaii to commit itself to universal health access, something that seemed impossible to achieve on the mainland of the United States. Under the leadership of the DOH, Hawaii developed the SHIP health insurance program for the remaining uninsured. This enabled the state's overall health insurance coverage, already higher than the rest of the country, to reach 97 percent of the population. The DOH then proposed and succeeded in greatly expanding mental health and clinical preventive services. The nation noticed; and in 1992 President Bill Clinton used Hawaii as the basic template for a proposed national health reform strategy. The Hawaiian public noticed too; and the DOH became a source of inspiration and leadership again. In this case, a little vision, developed and shared by both employees and the public, went a long way.

Instilling Hope

Once consensus has been reached on the need to change, and better futures have been envisioned, leaders must instill a sense of courage and confidence that the new visions can be realized. At this point, there can be absolutely no room for doubt. Management must vaccinate the entire workforce with hope and use the positive momentum to forge the path to a better future.

When milestones in the new business plan are reached, or when media or community leaders praise and express confidence in changes taking place, leaders should hold small celebrations for the staff involved. Updates on the progress of initiatives, distributed via E-mail, and personal meetings with small groups of staff are opportunities to instill hope and keep feedback channels open.

CREATION OF AN INFRASTRUCTURE FOR CULTURAL CHANGE

As Stephen Covey, author of *The Seven Habits of Highly Effective People*, has said, "Wars are won in the general's tent."[3] Although development of a new culture may not involve a traditional planning process, certain measures must be taken in order to succeed. Leaders must establish a critical mass of support for change, provide channels for people on all levels of the organization to participate in the change process, and move the organization from a hierarchical chain of command to a horizontal one. These measures will create a strong infrastructure on which to build the new culture.

Establishing a Critical Mass of Supporters

The first step in the change process is to identify and develop a critical mass of supporters to provide a catalyst for changing old ways of thinking and behaving. Assuming that the majority of employees have recognized the need for change, it will soon be apparent that most will have accepted it, while others will be excited about the prospects. Clearly, the latter group must be identified and involved in moving the process of change along. Even among those willing and ready to change, a variety of different personality types will be involved, the recognition of which is essential to successfully moving further in the process of cultural change.

Differentiating between Maintainers and Creators   Some people are more comfortable maintaining and supporting a known and relatively stable set of circumstances—these are the "maintainer" types, those who like predictability and who keep things going along smoothly and reliably. These kinds of people dislike uncertainty, surprises, and lack of structure or clear lines of authority. On the other hand, every organization also contains "creative" types who thrive on change and uncertainty. These people find the status quo dull.

Utilizing the Talents of Both Groups   To utilize the talents of both groups, leaders must maintain a balance between creators' desire for change and maintainers' need for stability and order. The challenge is to organize creative types into a cohesive catalyst for change while avoiding unnecessary anxiety and decreased productivity among maintainers.

It is likely that executives and managers with maintainer personalities will resent creative subordinates who take an active role in creating the new organizational vision. To avoid conflicts and facilitate an open, honest approach to creating the new vision, leadership must assure that the creative types have the opportunity to contribute their ideas and energy to the change process, yet, at the same time, position the maintainers to provide stability and ongoing oversight of existing operations. An excellent means for striking this balance is the creation of temporary advisory committees.

Establishing Temporary Advisory Committees   Temporary advisory committees can not only provide creators and maintainers with a common ground for using their talents, but also provide a forum for all organization members to participate in the change process. For these reasons, the formation of transitional committees should be looked upon as another important step in the change process.

Note that the committees should be interdisciplinary and include members from all organizational levels. In this way, all interested members have a chance to participate, and the needs and ideas of every group in the organization can be addressed. Leaders can appoint these committees from a request for volunteers from the entire organization, or if the number of interested persons is not too great, the committees can consist of all who volunteer. It may be necessary to recruit a few key people for each committee to assure a genuine balance of talents and perspectives. In addition, leaders should make it clear that the committees are temporary and intended to serve only during the period of transition. If, however, the committees work well, the organization may wish to retain some interdisciplinary committees as a way of providing continuous input to the CEO and top management in the new structure.

Organizing Committees by Task   For advisory committees to work effectively, they must have a clear sense of purpose and clear goals. Typically, in an organization that anticipates significant change, a committee might be assigned the task of integrating present and potential business goals into the context of the new vision. Another committee might be formed to deal with employee morale and issues of organizational restructuring related to anticipated personnel changes and needs. Other committees might evaluate the strengths and weaknesses of existing operations and services, seeking more efficient means of dealing with existing programs that are certain to be part of the new vision and structure. Yet another committee could define, articulate, and advocate common values for the organization. These common values should follow from the elaboration of the new vision and be incorporated in orientation and periodic reorientation programs for all employees, volunteers, and board members, as well as into existing quality assurance programs and employee job satisfaction surveys.

Encouraging Lateral Thinking   "Lateral thinking"—thinking that departs from typical linear progressions and conventional wisdom—must be encouraged through such techniques as brainstorming sessions. Committees and staff need permission to entertain seemingly wild and irrelevant ideas, and nontraditional products, services, and organizational structures. Ideally, committees will have the skills and means to survey the customers the organization serves—patients, businesses, and community leaders—and consider their input during the process of effecting change. Such surveys need to encourage external stakeholders to open their minds and imaginations to provide ideas and feedback about how the changing company can meet evolving or new community and business needs.

Promoting the Participation of Staff   To prevent suppression or fear of open communication, leaders would be wise to prohibit managers from serving as committee chairs. Rather, managers should be encouraged to participate as equals with the rank and file. In addition, top leadership should attend as many of the sessions as possible to ensure that open and honest deliberation takes place and that discussion focuses on the task at hand. Finally, committees must be assured that their recommendations will be seriously reviewed and either integrated into the new vision of the organization or, if not included, rejected for clearly stated and openly discussed reasons. In fact, to generate enthusiasm and support for committee work, leaders should make every effort to implement a few early recommendations as soon as possible.

Moving from Hierarchy to Interdependence

Any company or organization that seriously desires to effect a shift in culture and a shared vision is, of necessity, committing itself to a more horizontal management structure. In essence, this consists of reducing hierarchy and strict vertical chains of command and replacing them with a greater reliance on teamwork, group accountability, and a sense of interdependence. A restructuring of this sort will pose a threat to most managers unless they are assured that their jobs are secure and that a more flexible, dynamic organization should increase the potential for growth, leading to higher salaries and better working conditions. If some managers are clearly uninterested or incapable of participating in the new culture, it may be best to develop generous severance packages and outplacement programs and to encourage such individuals to move on before major workforce changes are actually implemented. This approach allows people who do not see a place for themselves in the new structure, as it is gradually articulated, to gracefully and voluntarily leave or retire early. As Stephen Covey points out, a highly effective organization requires that key staff evolved from "dependence" to "independence" on the path to "interdependence."[4] While visionary leadership will help managers make this transition, not all will be willing or capable.

Definite steps need to be taken to prepare managers for more horizontal structures. A new context for decision making and intrastaff communication is required and must be clearly spelled out. As noted, the change from a reactive to a proactive organization begins with the creation of a new and shared vision, but then must proceed directly to development of a philosophy of greater inclusiveness in decision making and policy development. If, for example, the organization's security officer has an idea about how to improve service quality or staff morale (the improvement of which will undoubtedly improve service quality), why suppress it? The tyranny of "the way things have always been done" precludes this kind of feedback. It also sends the strong message that a security officer's ideas are unworthy of consideration unless they are related to security. How can an organization get around these kinds of "chain of command" inhibitions and involve the whole organization in the development and sharing of a vision, common values, and quality improvement?

Expanding Delegation via Decentralized Policy Development

Horizontal communications—those that occur between employees in different units, divisions, or aspects of the organization—break traditional vertical chains of command. This obviously threatens many managers; conversely, managers' concerns are fueled by less scrupulous employees who would bypass the chain of command for other than efficiency-related or honorable reasons. For horizontal communications systems to work, they must *be* systems, based on accountability, trust, and overall company policy. One way to overcome these obstacles is to emphasize the delegation of authority based on a mutually developed policy between managers and subordinates. If policy decisions by top management, based on feedback and review of the committee input structure, can be made general enough to allow for flexibility in different aspects of the organization, then local managers and their subordinates can participate in making decentralized policy decisions for greater efficiency and improved morale.

Suppose, for example, that after a top-level decision to implement recommendations for an employee wellness and fitness program, an assistant to your organization's vice president of human resources presents a proposal for such a program that includes representatives of every division and can be implemented within budgetary constraints. After the vice president reviews the elements of the proposed plan and the related policy governing the implementation of the program, he or she might delegate to the assistant responsibility for overseeing and managing the new program within the specific, agreed-upon terms, policies, and outcomes requirements. Ideally, the delegated policies and outcomes should be proposed by the subordinate and accepted by the manager. Both parties might agree to meet and resolve together any changes, new elements, or different circumstances that might later develop. With those understandings in place, the staff person would be authorized to speak as required about the project with any employee in the organization, including those in other divisions—even the CEO. This puts the employee in charge.

This kind of arrangement can work well only if a relationship of trust, integrity, and good communication exists between the supervisor and employee. And if it *can* work, it allows for not only the development of a shared vision, but also a structure that is both more flexible and change-friendly.

Linking Performance to Results   The more flexible and creative an organization wants to be, the more it must hold its employees to mutually agreed-upon performance indicators and specific results. Short of violating ethical, legal, and core company policy actions, employees at all levels must be involved not only in sharing the new vision but also in implementing it. This can be done by minimizing bureaucracy and maximizing decentralized decision making through delegated policy and results-oriented performance indicators. Organizations that are truly serious about moving faster and smarter in their marketplace will encourage employees to consider the basic parameters of their jobs and create their own annual work plans, as well as develop their own performance indicators and defined results.

Once employee-generated work plans are approved by the manager, the employee is empowered to act as the decentralized leader of his or her own work activities in a structured fashion. If the results are not achieved or periodic benchmarks en route to such results are not met, the manager and employee must work together to eliminate whatever barriers are in the way of desired progress or realistically redefine the timing or nature of the results and related performance indicators to what is achievable.

The manager in a decentralized workplace will become accountable for assisting subordinates in defining and organizing their work plans and then in assuring that the agreed-upon progress is being made. The manager becomes responsible for articulating and producing the sum of the results of those in his or her purview. On occasion, an employee's project will straddle the overall responsibilities of more than one division or manager, meaning that several managers may need to be involved in overseeing the employee's overall performance. If so, these areas must be clearly defined in the work plan and in the development of the performance indicators for that project. And, in rapidly changing organizations, leader-managers must schedule their priorities rather than prioritize their schedules to achieve new objectives and real results.

Providing Incentives to Change

As a final step in the change process, leaders must look at the feasibility of developing incentive plans. It is unreasonable to expect managers and employees to change their long-standing habits and practices without offering some kind of monetary rewards or other benefits in exchange. An exhaustive analysis of physician behaviors in different modes of practice and reimbursement systems—published in 1996 by the Advisory Board Company, a Washington, D.C., consulting firm—attempted to compare productivity of managed care physicians with their traditional fee-for-service counterparts.[5] Fee-for-service physicians earn more as they work more; and while they may tend to overorder expensive diagnostic and therapeutic services, they are, on average, more productive than their managed care counterparts in terms of the numbers of patients they see, the hours they work, and, likely, their willingness to be on call during the night and to make house calls. These conclusions should not be terribly surprising. Managed care physicians are paid by salary or on a flat per member/per month capitation basis, regardless of how much or how little care is required. To approximate the productivity of fee-for-service physicians, the study concluded, would require that incentive pay for managed care physicians be 50 percent or more of the total reimbursement. While there are consumer/patient concerns about how physician pay incentives affect quality of care—quite a different subject from volume- and gross earnings–related productivity—the study makes it clear that incentives can affect the quality and volume of work produced by professionals.

When creating incentive plans, three things need to be considered. First, if productivity is incentive-based, it must be related to quality of work as well as volume. Second, pay incentives are more easily designed for certain classes of employment than for others. For example, the volume of work produced by such employee functions as accountancy, visitor reception, and clerical work can be difficult to quantify in relation to increased income for incentive development purposes. Finally, every organization includes jobs that offer greater potential for new income generation than others. Thus, a mechanism is needed to equitably reward efficiency, creativity, quality-controlled productivity, and improved customer (patient) satisfaction. Incentives based on increased business revenue or administrative savings may need to be prorated across an entire division of work teams to be fair and to improve overall organizational morale. This is not only a fairer approach, but it also promotes a team effort.

THE CORNERSTONES OF THE NEW CULTURE: VISION AND VALUES

Without shared values among leaders, staff, and the governing body, cultural change cannot be sustained. Health care organizations, like those in other industries, more than occasionally suffer from the perception among employees and clients that the verbal statements of values in promotional materials do not necessarily reflect the true values of the organization. Of course, every health care organization professes to be dedicated to improving quality, but many consumer advocates, physicians, and other caregivers increasingly question whether health care organizations are not actually dedicated to maximizing profits.

To sustain cultural change, it is absolutely critical that statements of organizational values truly reflect policies, attitudes, and behaviors. Nothing is more demoralizing and inflammatory to employees than external pronouncements of organizational values that have little or no relevance to internal behaviors or to actual company culture. Employee attitudes profoundly affect the quality of products or services. Organizational or corporate doublespeak will be rapidly transferred, directly or indirectly, from disenchanted and cynical employees to customers, the public, and the media.

On the other hand, an organization that makes consistent values known to both the public and its employees, that creates internal policies supporting those values, and that engages its workforce in articulating, improving upon, and implementing such values has substantially better chances of successfully communicating those values to customers, new employees, and into the quality of products and services. The common values need to be *lived*, not just spoken.

In addition to the need for honesty and consistency, clarity and focus of vision and values are critical to success. For example, a health care organization's statements of values might include "consistent quality patient care, excellent patient communications, caring and compassionate attitudes, and innovation in prevention and wellness."

Achieving clarity in focusing and articulating vision and values will have a powerful and positive impact on any organization. And, in times of tumultuous change, clarity of vision and values will allow the organization to see the opportunities in a crisis by anticipating and adjusting rapidly to external events while other organizations flounder. The advantage of knowing who you are and who you aspire to be in the individual sense is the power equivalent to clarity of vision and values in the organizational sense.

Distinguishing between Values and Goals

Doubtless, priorities and goals will frequently need to be adjusted as external events change. For example, in the mid-1990s the conventional wisdom of health care consultants was that for-profit HMOs and related physician and hospital reimbursements by capitation would dominate the future and that, sooner or later, everybody would need to "get in line." But just a few years later, we are discovering that managed care is far from mature. HMOs will either be replaced with a new form of health care delivery, or they will change to become more sensitive to patient concerns about choice, continuity of care, and the preservation of the physician-patient relationship, as well as become more attentive to physician concerns about preserving quality of care and the health of the population.

In short, every health care organization will likely be changing its goals, priorities, and internal structures, perhaps frequently, during these times. But the organizational vision and values—including a commitment to patient satisfaction; quality of care; excellent patient communication; and promoting prevention, wellness, and the health of the surrounding community—not only stays constant but also serves to guide the organization through multiple changes in economic, marketplace, and regulatory conditions.

Creating Synergy among Key Stakeholders

Change is least painful and most successful when we build the future on top of what works well in the present. Conversely, identifying and replacing aspects that are *not* working well is the next step. Decisions regarding what to protect and what to replace should emanate from the development of a shared vision and common values. But such considerations must, in a practical sense, be considered from the often differing vantage points of three key internal stakeholders: executives and managers, the nonmanagerial staff, and the governance members—typically the board of directors.

Until there is synergy among these stakeholders, there will be little coordinated movement and, in fact, the old hierarchy will persist. Once internal synergy has been achieved, the team must then project the new vision and values outward to the customers and clients—patients and employers in the health care model. This certainly occurs through marketing materials and messages, but also through consistent expressions of the theme in every opportunity for communication or personal contact of employees with the public.

Typically, the development of a new organizational vision stems from subjective or, even better, objective feedback from such external sources in the first place. This can occur in the form of decreasing business, negative publicity, focus group feedback, or surveys of various types. However the impetus for definition and redefinition of the vision of a dynamic organization comes best from continuous monitoring of such external feedback. The dynamic organization is constantly learning from its environment and reprogramming its behaviors to achieve and sustain internal synergy among employees and governance, and external synergy with the customers, essential business partners, and communities of primary importance. The entire team must then be committed to transforming the feedback it receives externally into continuously updated internal reeducation processes.

Assisting Naysayers to Depart Gracefully

Finally, and usually with great difficulty, dynamic organizations desiring to develop a team approach to implementing a common vision and values must weed out those persons who will not or cannot embrace these changes. Everyone in the organization will not realistically survive or desire to work in a more participatory system. However, individuals whose productivity levels or attitudes are not consistent with the new vision and values should first have been given a fair and thorough opportunity to understand the changes proposed.

Providing a Severance Program   Even with a major effort to bring everybody on board, it is desirable to anticipate the need for a voluntary severance program. It should be generous enough to provide an incentive to depart for those who desire this, and it should have a clearly defined deadline for eligibility, so that people can make up their minds early on as to whether they are going to embrace the future or leave.

Providing Outplacement Services   In addition to the severance incentive, it is also desirable and smart to offer an outplacement service to relocate individuals who recognize that they don't fit into the new future. This sends an important message to all employees that the change process is caring and sensitive. It is also likely to get the naysayers and the underproducers to move on voluntarily. It follows that individuals who did not avail themselves of this opportunity, yet who cannot support the overall effort in attitude or performance, must then expect to be asked to leave eventually. Real change requires that the whole team be committed to each other and to the vision.

That kind of coordinated commitment is contrary to human nature, and thus it is more than just difficult to achieve or maintain. Pleasing all customers (or patients) is also next to impossible. But attempting to achieve that level of both internal and external synergy is the goal. If we really expect employees to support this kind of promise, then the managers and executives of the organization must exemplify it. Leaders must be more than maintainers. Period. And, as a corollary, institutionalizing change is far more important than changing the institution.

THE RENAISSANCE OF THE CMA: A CASE STUDY

Many organizations have successfully reinvented themselves through the creation of a shared vision and cultural change. One such organization was the California Medical Association (CMA).

Setting the Scene

The rapid transformation of the health care marketplace in California took many physicians by surprise. The new concept of managed care, just beginning to be felt strongly in the rest of the country, dominated the California health care environment. Nearly two-thirds of the population were enrolled in HMOs by the mid-1990s, including the nation's highest percentage of seniors enrolled in Medicare HMOs. More than half of managed-care physician reimbursement was by capitation (a per member/per month fixed-payment formula), rather than by the traditional fee-for-service approach. Quality of care decisions and the design of benefit and reimbursement strategies became the domain of non-physician M.B.A. types. Relentless pressure from employers to reduce premium costs, coupled with increasing demand for profits from investors in corporate health care, resulted in a trend toward "proletarianism" of physicians, nurses, hospitals, pharmacists, and most health care professionals. These were the easiest targets for squeezing money out of the old "nonsystem" of community hospitals and entrepreneurial individual and small group physician practices.

In response, more hospital chains and larger physician groups formed to confront larger and more autocratic HMOs and health plans, as well as marketplace demands. However, the historic divisions of physicians into groups and independent practice associations (IPAs), county and state societies, specialty societies, and competing hospital staffs created a situation in which managed care organizations could easily conquer. Physicians lost their historic position of leadership of health care. Instead of pulling together as a profession to reassume the control of patient care and quality, physicians have actually tended to abandon the only organizations capable of being reactivated to effectively represent them politically and legally, namely the state medical associations and the American Medical Association (AMA). Certainly, these organizations had their significant flaws, and in the minds of many physicians, they were "asleep at the wheel" in the face of the marketplace changes. But they offered the potential of unifying the existing fragmentation of physicians.

A key to viability for state medical associations relates to attracting the knowledge and experience of doctors who are practicing at the cutting edge of medicine, both to help their colleagues get up to speed and to propose and implement solutions to some of the glaring weaknesses of the current transitional phase. But organized medicine, trying desperately to hold on to the status quo, was inadvertently repelling the very expertise it needed. Meanwhile, the physician leaders in managed care organizations failed to understand that they needed the numbers, clout, and legislative power of organized medicine to maintain physician leadership of health care and to accomplish their own objectives. An unlikely marriage was indicated.

While managed care created some significant problems for doctors, hospitals, academic centers, and patients, the old nonsystem had to be replaced. New diagnostic and therapeutic technologies were remarkably effective at increasing the life expectancy and survival of patients with chronic illnesses, but the relatively indiscriminate application of these innovations proved expensive indeed. Costs were soaring.

Nobody can deny that managed care has been remarkably effective at cutting costs and improving efficiency. It has forced the necessary integration of systems, stimulated greater interest in quality of care, and, theoretically at least, has promoted prevention strategies. But the emphasis on costs and profits has resulted in a significant reduction of patients' choice of physicians, continuity of care, and communication with physicians. The public has recently begun questioning the values of some managed care health plans, particularly the for-profit versions, in which profits seem a higher priority than patient care. Quality of care, once the domain of physicians, is now often controlled by business interests in the marketplace. Those kinds of problems must and will be corrected, and physicians have been called to "step up to the plate" to reassume leadership of health care in order to move managed care from an awkward adolescence on to a more responsible maturity.

Analyzing the Situation at CMA

It was in this tense environment that I became the first physician executive vice president and CEO of the CMA and its various subsidiary companies. While the organization was still certainly viable with over 35,000 members and possessing powerful legislative and legal clout, membership was slowly declining, particularly among younger physicians, and physician leadership of health care was rapidly eroding. Dramatic and immediate action was needed.

The leaders of the CMA, namely the board of trustees and its executive committee, were progressives who had already recognized the need for this kind of change and had begun preparing for it. They had determined to restructure the governing bodies of the association, the board itself, and the annual policy-setting congress known as the House of Delegates, to incorporate medical groups, academic and public health physicians, administrative physicians, and specialty societies into the power structure.

They had begun serious discussions about becoming aggressive in rekindling leadership in the marketplace by (1) establishing a health insurance company; and (2) in the area of quality of care oversight, establishing an accreditation agency for health care professionals, facilities, and even HMOs. They had recognized that indiscriminately opposing all aspects of managed care was ineffective and irresponsible. Instead they had begun to differentiate the positive aspects from the undesirable, unethical, and unnecessary aspects. The entire transformation was based on a change in both vision and values.

The CMA's leaders had realized that physicians were not merely victims of change, but also victims of ignorance, arrogance, and apathy. Doctors and hospitals had ignored many opportunities to address the concerns of business, labor, and families about health costs that were rising faster than society's ability to pay. Physicians had often failed to act as a profession to address rare but real fraud abuse, and poor performers, and to ferret out, as only physicians can, hundreds of billions of dollars of ineffective, inappropriate, and futile care. We could easily blame lawyers, malpractice threats, government regulators, and patients who demanded everything to cure them of their own unhealthy lifestyles for the woes of the profession. But that made us victims. Responsibility meant taking action to identify and solve the problems. It meant leadership.

Choosing between Self-Interest and Health

Perhaps the most significant aspect of trying to achieve clarity in terms of values related to the split among physicians over whether organized medicine should be focused on income protection, in the manner of a guild or trade union, or on the principles of professionalism, as symbolically embodied in the Hippocratic oath. In essence, the choice was between self-interest and the health of patients and society.

The new executive vice president/CEO, picking up on the vital groundwork of the elected leaders, was charged with preparing a large and talented staff for new challenges, as well as preparing the membership for reassuming leadership of health care. Based on the guidance of the board and the information gained from physician attitude surveys, the staff was educated, down to the level of secretaries and clerks, that bold changes were needed to avert a long-term disaster.

This process of diagnosis of the reality of the problem was difficult because many physicians and staff members chose to believe that the membership downturn and the rise of managed care represented only a passing anomaly in the course of things and that all would improve if the old formats were pursued more effectively. A shock was definitely needed to capture the attention of both members and staff. But the staff needed to be repositioned immediately in order to assist members in negotiating the waters of unprecedented change.

Administering an Artificial Shock

A shock was not hard to create since the existing staff pension plan was in imminent danger of underfunding, the association's reserves had been reduced significantly, and gradual membership declines would force major staff reductions in the near future. Once staff recognized the problems were real, several ad hoc committees were formed to rethink and restructure the organization in order to meet the future, rather than the past, needs of physicians. Managers were certainly involved, but the staff advisory committees, which blended employees of all levels and divisions, were chaired by nonmanagers and created most of the concepts that resulted in the new organizational structure and culture.

Creating the Vision

The vision of the restructured organization was based on the long-valued principles of physician professionalism. The focus would be on quality of care, the physician-patient relationship, the integrity and design of the health care system, health care ethics, and the health of populations and communities. Protection of physician income and autonomy were not to be abandoned, but were seen to be dependent on the respect and trust of the public and businesses, which in turn, would only support physicians if professional values were clearly their top priorities and if physicians recognized that costs had to be checked while quality was preserved. It became apparent that taking the "high road" of advocating quality care for patients was the best way to protect physician autonomy in the long run.

Restructuring the Organization

The CMA reduced its staff by 30 percent before it was economically forced to do so. We then restructured the organization from an unmanageable number of diverse goals, priorities, and staff units into four centers focusing on legal advocacy, legislative advocacy, policy analysis and research, and communications. A statewide Internet communication network, CMAnet, was constructed, and all the business systems of the company were reengineered and brought up to date technologically. Relationships with the county medical societies, the specialty societies, and medical groups were emphasized, and attempts to coordinate and streamline overlapping and duplicative services were undertaken. In the old structure, these groups had been treated as competitors, not as partners.

Managing the Pain of Change

None of these changes were easy. The compelling nature of the status quo—including the strong preference for the "way things have always been done" and the frequently cited "We've tried that and it doesn't work here"—was very apparent. Combining those elements with fear of job loss as part of the impending major changes made this an unwelcome and suspect process. However, the staff reductions occurred without firing long-standing and loyal employees, and this approach avoided ill will and strengthened trust. The downsizing was effected by offering a generous one-time and time-limited severance package to all employees, in addition to quality outplacement assistance. People who perceived that their function was not likely to be emphasized in the new structure, who did not harmonize with the changes planned, or who were ready to leave anyway, voluntarily left.

The voluntary severance approach bore a risk of losing the best and the brightest employees, so it was important to have developed strong engagement and commitment from key and potential new staff leaders to remain and build the future before instituting the severance arrangement. Even with these efforts, a few vital people left. The reality is that these people would very likely have done so anyway, either to accompany a relocating spouse, to pursue a graduate degree, or to take advantage of a special career opportunity. But those employees who constituted the critical mass were already enthusiastically incorporated into the redesign process and desired to stay. Those who stayed were willing to work with leadership teams, more horizontal management systems, and change that needed not only to keep pace with the marketplace, but to move fast enough to get one step ahead of it.

Implementing the Vision

Whereas CMA staff had traditionally been able to wage political and legal battles with its own muscle, a sustainable vision required a process of building and rebuilding constituencies of support and common interest among hospitals, nurses, business, labor, government, and the public. These were major cultural changes, both for the CMA and for the other constituencies.

Within one year of the restructuring, many new and creative projects were under way, and membership recruitment had been made an all-staff focus. The CMA employees had developed and launched a unique health insurance company, CalAdvantage, which began building its own staff and influencing real changes in the competitive marketplace. Many new members joined just because of this effort.

Within its first year of operation, CalAdvantage had over 26,000 physicians on its provider panel and had made its unique managed care products available in 55 counties. The company goal was to create products that compete on the basis of price with other managed care plans but also provide higher quality and greater choice, all in a more patient- and physician-friendly manner. It is growing, despite the fact that many seasoned observers doubted that any new players could survive, even briefly, in the tough California marketplace.

Another CMA subsidiary company, the Institute for Medical Quality (IMQ), was developed and launched by CMA employees. Devoted to quality of care and accreditation, the IMQ has its own independent board. The IMQ soon successfully competed with national competitors to land the contract from the state of California to perform the quality reviews of state-licensed HMOs.

Simultaneously, other exciting new projects emerged from a reduced but restructured staff: (1) a new leadership academy, with the purpose of educating doctors about the new medical economic reality; (2) the "health plan report card" project, which, with business and other partners, will assist patients and employers in making more informed choices about the quality of health plans they choose; and (3) several new public health initiatives targeted toward increasing access to care for the uninsured, fighting tobacco addiction, and improving the health of adolescents. To make these things happen with fewer staff, forming partnerships with outside constituencies was essential.

Physicians, members and nonmembers, have responded positively to these organizational changes, as have members of the public and the media. Group practice, academic, and student physicians, traditionally not attracted to organized medicine, have become interested in membership. In just 18 months, the staff, though fewer in number, have produced more new products and services and new value for members than had occurred in the previous ten years. There is talk that a "renaissance of profession" is occurring. And physicians are reestablishing themselves as leaders in the ongoing debate about how to accomplish necessary health system reform and achieve universal coverage.

There is no guarantee of success here, and many adjustments and course corrections will be needed for the CMA to continue to change as quickly as the environment. Yet an organization that was threatened with gradual extinction is revitalizing itself and expanding its domain far beyond its traditional boundaries. It started with a vision based on shared values, first recognized and articulated by progressive elected physician leaders. It spread quickly to a reconfigured staff; and it increasingly harmonizes with business, labor, hospitals, other health care professionals, and, most importantly, members of the public, who are, after all, patients from time to time.

CONCLUSION

Although change is the norm in health care, most of the industry, be it physicians, hospitals, nurses, pharmaceutical businesses, or insurance companies, have responded to employers' and the public's calls for change only when absolutely necessary—only when up against the wall. To remain successful in the future, health care organizations must create change-friendly, fast-moving cultures.

A shared vision is the foundation for cultural transformation. The next decade in health care will be an exciting time in which to participate because it will produce an entirely new system with exciting new opportunities. While Providence likely holds the key to many of the unforeseeable aspects of the future, a shared vision in an organization united by common values and an ability to thrive on change is the best formula for both a lucky and a successful future.

References

1. Sarita Chawla and John Rensch, eds., *Learning Organizations* (Portland, Ore.: Productivity Press, 1995).

2. Ibid.

3. Stephen R. Covey, *The Seven Habits of Highly Effective People* (New York: Simon & Schuster, 1989), p. 296.

4. Ibid., p. 185–203.

5. Advisory Board Company, *Rewarding Cost-Effective Medicine— Aligning Physician Incentives under Managed Care* (Washington, D.C.: Advisory Board Company, 1995).

5

Managing Change through Effective Communication

Michael B. Green

H ow in the world did we get here and what do we do now? This question resonates in the minds of many health care leaders as they ponder how best to guide their organizations through cultural change. Of course, organizations can survive change; the best actually thrive on it. Key to managing change is effective communication.

This chapter examines the two kinds of change—continuous and discontinuous—and explains why discontinuous change often results in culture clash. The chapter then analyzes the "either/or" thinking behind culture clash and presents an approach that many successful organizations have used to overcome it. The chapter closes with an overview of practical communication techniques that foster understanding and unity among internal and external stakeholders of health care organizations.

CHANGE AND THE PERCEPTION PROCESS

In health care, culture clash is a fairly recent phenomenon. Over the past several decades, the industry has seen many changes, yet few have resulted in significant disruption or conflict. Why, then, are the changes health care is undergoing today received so differently? The answer lies in the type of change the industry is seeing and the manner in which people perceive change.

Perceptions of Continuous and Incremental Change

It is interesting to note that such programs as total quality management (TQM) and continuous quality improvement (CQI), mainstays of the health care industry for many years, have not resulted in profound conflict or significant culture clash. TQM and CQI most definitely involve change, but the change is continuous and incremental—implemented in relatively small steps over time. In many ways, continuous and incremental change is analogous to a small differential in the size of graph bars, a difference so small that under the right set of circumstances, it appears to be negligible.

Classic psychological studies of the perception process have demonstrated that when presented with a number of bars on a page (figure 5-1), individuals will more often than not say they are of equal length if their peers have proclaimed them to be so, even though when measured one is clearly longer than the others.[1] This phenomenon, called cognitive dissonance, has important implications for change leaders, because it suggests that people have a propensity to avoid inconsistency and conflict. It also suggests that perceptions of differences can be minimized or eliminated if the majority of people in an organization share the same vision.

Perceptions of Discontinuous and Sudden Change

In contrast to such incremental change processes as TQM and CQI, restructuring and reengineering are discontinuous and sudden changes.

FIGURE 5-1.   Cognitive Dissonance

If eight peers in a room agree that the bars are of equal length, the ninth peer will more often than not also agree, even though one bar is longer. Perception is as important as fact and can be influenced by the opinions of others.

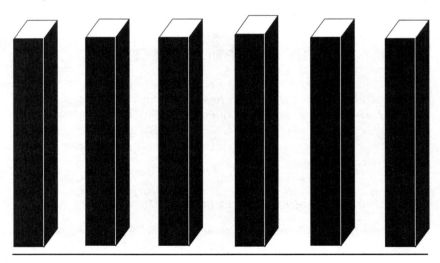

Figure 5-2 depects incremental or CQI change as a line with minor fluc-tuations. These changes do not usually result in dissonance. In figure 5-3, the change in the line graph is obvious, representing discontinuous, dramatic change—dissonance is unavoidable. As Michael Hammer and James Champy point out in *Reengineering the Corporation: A Manifesto for Business Resolution*, business reengineering requires "starting over." They further state that reengineering "doesn't mean tinkering with what already exists or making incremental changes that leave basic structures intact. It isn't about making patchwork fixes—jury-rigging

FIGURE 5-2.   Incremental Change

Incremental change can be used to avoid dissonance. Incremental change is not perceived as disruptive.

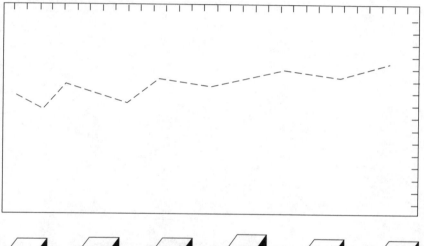

existing systems so that they work better. It does mean abandoning long-established procedures and looking fresh at the work required to create a company's product or service and deliver value to the customers."[2]

This kind of massive and swift change often results in psychological dissonance, a state of inner conflict in which new objectives and ways of doing business are perceived as inconsistent with long-held values. Compounding the dissonance caused by restructuring is the implication that the way things have been done is not the way things should be done. This per-

FIGURE 5-3.   Discontinuous Change

Discontinuous change will most likely lead to cognitive dissonance. Discontinuous change is disruptive, and no matter how many people try to minimize the change, it is apparent to all.

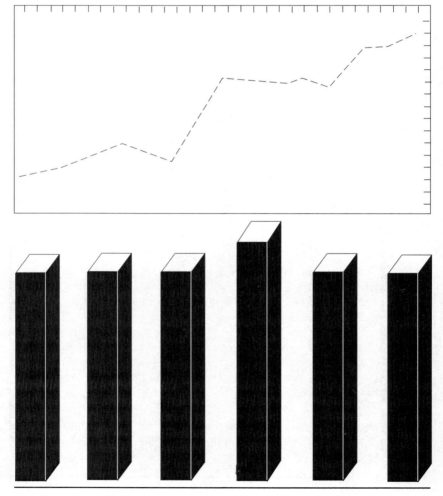

ceived gap between actions and beliefs is at the root of the culture clash from which the health care industry is currently suffering. In the absence of effective, timely communication to close the gap, reengineering or other euphemistically phrased dramatic change can have disastrous results.

Dissonance and the "Tyranny of the Or"   In *Built to Last: Successful Habits of Visionary Companies*, James Collins and Jerry Porras point out that dissonance can lead to "the tyranny of the or," a destructive mind-set in which people believe that the old and new cannot be reconciled. For example, when dissonance is present, people may believe that an organization can

- Have change *or* stability
- Be conservative *or* bold
- Have low cost *or* high quality
- Have creative autonomy *or* consistency in control
- Be values driven *or* financially driven[3]

In health care, the tyranny of the or is seen in many quarters—for example, among managers who believe that greater staff autonomy leads to chaos and among care providers who believe that cost containment and traditional health care values cannot be reconciled. Clearly, this either/or mind-set is a barrier to successful change. The tyranny of the or is especially problematic in today's environment, because payers, patients, and other external stakeholders demand health care that is both affordable *and* of the highest quality.

Constructive Dissonance   Collins and Porras make a strong case that the most successful companies differentiate themselves from the pack by their ability to deal effectively with seemingly contradictory forces simultaneously, thereby constructively dealing with dissonance. According to Collins and Porras, successful organizations embrace the Chinese dualistic philosophy of the yin and the yang. These companies find a way to succeed with objectives that appear to be paradoxical. In short, they can

- Have purpose beyond profit *and* pragmatically pursue financial goals
- Have a relatively fixed ideology *and* pursue vigorous change
- Be conservative around the core *and* make bold, risky moves
- Have clear vision and sense of direction *and* be open to new opportunities
- Select managers steeped in the core *and* managers that induce change
- Maintain ideological control *and* operational autonomy
- Invest in the long term *and* demand short-term performance

- Be philosophical, visionary, futuristic, *and* superb with daily execution
- Be an organization aligned with a core ideology *and* an organization that continually adapts to its environment[4]

In some ways, the health care organization is an ideal setting for the development of constructive dissonance because the essence of the organization—the delivery of high-quality, compassionate care—should remain the same, regardless of dramatic changes in reimbursement systems, organizational structures, and staff roles. But the health care organization also has special barriers to overcome because it involves divergent constituencies—from internal stakeholders, such as governance, medical staff, management, and line staff, to external stakeholders, such as patients, patient families, and the community. These stakeholders are often like overlapping circles: while they have some common interests, their interest can also differ greatly. For example, management and line staff are vitally concerned about job security and the work environment. In contrast, medical staff are concerned about access to the resources needed to support professional activity and personal satisfaction, while governance is concerned about fiduciary responsibility, public perception, and the mission of the organization.

Although stakeholders' diverging interests always make consensus difficult to reach, sudden and massive change greatly compounds the problem. It takes leaders with excellent communication skills to find the points at which stakeholders' "circles" intersect and to show that seemingly contradictory objectives and forces can coexist. Although it is impossible to meet everyone's expectations and perceived needs, it is very possible to understand the basis for them. Through empathic communication, leaders can show concern and minimize destructive dissonance.

THE IMPORTANCE OF EMPATHIC LISTENING

Empathic listening in which, as Stephen Covey has put it, leaders "seek first to understand . . . then to be understood"[5] is, perhaps, the most important communication skill leaders can develop. Covey identifies five levels of listening, with empathic listening as the highest and most difficult to achieve:

- *Ignoring:* Not really listening at all
- *Pretending:* Acknowledging feedback without hearing it
- *Selective listening:* Hearing only certain parts of the conversation
- *Attentive listening:* Focusing and paying attention to the feedback
- *Empathic listening:* Listening with the intent of understanding[6]

Empathic listening is essential during times of change because it helps leaders to identify common ground and to build consensus. Empathic listening also provides essential information for decision making and implementation of difficult management decisions. Perhaps most important, empathic listening helps forge strong bonds between people. As Covey explains, "empathic listening is a tremendous deposit in the emotional bank account."[7] When people understand that their leaders really care about them—about how they feel, what they need, and how change affects their lives—they are much more likely to "cut them some slack" and accept them as human beings rather than view them as "empty suits."

Tom Peters and Nancy Austin also talk about the important role that listening plays in understanding other people's perspectives. They suggest that leaders must set aside preconceived ideas, biases, and even scientific data in order to listen in a more pure—even naive—manner.[8]

Empathic listening isn't easy. It requires the listener to see the world through another's eyes and to give thoughtful consideration to that person's ideas. While it doesn't require listeners to agree with speakers, it does require that they acknowledge that other people's thoughts and opinions are just as important as their own. Listening to understand— particularly to understand the magnitude and the cause of dissonance— is critical.

Empathic Listening and the Medical Staff

Empathic listening skills are of tremendous value when dealing with individual members of the medical staff and the medical staff as a whole. Far too often, lay administrators tend to judge members of the medical staff without a real understanding of their paradigm of the world.

It is of paramount importance to recognize that the changes buffeting the health care industry often affect physicians in very personal ways. In many cases, the economic equation has changed. Some physicians, particularly specialists, built their lifestyle around certain income expectations that may now be unattainable. At the same time, many primary care physicians are experiencing greater income, power, and influence— changes that can affect interpersonal relations among medical staff as well as between staff and leaders.

For most physicians, loss of autonomy has had an even greater impact than loss of income. Many physicians are now employees either of a large group practice, an insurance company, or a hospital. Because most leaders have known for their entire career what it means to be an employee, they tend to forget the transition physicians must go through as they move from independent practitioner to salaried staff. As an example, consider the manner in which employee physicians were treated during the recent construction of two medical office buildings. One was to be predominately occupied by independent physicians practicing in small groups; the other was to be occupied by physicians employed by a large HMO. All stages of the construction project for the building to be occupied by independent physicians were complicated by the almost constant need for communication with each physician (or each small group) as the office suites were being designed. For the building that was to be occupied by HMO physicians, the process was much easier because the contractor dealt exclusively with a management representative of the HMO. Thus, the physicians had very little input into their own office space. The point is not that one approach was wrong and the other right, but that the employed physicians felt slighted, particularly since not that long ago they were independent practitioners.

Even those physicians who can remain in independent practice are affected by the dynamics of managed care. Their reimbursement may be arbitrarily reduced by the insurer. It may be much more difficult to acquire patients as insurance companies and primary care physicians steer patients in different ways. The practice of medicine has always been stressful; the nonclinical pressures have never been greater. Covey's conclusion that seeking first to understand is the key to effective interpersonal communication is most assuredly applicable to an administrator's relationship with physicians. On many occasions, employees complain that they have heard of a physician group taking business away from a hospital. One can be unequivocally committed to retaining volume at the hospital while understanding that a shift in volume from the hospital to a physician-controlled setting may be an attempt to retain an income level that is otherwise eroding. This understanding can be the basis for a dialogue with employees about the situation and with the physicians about how a more mutually beneficial situation can be pursued.

In short, it is important to recognize that when changes are implemented in the health care setting, these changes affect physicians' workplaces too. Because the physicians are not ultimately answerable for resource consumption or financial performance, it is unreasonable to let them dictate resource allocation decisions. Nevertheless, physicians should have input into decisions before they are made. Leaders cannot expect physicians to understand their perspectives unless they have made an effort to understand the physicians'.

Empathic Listening and Other Stakeholders

Many leaders base the amount of time and attention they give to various stakeholders on "clout." Because effective communication with governance and the medical staff can lead to greater job security, leaders tend to listen most carefully to these two groups. That is a mistake. All stake-holders are concerned with the ultimate success of the organization and will have an impact on that success. Particularly during periods of dramatic change, effective communication with management and line staff—the individuals who will be charged with the responsibility of carrying out change—is essential. Thus, leaders must create opportunities to communicate—particularly opportunities for two-way communication.

METHODS THAT FOSTER TWO-WAY COMMUNICATION

There are a number of ways that leaders can create opportunities for two-way communication to occur. Most informal methods, such as management by walking around, require little or no preparation. Other, more formal means, such as meetings and interviews with the media, require advance planning.

Informal Methods

Because informal communication is spontaneous, it is often the most honest and informative. In addition, informal communication helps leaders overcome the barriers of physical and psychological isolation. Three methods for promoting informal communication are management by walking around (MBWA), an open-door policy, and shadowing.

Management by Walking Around   The most direct way for leaders to encourage two-way communication is to initiate it themselves. By strolling around the organization on a regular basis, leaders invite open conversations from which they can learn much about staff's problems and concerns.

In their book *A Passion for Excellence*, Tom Peters and Nancy Austin state some of the advantages of MBWA, pointing out that it "is at once about common sense, leadership, customers, innovation and people. Simple wandering—listening, empathizing and staying in touch—is an ideal starting point."[9] Indeed, during periods of dramatic and traumatic change, MBWA and the listening, empathizing, and talking that go with it take on even greater importance.

MBWA should give leaders a good feel for the organization and help them assess the organization's readiness for change. However, MBWA has limitations. Given the relatively large number of employees in most health care organizations, it is impossible to reach the majority of people directly. Thus, leaders may wish to supplement MBWA with an open-door policy.

Open-Door Policy   Effectively implemented, an open-door policy can symbolize leaders' receptivity to new ideas. For the policy to be effective, leaders' offices should be easily accessible so that staff members feel welcome to drop in. When individuals do visit, it is important that leaders promote conversation by giving them their undivided attention. The leader should stop working, get up from his or her desk, invite the listener to sit down, and listen empathically. After the visit, the leader should thank the staff member for stopping by. It is important to remember that some staff feel intimidated by the prospect of dropping in on leaders. Therefore, to encourage future visits, it is important to show sincere appreciation when staff do summon up the courage to stop by.

Shadowing   "Shadowing"—spending concentrated time (four to eight hours minimum) observing, participating in, and discussing the work of another individual—is a more intensive approach to facilitating two-way communication. A major advantage of shadowing is that the staff member is on his or her own "turf," which increases the odds that the person will be more relaxed and less guarded. Through observation and discussion, the leader can learn what the person does and how change is affecting his or her job. Even more important, the leader can learn how the person *feels* about his or her job and the organization. This knowledge will, in turn, allow the leader to listen with genuine empathy. Although shadowing may ultimately not influence any business decisions, the opportunity to listen provides insight into the complexity of the environment and a better sense of the organization as a whole.

For example, spending time with caregivers on clinical units can help leaders realize the importance of supporting management and human resources development. Some leaders who have practiced shadowing on the clinical side have noted that outstanding clinical nurses are not necessarily comfortable in a team environment and, following the traditional hierarchical management model they are used to, frequently pass problems on to "managers." If, through shadowing, a leader finds that this is the case, he or she might send teams of caregivers to a ropes course to help them develop team and problem-solving skills in an environment in which interdependence is critical to success. A ropes course is a physically, emotionally, and mentally challenging series of outdoor obstacles or puzzles that requires individual athleticism, confidence, and teamwork.

As a follow-up measure, the leader might wish to chronicle shadowing experiences in a newsletter to staff. By describing what he or she observed and felt, the leader can publicize his or her concern for staff and a commitment to learning about them.

Formal Methods

To supplement information gathered through informal means, it is important to make judicious use of more formal methods of two-way communication—methods that are scheduled in advance and that require preparation. These include small and large group meetings, meetings with standing committees, and interviews with the media.

Small and Ad Hoc Group Meetings   During periods of rapid and dramatic change, leaders may wish to talk to all or most employees through the use of small group meetings (15 people or less). These meetings, though time-consuming and difficult to schedule, can provide both leaders and staff with certain advantages. For staff, the meetings provide an opportunity to meet with leaders and ask tough questions. For leaders, the meetings provide a forum for discussing the challenges that the organization faces and the substantial change that is on the way. Through face-to-face communication, leaders can correct inaccurate perceptions and lay rumors to rest.

During the meetings, leaders should remind themselves that the purpose of meeting is to create an opportunity for two-way communication. Leaders should not allow the meetings to become just a series of announcements. Leaders also should listen empathically and observe nonverbal feedback—body language and tone of voice—that can provide clues about staff's real feelings. Most important, leaders should not seek to avoid answering tough questions. Evading questions about layoffs or other difficult topics is, perhaps, the quickest way for leaders to lose credibility in staff's eyes.

Small ad hoc groups can also be used effectively as work groups to assist with the change process. Work groups with clear objectives can provide input into change. Individuals become invested in the change and, because of personal involvement, may come to champion it. In addition, the use of small work groups assures two-way communication regarding proposed changes. (For a more complete discussion of the role of work groups in facilitating change, see chapter 4.)

Large Group Meetings   Although large "town-style" group meetings are not always the most effective vehicle for two-way communication, they can work well if they are held on a regular basis. As in town meet-.ings, people can, over time, feel comfortable enough to participate, and if the fear of retribution is eliminated, learn to ask probing questions and to challenge decisions. As with small group meetings, leaders build credibility by being honest and leaving themselves open to criticism. To maximize the benefits of large group meetings, someone should take minutes and distribute them to all staff. In this way, those who were unable to attend can be kept up to date, and those who did attend have a written record of the proceedings.

Standing Committees   Meetings with standing committees can be used to provide opportunities for two-way communication with other stakeholders. For example, monthly board and committee meetings can be used to help governance understand rapid changes in the environment and their impact on the organization. Apprising the board of progress in the strategic planning process can help educate it about the pace and magnitude of change. And providing data and other information about national, regional, and local trends can help prepare the board for major changes, such as dramatically declining patient populations. Monthly medical staff departmental meetings can be used in a similar fashion. Although these types of meetings are apt to result in one-way communication rather than the give-and-take characteristic of two-way communication, they can create a level of comfort that will eventually lead to more open and relaxed communication.

Interviews with the Media   An excellent method for promoting two-way communication with the community is to schedule time with the local media. The organization's public relations staff will be able to help with suggestions for and coordination of media interviews. Radio interviews with question-and-answer sessions can work very well, as can talk radio programs where listeners call in with questions. In addition, many cable television services broadcast community programs on which leaders might discuss changes taking place at their health care institutions. Although many leaders are concerned about being misquoted or quoted out of context, it is important to recognize that newspapers can also be valuable allies. Editors and editorial boards are often willing to listen to well-documented rationales for change and the impact that change will have on the community.

ONE-WAY COMMUNICATION TOOLS

Sophisticated and successful two-way communication should and must be supported with one-way communication tools such as press releases; newsletters to board members, employees, medical staff, and the community at large; minutes of meetings; and, on special occasions, advertising campaigns. One-way communication can be used to reach a broad audience. In addition, it is an effective way to document the substance of two-way communication. Not everyone has the opportunity to participate in two-way communication sessions; one-way communication can provide information to interested parties who are unable to attend two-way sessions.

Press Releases

Press releases are perhaps not the best mechanism for providing in-depth information with regard to change. However, they can be very effective catalysts for alerting the media and the general public that a specific change has, or will, occur. The press release thereby becomes a mechanism for creating a dialogue. If the press release succinctly identifies the nature of the change, the magnitude of the change, whom the change will affect and how it will affect them, it becomes a stimulus for reaction. And that reaction, when properly anticipated, opens a dialogue for more effective two-way communication.

Newsletters

Newsletters can be very effective for providing timely information about change to a wide variety of stakeholders. However, to be truly effective, newsletters may have to be tailored to the interests and needs of different groups. For example, physicians will be more inclined to read a newsletter that they believe has been developed specifically for them than to read a generic newsletter intended for all employees.

Effective newsletters are short (one to three pages), timely, published on a regular basis, and effectively distributed. In today's world, newsletters can be distributed outside the organization via the Internet or within the organization via an intranet. Newsletters should always include an address (Internet address if available) so that readers have an opportunity to respond.

Minutes of Meetings

Minutes are a good way to document that an attempt was made to inform an audience of change and to record discussions about the anticipated effects of the change. For minutes to be an effective medium of communication, they must be effectively distributed. Paper copies should be delivered to all interested parties and posted in convenient locations. In addition, minutes can be distributed via E-mail.

Advertising Campaigns

Advertising campaigns can be used successfully to help convey the message that change will be constructive. Advertising, if properly designed, can help lessen the fears about change and can reinforce the importance of such issues as quality and compassion. Advertising is most effective if it is presented in a manner that educates and informs. Regardless of the advertising medium, the concept of the "infomercial" can be used to support both the rationale and the benefits of change.

CONCLUSION

Many health care organizations are undergoing the kind of swift, discontinuous change that results in culture clash and either/or thinking. With the right communication strategies, such as empathic listening, leaders can break the shackles of the "tyranny of the or" and create constructive dissonance.

To be effective, communication must be honest and frequent. Leaders should create opportunities for formal and informal communication to occur with stakeholders on a regular basis. In this way, they can assess stakeholders' reactions to change and move the organization toward a successful future.

References

1. Kenneth Burke, *Permanence and Change: An Anatomy of Purpose*, 3d ed. (Berkeley, Cal.: University of California Press, 1984).

2. Michael Hammer and James Champy, *Reengineering the Corporation: A Manifesto for Business Revolution* (New York: Harper-Collins, 1993), p. 31.

3. James C. Collins and Jerry I. Porras, *Built to Last: Successful Habits of Visionary Companies* (New York: HarperCollins, 1994), p. 43.

4. Ibid., p. 44.

5. Stephen R. Covey, *The Seven Habits of Highly Effective People* (New York: Simon and Schuster, 1989), p. 237.

6. Ibid., p. 240.

7. Ibid., p. 241.

8. Tom Peters and Nancy Austin, *A Passion for Excellence* (New York: Random House, 1985).

9. Ibid., p. 13.

6

Forging Strategic Alliances among Stakeholders

Matthew J. Lambert III, M.D., M.B.A., F.A.C.S.

For many years, physicians, hospital administrators, and boards of directors operated relatively independently. Today, however, with the advent of physician-hospital organizations (PHOs)—most usually developed, funded, and controlled at least 50 percent by hospitals—there is a pressing need for cooperation and collaboration among these groups.

At the same time, a greater need for collaboration between hospitals and community leaders has arisen. Under threat of loss of their not-for-profit status, many hospitals have sought to document their efforts at improving the health of the communities in which they reside. However, many of these undertakings have less to do with community benefit than with marketing and an attempt to gain market share.

Meanwhile, relations with payers remain adversarial and antagonistic. Most physicians deal at a distance with managed care providers, and hospital efforts are directed at extracting the most revenue from the tightly closed fist of the HMO or insurance executive. While there is much talk about building integrated delivery systems, the actual goal often seems to be to wrest control from payers and gain market share or dominance rather than to improve the health care system or the health of the local community.

This chapter explores, through the use of case examples and practical methods, how to move beyond the rudimentary and often self-serving efforts at collaboration among the traditional components of the "three-legged stool" of the health care system: (1) the hospital governing board, (2) hospital administration, and (3) physicians. In addition, the chapter looks at ways to increase collaboration with payers and the community, two groups whose importance to the health care system has grown in recent years. Finally, the chapter reviews barriers that must be overcome before these groups can be aligned in efforts to improve health care access, cost-effectiveness, and quality. By collaborating in a climate of trust and seeking solutions that benefit all concerned, these groups can define and shape the new world of American health care.

THE SHIFTING ROLE OF THE GOVERNING BOARD

In the past, hospital board members were selected for their prominence in their communities and their ability to supply or raise capital for the institution. Increasing hospital costs resulted in the patient being financially responsible for more of the care, and the physician (with the ability to admit and treat patients) became more important to the hospital's future and, indirectly, the chief source of hospital income.[1] Because the complexity of the environment required specialized administrators, the board became largely passive—a "rubber stamp" for administrative initiatives. It was a sufficient membership criterion to be prominent in one's community, although wealth was certainly always welcome.

A New Role for Board Members

Today the litigious nature of our society, the increased regulation of the hospital industry, and augmented competition demand a more active, involved, and specialized board of trustees. New criteria for membership include established success in business, excellent judgment, dedication, motivation, and community orientation. The effectiveness of a board is judged by how well it satisfies its community and how completely it attains its own goals and objectives. The stresses of the current marketplace and the responsibility to be stewards to the community dictate that board members participate actively and frequently in formulating the institution's vision and strategic plan. It is the board that must drive the development of an integrated delivery system and seek to define areas of commonality among its constituents. Yet board members often have little contact with hospital physicians, and many boards lack physician members. This deficiency should be remedied to improve understanding between the board and medical staff.

A Board of Trustees That Thrives on Collaboration: Case Example

One organization that has made great strides in collaboration between the board and medical staff is Martha Jefferson Hospital, a central

Virginia not-for-profit facility that shares community health care responsibility with the University of Virginia Medical Center. Martha Jefferson's board of directors is composed of six actively practicing physicians and six community leaders. Physicians are prepared for this role by obtaining experience as committee chairs, members of the medical executive committee, and officers of the medical staff. By the time a physician is selected as a board member, he or she has had considerable leadership experience and has been exposed to all aspects of hospital operations from finance to strategic planning. Community members are selected for their expertise in business, finance, law, or community activities and involvement. An annual board retreat includes administrators and an open invitation to physicians to discuss strategic planning and to offer suggestions or raise concerns. The board members remain actively involved in quality-assurance activities and collaborative efforts with other health care facilities. The open nature of the governance structure has created an environment that delivers high-quality, low-cost care, continues to attract superbly trained health professionals, and receives excellent feedback from patients and their families.

THE SHIFTING ROLE OF HOSPITAL ADMINISTRATORS

In the post–World War II era, technological advances and adequate funding led to the substantial growth of new and existing hospitals. Community hospitals were able to offer services that had previously been limited to only the largest and most advanced health care facilities. The passage of Medicare resulted in a cost-plus reimbursement environment that fueled expansion and acquisition of new technology. Administrators presided over facilities that were the pride of their communities and were financially sound. Although physicians and administrators operated within the same environment, there was little reason for interaction—or conflict. Each profession was thriving, and patients were satisfied.

The Schism between Administration and Medical Staff

The advent of prospective payment for hospital services by the federal government signaled an end to the easy living enjoyed by hospitals for almost a generation. Administrators watched their fixed diagnostic-related group-specific payments erode rapidly as physicians conducted business as usual, caring for patients without regard to length of stay or level of resources consumed. That is the way medical schools and residency training programs had taught them to behave, and that was the way they were reimbursed.

Administrators, seeing profit margins decline, instituted aggressive utilization review programs. Physicians accused CEOs of being concerned only about costs, not quality. In addition, they were charged with meddling in the practice of medicine and attempting to usurp physician autonomy. Administrators, on the other hand, viewed physicians as unwilling to address the realities of a changing environment and unreasonable in their demands to use unlimited hospital resources without fiscal responsibility. Meanwhile, managed care continued its inexorable penetration of virtually every market, and constrained payments, along with intrusive third-party utilization review parameters, became the rule rather than the exception.

Challenges of Operating in the Newly Competitive Environment

CEOs sought safety and strength in numbers by abandoning the typical stand-alone posture of most health care facilities and by forming networks, alliances, mergers, and a variety of other arrangements with other similarly affected institutions. But as early as 1988, a mere five years after prospective payment was instituted, it was recognized that the development of hospital systems had not added value or achieved goals, such as economies of scale, greater profitability, and improved quality. In addition, many CEOs, anxious for a quick return to profitability and stability to keep their careers upwardly mobile, have focused only on short-term goals.[2]

The development of PHOs by hospitals served to provide vehicles to attract managed care contracts, to bring physicians into alignment with hospitals by offering financial incentives for lowered resource utilization, and to ensure a stable flow of patients to the facility. A further search for stability resulted in the purchase of physician practices. These efforts were often referred to as "integration," but that was far from the truth.

The CEO Who Saved a Hospital: Case Example

Stephanie Thompson* is a CEO who has successfully saved a failing hospital. She came to Chicago as CEO of one of its older facilities, where inpatient census had declined, quality had become tarnished, and physicians were increasingly disenchanted by the lack of stable leadership as three CEOs had come and gone within a period of several years. In

---

*This executive's name has been changed to protect the privacy of the people and organizations involved.

Chicago, 25 percent of the population is enrolled in managed care plans, and HMO volume has doubled in the last ten years. Chicago is significantly overbedded for its health care needs, and many hospitals have seen their bottom lines disappear.

Thompson's first priority was to reinforce the vanishing bottom line through aggressive, albeit painful, workforce reduction to bring full-time equivalents (FTEs) more in line with patient volumes. Trust was rebuilt with the physicians by the CEO's high visibility, honest and open approach to problem solving, and inclusion of physicians in decision making. Physician-administrators were replaced in several departments that had languished under indifferent chairs. This change created a climate that encouraged the applications of a number of young, highly trained primary care physicians and specialists interested in developing a meaningful quality-assurance program and establishing closer relationships with their colleagues.

The administrative team was reconfigured with the recruitment of key personnel in finance and information systems. Substantial efforts were made in articulating a vision and values for the hospital and making them known to all employees and physicians. Although there were acute problems, the focus was on achieving long-term viability and success by developing and refining a strategic plan. Partnering opportunities were explored with other acute care facilities, but it was elected to continue internal improvements and achieve greater financial stability before pursuing other relationships.

At the conclusion of the CEO's first year, the bottom line was again positive, relations with the physicians and employees had improved, and there was a sense of teamwork and ownership that had been decidedly lacking in prior years.

THE SHIFTING ROLE AND STATUS OF PHYSICIANS

Until recently, physicians maintained the power and prestige with which the profession has been vested for most of the twentieth century. That was the case despite numerous attempts to more tightly regulate medical care and institute some form of national health insurance. However, the continued steep rise in health care costs has had a profound effect on businesses and the middle class, leading, in turn, to the rise in managed care.

Physicians under Siege

Today physicians see their incomes declining, their prestige diminishing, and their practice overheads skyrocketing. There are more expressions of dissatisfaction among physicians, a greater number of early retirements, and fractures in the professional alliance as primary care physicians assume primacy under managed care at the expense of specialists.

Physicians are now expected to be resource conservationists (or risk being excluded by an HMO or PHO), to document their outcomes, and to share decision making with other health care professionals. In the new climate, physicians find themselves between Scylla and Charybdis—caught between the role of patient advocate and a seller of services financed and controlled by a third party who demands minimal cost expenditure per patient encounter.

Physicians are struggling to again control health care but without much success. PHOs are moderately successful, but physician autonomy remains constrained, and demands for better utilization continue. Physician organizations (POs) seek to eliminate hospitals from their mix of providers and gain control of the total managed care payment but have suffered from undercapitalization and a lack of business expertise and direction. Primary care physicians enjoy their new prominence and augmented incomes and seem disinclined to bridge the rift with specialists caused by these reversals of fortune. Physicians watch colleagues sell their practices to hospitals or for-profit physician management firms and wonder if they "have met the enemy and it is us."

Physicians Seek to Shape Their Own Future: Case Example

In 1993 physicians in a Michigan hospital that had enjoyed an excellent reputation as a prime referral facility sought to reevaluate their position as they looked to a future based on managed care and declining reimbursement. They had formed a PO in 1986 and subsequently a small regional HMO was developed with about 100 shareholders. The initial review suggested that the HMO should be open to the entire medical staff as well as regional physicians. It subsequently attracted about 400 physicians from multiple counties in the area.

The physicians decided to evaluate each of their clinical departments to see how they were positioned for the future. With the assistance of an outside consultant, the physicians formed a medical advisory council (MAC), which considered the broad range of contractual, financial, and organizational issues that formed the basis for planning and operation of their clinical programs and resources.

The MAC, in turn, required that all clinical departments and sections meet to discuss how to optimize their respective specialties and develop future plans that included anticipated resource requirements. Each department then presented its findings to a clinical priority task force (CPTF) composed of 10 to 14 of the staff's best and most widely respected physicians. The CPTF listened to each presentation, evaluated the arguments, and synthesized a comprehensive recommendation on clinical priorities for the MAC and the hospital's board of directors.

These recommendations were then reviewed and integrated into the hospital's strategic plan. Approximately 80 to 85 percent of the recommendations were acted upon, and the hospital and physicians have found that their overall cost position has improved, along with its statistics for lengths of stay. This process allowed the medical staff to directly evaluate and prioritize requests by colleagues for resources and to help shape the planning of the organization. Although managed care still covers a relatively small percentage of the population, the hospital and medical staff have improved their collaboration and strengthened their ability to compete in an environment that rewards cost-effective medical care.

Such a cooperative undertaking between a hospital and its physicians has significant benefits that accrue to both parties. In the preface to their text *Integrated Health Care*, Coddington, Moore, and Fischer note:

> In our consulting practice, we have observed that physicians and hospitals working together almost always increase their market share, provide more coordinated care and better access to patients, have more favorable economies of scale, and are better positioned for the future. And they are more likely to listen to their customers and promptly implement the changes needed to enhance their customer relations.[3]

THE SHIFTING ROLE OF THE HOSPITAL

For many years, not-for-profit hospitals focused on the delivery of health care to the members of communities. This was their major contribution to the community good. However, with the advent of more aggressive for-profit institutions, a great debate began over the validity of this role to the towns and cities hospitals served. The for-profit corporations deflected the debate somewhat by demanding that not-for-profit facilities document the community benefit they provided in order to justify their tax benefit.

Hospitals as Community Stewards

Hospitals began to try to compile the positive impact they had on their communities above and beyond the medical care they provided. For some it was a rude awakening that prompted more attention to community health and wellness. Unfortunately, a number of recent efforts under-taken by hospitals to emphasize their community commitment have been nothing more than advertising campaigns or attempts to increase market share. Aiding in the development of a healthy community is more than just the delivery of care to the sick; it is participating in an assessment of community needs, such as literacy and employment, that may ultimately have a greater effect on illness and disease.

A Pillar of the Community: Case Example

Saint Anthony Hospital on Chicago's southwest side celebrated its cen-tennial in 1997. Over the years it has served an immigrant community that has changed from Irish to Bohemian to Mexican. Throughout all these changes in the community, it has continuously adapted its ser-vices to the needs of its physicians and patients and sought to integrate itself into the everyday life of the area it serves.

Many of the hospital's employees are from the immediate area. Those who are not are encouraged to work with community organiza-tions and serve on their governing bodies. A group of senior citizens from the community meets at the hospital on a regular basis and receives updates on the hospital's plans. The hospital is a central site for cultural and religious celebrations. The Friends of Saint Anthony is a group of business and community leaders who are intimately involved in the hospital's growth and development.

The hospital recently embarked on a collaborative project with Cook County Hospital that will allow certain of the county hospital's patients who wish to deliver their babies at Saint Anthony to still be cared for by Cook County physicians. In turn, Cook County pediatric specialists will staff clinics at Saint Anthony, which will allow patients to be evaluated at one site rather than having to travel to another hos-pital. In addition to helping patients, such collaboration eliminates cer-tain duplicative services, which should lower the community's health care costs.

The hospital supports other efforts, such as an intensive outpatient counseling program for mothers with substance abuse problems. It also recently received an empowerment zone grant that would have allowed it to develop its own medical assistant training program. How-ever, it elected instead to support a community job training effort that was already in existence and in need of additional support. Other areas in which the hospital can assist the community are being explored. They include reducing the incidence of adolescent pregnancy and gang violence and encouraging job training and improved educational opportunities.

ERODING RELATIONS BETWEEN PAYERS AND PROVIDERS

In many cities, a small number of managed care organizations (MCOs) dominate the market. Their stringent and, at times, arbitrary rules and decisions, coupled with their cost control efforts, have been met with hostility on the part of providers, especially physicians. Yet MCOs are successful because the market remains dissatisfied with the efforts (or nonefforts) of health care professionals to control the costs and quality of their services.

Had physicians and hospitals paid greater attention to these fundamental concerns, MCOs would not be having such a significant impact. It is more likely than not that reimbursement will continue to decline and more people will participate in managed care plans. It seems a waste of time and energy to continue an adversarial relationship with organizations that are selling a reimbursement and utilization product that the market wants. It would be better to determine how one can be successful under these conditions and how such efforts might also benefit the MCO.

Payers as Customers: Case Example

Richard Bell* is the chair of the section of thoracic and cardiovascular surgery at a community hospital in a city dominated by five MCOs and possessing a substantial number of competing cardiovascular surgical programs. He has worked diligently to garner additional referrals, and the program's volumes now exceed the threshold that allows it to compete for managed care contracts.

Despite his clinical activities, Bell returned to graduate business school part-time to acquire expertise in management and finance, and he recently received his M.B.A. It was his feeling that such education would enable him to lead the program more effectively and to be better prepared for the future. In creating a business plan for his division, he operated under the assumption that reimbursement would continue to decline and managed care would remain a significant part of the city's landscape. In addition, he emphasized that all members of his team should treat payers as customers rather than as enemies.

Bell went out of his way to visit with executives of MCOs and to establish relationships with each organization's medical director. He learned the criteria for successfully obtaining contracts and incorporated

---

*This executive's actual name has been changed to protect the privacy of the people and organizations involved.

them into the program. During every managed care negotiation, he and his team gave a presentation that outlined their most recent results, including costs and outcomes, and that reviewed their plans for quality improvement activities. Since its inception, Bell's program has participated in a national database that allows its outcomes to be compared with similar-size hospitals across the country.

Bell and his team are constantly seeking to improve their service and have received commitments from other specialists involved in the care of cardiovascular patients to accept capitated payments. He has worked with the hospital's finance department to develop package prices for all cardiovascular services. A nurse case manager is responsible for ensuring that clinical pathways are followed, that data are collected, and that communications with MCOs are up-to-date.

This attention to detail and Bell's attitude toward payers has resulted in the program gaining additional credibility and contracts while at the same time lowering costs and improving quality.

FORMING STRATEGIC ALLIANCES

The hallmark of each of the successful examples noted previously has been the ability to form alliances to improve the outlook for each interested party and the combined enterprise. Strategic alliances can be considered as any one of a number of formal arrangements between parties for purposes of cooperation and mutual gain. Some of the stimuli for alliances are a desire to expand one's business, to pursue additional competencies lacking in one party's enterprise, to reduce risk in an uncertain market, to lessen constraints on capital, to develop organizational standards, and to favorably influence potential customers.

Strategic alliances often form when potential partners relate to one another symbiotically as well as competitively. In other words, alliances are more likely to emerge when one organization uses the services or products of another as opposed to situations in which organizations are competing for similar resources.

The high failure rate of strategic alliances (50 to 80 percent) is related to inadequate planning and analysis or attitudes that remain more competitive than cooperative. The partners need to recognize that each must facilitate the attainment of mutual objectives if they are to achieve the win-win endpoint that marks success.[4]

It cannot be emphasized too strongly that to be successful, strategic alliances in health care cannot be generated out of the current mind-set that affects the majority of board members, hospital administrators, and physicians: "I'll do it my way." To paraphrase Albert Einstein, none of the current health care problems can be solved by the same thinking that created them.[5]

Build a Climate of Cooperation

The fundamental element required to promote and focus strategic alliances is cooperation among the involved parties. One of the major problems in health care today is the self-interest of the various participants—physicians, hospitals, and payers. Although one might argue that each has become enormously profitable with this approach, research would suggest that in the long run, such unbridled competition leads to a worse outcome than could be achieved by mutual cooperation.[6]

Certain approaches should be employed by parties seeking a cooperative relationship that could evolve into a strategic alliance. These include creating a shared vision, building strong relationships, and fostering regular communication.

Have a Long-Term Focus or Vision   If potential partners are only interested in the next quarter's results, each is likely to do whatever it takes to maximize personal gain. It is only by making the probability of future interactions important relative to the present that a more cooperative posture is likely. In addition, many initiatives, especially those dealing with process improvement, may require substantial investment and a relatively long timeline before they bear fruit. Participants have to be willing to take risks in these areas in order to move the organization forward. Those who continue to pull back in the face of increased competition and more restrictive payment schedules are likely to send the organization into a death spiral from which it will never recover.

Improve Relationships among Involved Parties   It is only by frequent interaction and small successes that a climate of trust can be developed among individuals and groups, allowing larger decisions and initiatives to be undertaken. It is helpful to try to understand the other individual's position before you insist he or she understand yours. This promotes a more critical look at one's actions and how they affect others. Respect for another's point of view is fostered by spending time with that person in his or her operational area.

Board members and administrators can acquire a greater understanding of clinical care processes by allotting a certain amount of time during the year and spending it in clinical care areas or by shadowing a nurse or physician. In addition, physician-administrators, such as department chairs, should be afforded the opportunity of having an administrative mentor during their tenure to assist them in acquiring additional management expertise. Many hospitals are developing formal management programs for their physicians that will enable them to better understand the challenges facing health care professionals, especially those charged with the responsibility of leading health care institutions.

Encourage Regular Communication   Open and honest communication is the sign of a healthy organization. In times of rapid and tumultuous change, communication must be multidimensional, clear, and frequent. Otherwise the information gap will be rapidly filled by rumors.

Trying to manage information by limiting it to select individuals or groups is foolhardy. Ultimately, discussions become common knowledge, and those excluded withdraw from further interaction if they view such behavior as untrustworthy. Attempting to repair such damage to relationships is time-consuming and may, in some cases, be impossible.

In some circumstances, it may be necessary to engage in one-on-one dialogue if issues are particularly difficult or troublesome. Although this will be labor-intensive, it may be critical to the success of the new enterprise in demonstrating commitment to entertaining all points of view as well as a willingness to address concerns on an individual level.

Build the Alliance Brick by Brick

Building an effective, secure, long-term relationship between boards, hospitals, physicians, communities, and payers must proceed brick by brick. In evaluating our current health care system, many would agree that a cooperative attitude would be more likely to conserve resources, lower costs, improve outcomes, and provide greater access to care than our current dog-eat-dog environment. Despite the intuition that cooperation trumps competition, it is necessary to convince others that change is required.

Gain Organizational Commitment for Change   Any effort to promote a philosophical shift and dramatic relationship restructuring must encompass a number of related activities that require the commitment of the leadership of the potential partners.[7]

Motivate Individuals to Change   It is a human characteristic to avoid change unless compelling reasons exist to do so. The significant pain inflicted on providers by external forces should have sensitized most of them to the pressures for change, but they may need additional stimuli. Leaders should encourage a comparison between the current state of functioning and one that would be considered desirable and then communicate realistic expectations about the changes necessary to get there. At the same time, they must be empathetic and supportive and view the situation from the perspective of others by becoming active listeners.

Communication about planned changes is essential and can reduce unproductive speculation as well as calm individual fears. The more uncertain individuals are about the consequences of change, the more they will resist it.

It is also important to involve as many people as possible in change activities, especially those who are most critical of the process. It is better to have one's detractors on the inside where they can be influenced than to have them undermine the efforts from the outside.

Create a Vision   Creating a vision is a major challenge for any leader and requires creative and intuitive thought processes. It should not be the task of a small group, rather, it should be inclusive. A leadership retreat that includes board members, physicians, administrators, and other health professionals can be an excellent mechanism to build commitment and relationships as well as consensus about the direction of the organization. It is helpful if midpoint goals are established so that they can serve as milestones showing that the process is on track and moving forward.

Develop a Political Foundation   Although collaboration and cooperation are desirable characteristics of a strategic alliance, the change process does require a political power base to move it forward. Key stakeholders can be identified as those who have the most to gain or lose from the proposed changes, and leadership can target them to help them understand the importance of accepting and supporting the proposed changes. Again, it is important not to exclude vocal critics but instead bring them into the process and attempt to allay their concerns and obtain their support.

Move through the Transition   It would be wonderful if one could move from one's current situation to a more desirable state of affairs without any detours, but that is not possible. There will always be a transition period, often chaotic, which allows participants to learn the necessary techniques to successfully manage change.

This is the time when activities and events are laid out that will mark the passage through this process. New organizational structures may be required to deal with certain of the changes and, once again, stakeholders must be targeted to gain their support.

Keep It Moving   All of the elements of the change process must be constantly reinforced to all concerned. There is no such thing as articulating the vision once and then putting it on the shelf. It must be reviewed constantly and the desired behaviors manifested by the alliance's leaders. For the effort to succeed, resources must be provided to support the change process and to allow members of the organization to acquire new knowledge and skills. Formal recognition programs or individual support and praise can reinforce desired behaviors.

Learn the Art of Remodeling

The development of a strategic alliance with a creative vision requires remodeling from top to bottom—everything from structure to functions. The old organization should be taken down to its framework—including the history and values of the old culture. There must be a willingness to question everything through a thorough assessment: whether to retain or discard certain lines of business, maintain existing relationships or develop new partners, and how to creatively share risks and rewards among potential associates.

The following case study represents the process in evolution and highlights some of the key elements in developing strategic alliances and a cooperative rather than a competitive environment.

Competitors Become Partners: Case Example

In November 1995 Chicago's Saint Joseph Health Centers and Hospital sponsored by the Daughters of Charity merged with Columbus-Cabrini Health System of the Missionary Sisters of the Sacred Heart, forming Catholic Health Partners (CHP). The system comprised four hospitals. Two were located only a few blocks apart on the north side of the city in the affluent Lincoln Park area. The two remaining facilities were on Chicago's southwest side, served minority communities, and were designated disproportionate share facilities.

Shortly after the merger, one of the southwest side facilities was closed, and its services and medical staff consolidated at the remaining facility. On the north side, the board selected a consolidation model that moved all acute patient care to one facility and reserved the other for an existing neurosurgical institute, a world-renowned headache clinic, a skilled nursing facility, and certain types of ambulatory surgery.

The north side medical staffs were cross-credentialed at each hospital, medical staff bylaws were reviewed, an interim document was created to allow a merger of the staffs, and selection of departmental chairs and section chiefs was directed by a joint medical staff selection committee.

The board of directors was reconfigured to include half actively practicing physicians and half lay board members. Physicians were involved in the selection of the new chief nurse executive and all other clinical directors. In addition, physicians served on all functional consolidation teams to develop plans for the integration of clinical services.

Communication with employees, physicians, managed care executives, and the community was frequent and involved multiple vehicles. Physicians received updates through various newsletters, quarterly medical staff meetings, and open forums. Shortly after the merger was consummated, a physician committee was created that met monthly to receive updates on merger activities and to provide input to the CEO and the board.

On the southwest side, the community was apprised of changes wrought by the merger, and efforts were undertaken to rationalize community health care costs by collaborating with other area health care providers. Additional resources were provided to the community to address certain chronic problems, such as substance abuse and adolescent pregnancy.

On the north side, two employees have received fellowships to study initiatives to promote healthy communities, and the organization is exploring ways to assist communities in resolving some of their major concerns, such as poor educational resources, unemployment, crime, and drug abuse.

The organization's chief nurse executive and physician executive were aligned in such a way as to collaborate with the chief operating officers of the three facilities to develop consensus about personnel and resource allocation issues. This model was to be replicated throughout the organization at every level, on every patient care unit, and in each critical care area. A nurse, administrator, and physician would evaluate costs, quality, and resource use, and identify areas for quality improvement.

Additional meetings were held with payers to inform them of the plans for the merger and to present a strategic plan that demands substantial operational cost reductions over the first two years of CHP's existence. Individual departments continue to refine their efforts to deliver the most cost-effective and highest quality service. The physician hospital organizations of each partner merged, forming the third largest PHO in the city. The new entity continues to thrive and is well capitalized and supported by its physician members.

Although this merger is an alliance in evolution, it has attempted to benefit the community by eliminating unnecessary beds and consolidating clinical activities. It has developed a more collaborative governance structure and seeks to increase organizational participation among all its members. Its continued success is predicated on strengthening these new relationships and working together to eliminate additional system costs while at the same time encouraging continuous quality improvement efforts.

CONCLUSION

The American health care system is on a raft being swept down a river through the turbulent rapids of change. It would be ideal if there were calm pools ahead, but there is only continuous white water as far as the eye can see.[8] One group cannot bring the raft safely through; it requires everyone's paddle to be in the water steering, adjusting, and maneuvering the craft around obstacles to the shore.

Until the last decade, each element of the health care delivery system operated essentially independently, each competing to achieve its own level of success. The results have been a failure to control costs, lack of attention to quality, and an increasing number of citizens unable to afford even the most routine medical care. It is time to make a commitment to a new way of doing things in health care—a commitment to look at the long-term implications of decisions and to seek to bring others into collaborative, cooperative relationships that have the best chance of improving the system for everyone.

In his 1997 inaugural address, President Clinton identified the people, not the government, as the solution to many of the problems confronting America. In health care, professionals likewise hold the answers to the problems of access, resource conservation, cost, and quality, but they need to think "outside the box" and be creative in their approach to such problem solving. Creativity involves risk, but the rewards are potentially great. It will be bold leadership that plants the seed of true collaboration in our cities and communities; that seeks to create an environment that has as its goal the provision of quality health care for all people; that is willing to put aside ego and self-aggrandizement to achieve a higher good.

References

1. Paul Starr, *The Social Transformation of American Medicine* (New York: Basic Books, 1982), pp. 161–62.

2. Stephen M. Shortell, "The Evolution of Hospital Systems: Unfulfilled Promises and Self-Fulfilling Prophecies," *Medical Care Review* 42, no. 2 (1988): 177–82.

3. D. C. Coddington, K. D. Moore, and E. Fischer, *Integrated Healthcare: Reorganizing the Physician, Hospital and Health Plan Relationship* (Englewood, Colo.: CRACHA, 1994), pp. xvi–xvii.

4. E. Zajac, "Strategic Alliances: Developing Successful Interorganization Relationships," presented at the Future Focus Forum, J. L. Kellogg Graduate School of Management, Northwestern University, 1996.

5. M. Wheatley, *Leadership and the New Science: Learning about Organizations from an Orderly Universe* (San Francisco: Barrett-Koehler, 1992), p. 5.

6. Robert Axelrod, *The Evolution of Cooperation* (New York: Basic Books, 1984), pp. 7–10.

7. T. G. Cummings and E. F. Huse, *Organization Development and Change* (Minneapolis: West Publishing, 1989), p. 418–19.

8. P. B. Vahill, *Managing as a Performing Art: New Ideas for a World of Chaotic Change* (San Francisco: Jossey-Bass, 1989), p. 2.

7

Developing Work Relationships Based on Trust

Kenneth C. Cummings, M.D., F.A.C.P.E.

The subject of trust—once considered a topic of discussion for philosophers, poets, psychologists, and religious leaders—has now found its way into the boardroom. A stroll through the business section of your local bookstore will turn up a plethora of books on this subject, ranging from eminent economist Francis Fukuyama's *Trust: The Social Virtues and the Creation of Prosperity* to corporate turnover specialist John O. Whitney's *The Trust Factor: Liberating Profits and Restoring Corporate Vitality.*

Why is American business suddenly so interested in the subject of trust? The answer is simple: Even the best-laid strategic plans just won't work unless the organization's leaders, staff, and other stakeholders trust one another. In the health care setting, trust can spell the difference between a merger's success or failure, between a nurse manager's embracing or resisting the new patient-centered care model, and between staff's supporting or subverting work redesign. Because the failure of strategic initiatives can have a devastating effect on the bottom line, it is not an exaggeration to say that trust is essential to an organization's fiscal health.

This chapter examines how one organization built trust among leaders, physicians, and other stakeholders as it moved toward a systems approach to health care delivery. The chapter describes three key leadership traits essential to the building of trust—integrity, capability, and character—and discusses how leaders can display these traits in their day-to-day dealings with others. To help leaders resolve the conflicts that inevitably arise during times of change, the chapter also includes practical tips for building consensus among diverse groups.

THE IMPORTANCE OF TRUST IN WORK RELATIONSHIPS

For the purpose of this chapter, trust is defined as confidence in the integrity, capability, and character of a person, group, or organization. The degree of trust people or groups share—whether that level is zero or 100 percent—influences how they view each other and interact. Although trust is always an important factor in work relationships, it is especially important during times of rapid change, such as those currently being experienced by the health care industry. In stressful and uncertain times, people are apt to act out of self-interest rather than the best interests of the group as a whole. In the absence of trust, successful new relationships are unlikely to be formed and existing ties are more easily broken.

Take, for example, an attempt a few years ago to develop a regional alliance of eight hospitals in the greater Kansas City area. The effort ultimately failed because, to varying degrees, each facility perceived that there was too much to lose and too little trust to make the alliance work. Similarly, partners in a group medical practice linked only by legal agreement are much less likely to stay together when "predators" attempt to acquire the practice because the partnership is made vulnerable by the absence of genuine commitment built on trust.

In contrast, strong, trusting relationships help organizations survive tough times. When people trust their leaders to be open and honest, when people believe their leaders are acting out of a sense of stewardship, when people are confident that planned changes will genuinely improve the organization, then they are much more likely to give their enthusiastic support to initiatives and effect positive outcomes.

Such has been the case at Saint Joseph Health System, which in recent years has successfully implemented several politically charged strategic changes. Realizing the difficulty of aligning diverse groups, Saint Joseph actively sought ways to build trusting work relationships. The following case example provides an overview of techniques Saint Joseph used.

SYSTEM INTEGRATION AND THE BUILDING OF TRUST AT SAINT JOSEPH

Saint Joseph Health System in Kansas City, Missouri, is a two-hospital system that is part of the national Carondelet Health System. In 1986 a new CEO was hired and charged with the responsibility of implementing a strategically oriented systems approach. Under the CEO's leadership, the board of trustees redefined the organization's mission to state, "We will attract and support a staff of competent, caring, loyal physicians with state-of-the-art equipment and support services in a caring, responsive, and collaborative environment."

The new era began with the CEO's facilitation of a strategic planning retreat that included institutional trustees, medical staff leaders, and senior administrators. Among the major needs identified during the retreat were to hire a physician executive and to create a medical staff development plan (MSDP). When I joined the staff as vice president of medical affairs in 1989, one of my early responsibilities was to direct the MSDP process.

Setting the Stage

Recognizing the importance of building trusting work relationships during every phase of the initiatives, we began by inviting representatives of the major power groups—the hospital board, medical staff, and senior physicians—to form a consultant selection task force. The task force was cochaired by the leaders of the hospital board and the medical staff. To develop support for the MSDP, the task force decided to hire a consultant whose approach was to make the MSDP a grassroots effort. While the selection process was educational in and of itself, we realized a much larger benefit: By working together on a structured task, we had the opportunity to get to know and trust each other.

After about 10 months of working together, most of the physicians from the selection task force, board members, and senior administrators presented the MSDP proposal to the medical staff, the administration, and the hospital board of trustees, all of whom accepted it. During the development of the MSDP, there was ongoing, in-depth communication between the senior administrative staff and board members, medical leaders, and other key administrators. The intention behind these communications was to increase understanding and support and to raise our level of trust in one another. The participation of members of each of the major interest groups was instrumental to the plan's ready acceptance.

The MSDP recommended the development of four main elements: (1) a network of satellite primary care facilities (PCN), (2) a management services organization (MSO), (3) a primary care residency or affiliation, and (4) a managed care organization (MCO). The following discussion is limited to certain stages in the development of the PCN and MSO.

Designing the Carondelet Primary Care Network

During the early planning stages for the Carondelet Primary Care Network (CPCN), a major effort was made to communicate with specialty medical staff, a group of approximately 700 physicians, in order to build a strong relationship with them. The message consistently communicated was that the CPCN would bring a stable source of patients to the physicians' practices and that other specialists' needs would also be addressed. Additionally, it was agreed that the administrative staff would assist as much as possible in the development of their practices. By building on past positive interactions with this group, we were able to maintain an atmosphere of cooperation and communication.

The actual design, implementation, strategic guidance, and operation of the CPCN became a collaborative effort. Several individuals with a diversity of experience, knowledge, and vision were recruited to help, including the newly selected medical director of CPCN. He had been the department chair and was well liked, trusted, and respected by the medical staff and administration. With his collaboration, the planning team designed the clinical and medical contractual sides of the CPCN. Once the critical design elements were determined, the team looked for opportunities to implement key elements of the plan in a manner that would foster trust and lower the threshold of fear.

A Corporate Structure Built on Trust   It was decided that both the CPCN and the MSO would be independent of the hospital organizational structure. The MSO would have an independent board representing the shareholders (our holding company was a shareholder); however, the board was to be composed primarily of physicians. Although giving physicians control of the majority vote was somewhat risky, it was important to take the risk in order to send the message to physicians that they were trusted.

An Appealing Environment for Physicians   To create an appealing environment for CPCN physicians, we offered them a stable incentive-based income, close association with an excellent health care system with extensive resources and a dynamic strategy, and the ability to manage the clinical side of their practices with a minimum of intrusion. At the same time, it was made clear to physicians that the organization was actively preparing for managed care. As a result, the physicians and their medical directors knew in advance that they would be held accountable for clinical quality and outcomes, resource utilization and cost, patient satisfaction, and flexibility in testing new paradigms in a team setting.

An Appealing Contract for Physicians   Knowing that physicians struggle with the notion of employment contracts, the system decided to assume additional risk to build trust with physicians. A number of elements made the contracts "friendly," but the single most important one was that, except in very unusual circumstances, there is no non-compete clause. Our reasoning was that if the relationship didn't work out, we still wanted the physician and his or her patients to be associated with our system. Thus, if medical records of patients are brought to the relationship by a physician, they remain his or hers. A copy is required only for legal reasons. In this way, the physician experiences very little risk in joining the network, a philosophy that further encourages trust.

The Structure of the Management Services Organization   To quell medical staff anxiety over having physicians' office data available to the institution, and with the intention of sponsoring the establishment of a high-quality practice management capability, a for-profit, stock-capitalized corporate structure was selected. It was to be open to all active medical staff members and would be owned principally by them. A number of senior physician leaders participated initially, and as confidence and trust have grown, Cooperative Physicians Services, Inc. (CPSI) has raised capital by issuing additional stock. The physician network contracted with the MSO, thereby creating a wonderful synergy.

Assessing the Results of the Initiative

The first clinic satellite was opened in April 1992. To date, the network has grown to include 8 strategically placed clinic satellites in our market area, employing 22 physicians. We are currently in the process of integrating a primary care physician group and clinic satellites from our sister institution. This will bring us to a total of more than 40 physicians at 12 sites. By careful management and contracting, the PCN and MSO have been growing while turning a profit.

Based on our experience during this and other projects, we learned a great deal about building trusting relationships during change initiatives. The following list summarizes some of the most important principles we learned:

- *All parties involved in the initiative must be willing to cooperate.* Groups with different frames of reference, such as hospital boards and physicians, need to understand that they are not "natural enemies" but partners united in a common cause.
- *The organization must value and encourage open communication.* All parties (or their representatives) must be given opportunities to discuss their concerns honestly, openly, and with impunity. In this way, parties can overcome their fear of hidden agendas.
- *All parties must consider and respect each other's point of view.* Parties must be willing to listen to each other and respect the rationale behind each other's positions.

- *All parties in an evolving relationship must find a common ground.* Once parties are able to understand and acknowledge the legitimacy of each other's views, they must seek a common ground upon which to build.
- *All parties must be willing to relinquish some degree of control or authority to demonstrate trust in each other.* Participants must look at the big picture and realize that collaboration will reap more benefits than competition.
- *All parties must be willing to share risk.* As the case example illustrates, a willingness to share risk shows genuine concern for the welfare of all parties and therefore fosters trust.

LEADERSHIP TRAITS AND BEHAVIORS THAT BUILD TRUST

To build the kind of trusting work relationships Saint Joseph enjoys, leadership itself must be perceived as trustworthy. By displaying certain traits and behaviors, leaders can inspire trust in others and set the tone for the rest of the organization.

Displaying Integrity, Capability, and Character

As the definition of trust presented earlier suggests, trust is built by exhibiting three key characteristics: integrity, capability, and character. Each of these traits is essential; the degree of trust that people place in their leaders depends on the degree to which each of the traits is present.

Integrity   Integrity requires that each party in a relationship tell the truth, the whole truth, and nothing but the truth. This means that what one says in front of a person does not differ substantially from what one says when that person isn't within hearing distance. If, for example, a vice president of medical affairs (VPMA) plays the sycophant to his or her CEO, for example, praising the CEO's proposals for developing better relationships with the medical staff, then later denigrates the CEO's suggestions in discussions with the medical staff, neither the CEO nor the medical staff can be expected to trust the VPMA. Working relationships will be altered, and energy that could been spent on improving the organization will be wasted.

Capability   For trust to evolve, each party in a relationship must believe that the other parties are capable of fulfilling their parts of the task upon which the relationship is based. Failings are understandable (although still regrettable) *only* when they are unintended. Trust cannot survive if one or more of the parties in a relationship promises something undeliverable. As soon as the deception is uncovered, trust flees.

Consider, for example, a growing group of internists that joined a large network of physicians. The senior member of this group demanded to be identified as its local medical director. Over several years, it became obvious that, though an excellent physician, he had little management talent or motivation. As problems began to surface, it was evident that not only did this physician fail to perform his administrative duties (especially with regard to communication), but the decisions he did make were to his own economic advantage. By the time the extent of the situation was appreciated, the group was severely damaged through mistrust.

Character   The building of trust also requires that each party in a relationship believe that the other parties are committed to the relationship and that they will perform as expected, even when no one is looking or monitoring their behavior. The ethic here is one of being committed to the survival and enhancement of the relationship.

For example, a very senior-level medical manager was well-known for his keen intellect and his attention to details. He spoke eloquently of unity and cooperation when his superiors were present but changed dramatically in their absence. None of the physicians in the organization trusted him because he was considered to be ruthless, narrow-minded, and highly political in his interpersonal relations. His character deficits damaged the entire institution until he was removed.

Modeling Behavior That Inspires Trust

Trust takes hard work to establish and vigilance to maintain. Once initial trust is developed, certain practices can help keep trust alive. These practices include doing an assessment of potential barriers to trust, being open to all points of view, and showing a willingness to make the first move.

Assess Potential Barriers to Trust   One of the most important steps leaders can take is an honest self-assessment in which they analyze any personal barriers to forming trusting work relationships. Leaders should consider what goals they hope to achieve through the partnership—whether it is with employees, managers, or associates in business—and potential obstacles to the partnership.

For example, prior to assuming his new position with a large hospital, a VPMA went through the kind of personal self-evaluation just described. While he knew he was committed to working with all stakeholder leaders to create a patient-centered organization, he also realized that the culture shift involved in the VPMA role was a potential barrier to maintaining trusting work relationships with clinicians. The VPMA position requires the physician to move out of the clinician's role and into an administrative one. Although the VPMA may have been a long-time, trusted colleague on the clinical staff before accepting the new position, the change in roles from physician to administrator could cause clinical staff to distrust the VPMA. As a result of the self-assessment, the VPMA recognized the potential barrier and planned ways to overcome it.

Create Opportunities for Communication   In the absence of communication on an issue, people are inclined to suspect the worst. The rumor mill takes over and erodes trust in leadership and the organization. As organizations undergo change, the need for continual open communication at all levels is especially great. Thus, finding effective ways to keep communication lines open is crucial. Newsletters, more frequent and meaningful meetings, and informal coaching sessions all contribute to keeping the trust level high.

Be Patient   The development of trust takes time. Through continual testing and the accumulation of evidence that our trust is well placed, we arrive at a trusting relationship. Patience is essential to this process. In some instances it can take a long time and a lot of testing before certain individuals are willing to trust. Leaders must avoid taking this personally.

Value Other People's Ideas   Unfortunately, arrogance all too often accompanies high positions and titles. People higher in the hierarchy presume that their views are the "right" ones, and those below them acquiesce to that presumption. In the changing health care environment, those organizations that value everyone's ideas build trust and gain the benefit of the creative thinking of all stakeholders.

Be Willing to Make the First Move   Trusting relationships cannot be developed if no one takes the first step. Few would want to be part of an organization in which no one was willing to take the risk of trusting others. In good times, the lack of trust might be masked by good results having little to do with the quality of the organization. But in stressful times, the organization where there is little trust is vulnerable to being washed away by the first wave. It is up to leaders to make the first move.

Building Trust Where Disagreements Exist

Despite leaders' best efforts, there will still be people who are reluctant to support change. While detractors and naysayers can be hard to take, especially when the tremendous challenges confronting the organization require everyone to work together, it is important to do everything reasonable to bring these detractors aboard and to gain their trust in the process. Here are a few suggestions:

- *Look for something to respect in the other party.* All this means is that you trust the person in at least a small area. If you respect a person's technical competence, you may be prepared to trust his or her decisions and actions. That makes it a bit easier to then extend that trust to an action or decision outside the technical area.
- *State your intentions.* Signal your trustworthiness by indicating up front that you *can* be trusted. Statements such as "My integrity is not for sale" are a declaration that trust is an important value to you. Of course, a statement is not enough to guarantee acceptance by others, but it can pave the way. You have notified people that you want to be trusted. The consequence, of course, is that you must never be dishonest, duplicitous, or calculating.
- *Look for commonality of interests and goals and actively affirm them.* Determine where you share views and goals with others and concentrate on these common areas. The trust built here makes it easier to build trust in areas of contention or divergence.
- *Build a basis for trust.* Trust evolves over time, but its evolution can be managed. Strategize the priorities to develop trust. When I began my previous position as a VPMA, I found that there was no adequate eating facility designated solely for the medical staff. Realizing that physicians need time during the day to be separate from patients and other personnel, I established an attractive room with a buffet at a reasonable price for our physicians. To this day, physicians comment about our great lunchroom, and I am credited with the accomplishment. Early on, I was able to demonstrate to the medical staff that I had the physicians' interests in mind. It was a good beginning for developing a trusting relationship. Look for such opportunities.
- *Hold a stable vision.* When people are in the trust-building process, they will be focused and very sensitive to variations in message, actions, and words. They will be looking for consistency from you. This may be a difficult feat to pull off, particularly when rapid changes require rapid responses. However, a leader who appears to be hopping about on issues cannot expect to instill much trust in those who are being asked to follow.
- *Avoid prejudging people.* Try not to prejudge other people's motivations or capability of being trusted. It is prudent, of

course, to be alert, but prejudgments can stifle trust before it has a chance to develop. It is not uncommon for a new administrator to be "warned" about so-called "problem" physicians when they accept the job. By suspending assumptions and giving the alleged "troublemakers" a fair chance, leaders may find them to be honest and cooperative colleagues.

- *Be aware of body language.* Avoid words, facial expressions, gestures, and other body language that suggest suspicion, another agenda, or a lack of interest. Conversely, make use of friendly expressions and gestures—coming from a sincere intention—to encourage others to respond in kind.

CONCLUSION

The silver lining in the dark cloud of change is the opportunity to rethink, refocus, and recreate. New constructs of health care are causing professionals to challenge assumptions and redefine health care delivery. While this is a painful time, it is also an exciting time.

Establishing, growing, and maintaining trust is essential to the successful management of change in health care. Leaders have the opportunity to select one of several "futures" for our organizations. A clearly understood, creative, and well-implemented plan for building trust with stakeholders can be a central factor in the success and profitability of the organization. In short, trust is the currency of relationships.

Bibliography

Drucker, Peter F. "Post-Capitalist Executive" (interview by T. George Harris). *Harvard Business Review* 71, no. 3 (1993): 114–22.

Dwyer, Charles. *The Shifting Sources of Power and Influence.* Tampa, Fla.: American College of Physician Executives, 1991.

Fukuyama, Francis. *The End of History and the Last Man.* New York: Free Press, 1992.

Whitney, John O. *The Trust Factor: Liberating Profits and Restoring Corporate Vitality.* New York: McGraw-Hill, 1994.

8

Using Education to Build Support for Strategic Change

Gita B. Budd and R. Timothy Stack

In today's market, the most successful health care organizations are those that excel at identifying effective strategies and rapidly implementing them. Although strategy development is never easy, implementation of strategy is often the more difficult challenge. The magnitude of the changes that health care organizations are currently pursuing makes implementation that much more difficult. Key to successful implementation is developing stakeholders' understanding and advocacy of changes to be made.

This chapter describes the concepts involved in securing stakeholder understanding, support, and advocacy, and it identifies specific educational tools and techniques to use in the process. It is based primarily on the experiences of one organization seeking to improve its ability to effectively implement strategic change. This organization's improvement efforts were focused on the initiation and enhancement of both leadership development activities and widespread stakeholder education. Since leadership development activities are addressed more extensively in other chapters of this book, only an overview is provided in this chapter. The primary focus is on the various aspects of stakeholder education.

TWO MAJOR INITIATIVES

Developing stakeholder understanding, support, and advocacy requires a focus on two related but separate areas of activity—leadership development and widespread stakeholder education. (See figure 8-1.) Efforts in both of these arenas need to be integrated and coordinated.

FIGURE 8-1.   Selected Requirements for Strategy
Implementation Sucess

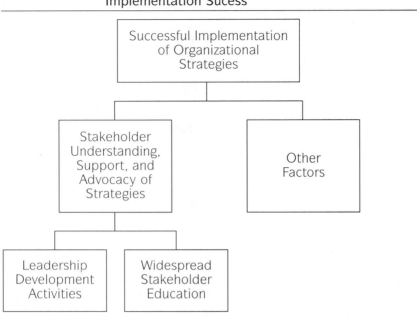

Leadership Development Activities

Because of the transformational nature of the strategic changes being pursued by most health care organizations, it is to be expected that the organization's culture will also change. In fact, changing the organization's culture may be required if the strategic changes are to be ultimately successful. The organization's management group must be in a position to practice and promote the type of organizational culture that will support the strategic changes being implemented. This generally requires organizations to undertake some type of leadership development activities.

Widespread Stakeholder Education

Because of the magnitude of the changes being pursued and the potential impact on every aspect of the organization, there is a greater need than ever for stakeholder education. All organizational stakeholders must be given opportunities to learn about the types of organizational changes that are being pursued. Specifically, stakeholders must be educated about the nature of the strategic changes, the reasons for these changes, and their potential and expected impact.

Borgess Health Alliance, an integrated health system serving southwestern Michigan, initiated its focus on leadership development and stakeholder education in 1993. Since then Borgess has continued to develop techniques within these two areas that have enabled the organization to consistently improve the effectiveness of its strategy implementation efforts.

Borgess's senior leadership remains committed to leadership development and stakeholder education. Anecdotal evidence and comparisons to past experiences are cited in support of the fact that these efforts have assisted Borgess in becoming more effective in its strategy implementation. However, the process through which Borgess has developed its leadership development and stakeholder education efforts has consisted primarily of trial and error. This chapter describes those processes, techniques, and tools that Borgess discovered to be most effective within its organizational context.

The lessons learned by Borgess Health Alliance are applicable to other health care organizations pursuing major strategic changes. The specific tools and techniques should be reviewed for appropriateness within each organization's specific context and be regarded as examples of potential approaches.

THE LEADERSHIP DEVELOPMENT PROCESS

In the context of implementing strategic change, the purpose of leadership development initiatives is to ensure that management's style and approach are promoting an organizational culture supportive of the types of changes being put in place. The leadership development efforts should focus on increasing the management group's personal capacities to change in a manner consistent with the desired organizational changes.

For example, leadership development efforts may need to focus on increasing the management group's knowledge in such areas as facilitating a change process, effective team development, and coaching and mentoring. To be successful, the development efforts must also ensure that increased knowledge is translated into changed leadership practices.

To ensure that the leadership development activities are focused on the appropriate skills and abilities, a determination must be made as to the type of organizational culture that will be necessary in order for the successful implementation of the organization's strategies. A variety of conceptual models and associated tools are available to help identify the type of organizational culture best suited to specific organizational and environmental circumstances. A review of current organizational development literature and discussions with organizational development consultants can be useful for identifying the various models and tools available. (See chapter 2.)

After determining the focus for the leadership development activities, the specific components to be included in the organization's leadership development process need to be defined. The components and the time frames in which they are to be accomplished will depend on the magnitude of the difference between the existing and the ideal cultures, as well as the pace at which the leadership development must occur relative to strategy implementation.

For example, if the gap between the existing and ideal cultures is small or the strategy implementation time frames are relatively long, the leadership development process can occur over a more extended time frame. On the other hand, if the cultural gap is large or strategy implementation is required to occur rapidly, leadership development activities must occur in a shorter time frame. At Borgess, both the cultural gap and the strategy implementation time frame dictated that the leadership development process needed to be initiated soon but could proceed on a measured (rather than an accelerated) pace. Table 8-1 summarizes the seven components included in Borgess's leadership development process.

Borgess's senior management is committed to leadership development as an ongoing process aimed at continuous improvement. Anecdotal evidence and comparisons to past experiences are cited in support of the effectiveness of these efforts and their positive impact on strategy implementation.

INTRODUCTION TO STAKEHOLDER EDUCATION

Stakeholder education seeks to give an organization's constituency groups the information necessary for them to understand, support, and advocate the organization's strategies. Traditional educational approaches, however, will *not* result in stakeholder support for strategic change. Many health care organizations have traditionally treated stakeholder education as single isolated events. But stakeholder education is effective only when the educational initiatives are directed at providing opportunities for ongoing learning. To have the greatest impact, stakeholder education must become an ongoing process within the organization.

Guidelines for Providing Education to Stakeholders

Through the trial-and-error development of stakeholder education and learning opportunities at Borgess, six guidelines were discovered and applied:

1. *Education and learning must occur broadly across the organization's stakeholders.* All of the major constituency groups should be included in the educational efforts. That includes the board, all levels of management, employees, physicians, network partners, and the community.
2. *Education and learning must create stakeholders who are knowledgeable about the opportunities and challenges faced by the organization.* Stakeholders must understand the environmental context in which the organization operates. Educational efforts, therefore, must include sessions focused on current trends and topics.
3. *Education and learning must address key aspects of the organization's strategies.* These aspects include a description of each strategy, the rationale for pursuing the strategy, the intended organizational impact, and the plans for implementation. In other words, the "what," the "why," and the "how" of each major strategy need to be explained in the educational program.
4. *Education and learning must address stakeholders' needs for information regarding their roles in implementing the organization's strategies.* Because of the magnitude of the changes being pursued, the roles of the specific stakeholder groups may be unclear. The organization's expectations with respect to the roles of each stakeholder group must be explained. Additionally, stakeholders will most likely need education aimed at personal skill development. This will enable them to better perform in their new and potentially expanded roles.
5. *Education must involve a process that goes beyond simple awareness building.* If stakeholders are to be in a position to provide support to the organization's change efforts, education must be translated into learning. These experiences need to be designed so that stakeholders are taken through a series of educational programs that first create awareness, then move to higher levels of increased comprehension and understanding, and finally result in the ability to apply, analyze, and synthesize the knowledge that is being shared. This implies that educational efforts will require traditional didactic sessions as well as varying types of experiential situations. Additionally, educational programming will need to include sufficient repetition of key concepts and additive learning opportunities in order to assist stakeholders in moving through the various phases of the learning process.
6. *Education and learning must be matched to the needs of the stakeholders.* Both the content and timing of specific educational efforts need to be tailored to the information needs of each

TABLE 8-1.   Summary of Leadership Development Process Being Implemented by Borgess Health Alliance

Component Focus	Process	Outcome
Development of individual manager profiles	360° assessment by superiors, peers, and subordinates using standardized evaluation tool	Profile of each manager's strengths and areas for improvement
Definition of desired leadership behavior profile	Identification of specific management skills and values-based behaviors	Specification of organization's expectations regarding management's behaviors
Comparison of individual managers to desired leadership profile	Setting of benchmark scores for selected items on standardized tool	Comparative assessment of each manager to desired profile and identification of gaps
Action planning with individual managers	Identification of methods to improve specific skills and behaviors	Plans for skill improvement to diminish each manager's gaps
Targeted leadership development education	Education focused on behaviors most needing improvement	Specific sessions on such topics as facilitation change, values-based leadership, and team development
Annual leadership evaluations	Ongoing 360° assessment process	Tracking progress both for individual managers and the management group as a whole
Incorporation of improvement targets in performance and compensation evaluations	Specific goals related to leadership improvement included in individual manager evaluations	Demonstration of organizational commitment to leadership development and improvement

stakeholder group. Different stakeholder groups will require different information at different times, based on their roles in the change process. To be most effective, appropriate education should be provided as close as possible to the time when the stakeholder group actually needs to use the information.

The application of these six guidelines is demonstrated in the following description of Borgess's experiences in the development of widespread stakeholder education.

"Just-in-Time" Learning

The process that evolved at Borgess can best be described as "just-in-time" learning. Consistent with guideline number six, the most significant element of this education and learning process was the attempt to carefully time the educational efforts so that the information needs of the stakeholders were matched closely with their roles in the implementation of the organization's strategies.

In the early development of its educational program, Borgess experienced the effects of educating stakeholders either too early or too late in the implementation process. Both of these situations resulted in less than optimal support for the organization's change efforts. As a result, significant emphasis was placed on carefully timing educational activities so that stakeholders were appropriately prepared for the types of changes that were occurring at any given point in time.

For example, the initial educational sessions held by Borgess for physicians regarding capitation were conducted too early when compared to the development of capitation in the local marketplace. This created difficulties because the information was not viewed as relevant by the majority of physicians and, therefore, was perceived as a waste of their time. Additionally, the information was perceived negatively by some physicians because they misunderstood the purpose of the education. They viewed it as an organizational endorsement, a promotion of the concepts and implications of capitation. The examples that follow indicate how Borgess learned to better match its educational efforts to the needs of both its stakeholders and the organization.

The content of the education and learning opportunities that Borgess created was wide-ranging. All stakeholders received information regarding such topics as:

- The employer's perspective on health care costs and quality
- Health care reform
- Managed care and capitation
- Work reengineering

- Network development
- Systems integration
- Current ethical dilemmas in health care
- The for-profit movement in health care
- Healthier communities
- Values-based leadership and decision making

The depth and detail of the information varied, depending on the strategy implementation roles of each group. Those groups that had more extensive implementation roles, such as management, received in-depth information. Those groups with less extensive implementation roles, such as board members, received broader overviews.

Additionally, everyone was provided with educational opportunities aimed at various types of skill development. These programs were tailored to the skills needed by each stakeholder group in their respective strategy implementation roles. Skill development sessions included such topics as fiduciary responsibilities for board members, team development skills for management and employees, and business management skills for physicians.

Borgess's just-in-time learning process sought to create education and learning opportunities for the broadest range of stakeholders. The constituency groups involved in the educational efforts included board members, executive and administrative management, departmental management, employees, physicians, network partners, and the community.

EDUCATIONAL OPPORTUNITIES FOR BOARD MEMBERS

The greater the amount of board understanding of and support for strategic initiatives, the greater the chance that the initiatives will be quickly and effectively implemented. For this reason, the information needs of board members should be given careful consideration. Board members should be provided with a variety of educational experiences and programs—from an orientation session for new board members to regularly scheduled continuing education programs for the board as a whole.

Orientation for New Members

Generally speaking, health care organizations place too little emphasis on the orientation of new board members. This oversight is unfortunate, because a well-prepared orientation session can be instrumental in helping the board function more effectively. The session, which generally requires a minimum of four hours, should include the following information:

- A description of the organization
- An introduction to significant environmental trends
- An overview of organizational strategies
- A review of the role and expectations of board members

The information presented during the session should be supplemented with written materials that new board members can use as a reference guide.

Ongoing Programs of Education

To build on the foundation created by the orientation session, the organization should provide board members with regularly scheduled continuing education. The primary purpose of these sessions should be to brief the board on significant internal or external environmental trends, such as managed care, network development, systems integration, and community wellness. Such information is important because it provides board members with an understanding of the context in which strategies are being pursued.

A secondary purpose of the sessions is to educate members about their organizational role. For example, sessions might cover such topics as board fiduciary responsibilities or the board's role in strategic planning, financial assessment, credentialing, and quality improvement. Equipped with this information, board members can more effectively assist the organization in overseeing strategic change efforts.

Examples of formats and approaches used at Borgess include the following:

- *National educational programs:* On an annual basis, senior management identifies those national educational programs of the greatest benefit to the organization's board members. Programs focusing on managed care trends, network development, systems integration, and board member roles in the new environment are emphasized. Board members are then required to attend one of these programs at least once every three years (more frequently if their schedules permit). Participation in national programs is required for two reasons: (1) to provide a "big picture" perspective on significant environmental trends and (2) to provide opportunities for networking with board members from different market areas.
- *Organization-sponsored educational programs:* To place the information received at national educational programs in the

appropriate local context, Borgess sponsors a number of different educational sessions locally. Speakers for these sessions are selected from among national experts, local experts, and experts internal to the organization. Borgess offers an annual two-day education retreat as well as quarterly lunch or dinner sessions. Topics covered at these sessions include the full scope of issues facing the organization—from health care reform, work reengineering, and systems integration to current ethical dilemmas in health care.

- *Issue-specific updates:* To supplement the various educational sessions that board members attend, Borgess has also developed a variety of mechanisms to keep board members up-to-date on current events that have an impact on the organization's strategies. These topics have included the impact of managed care on mental health services and board member conflict-of-interest responsibilities. Updates are provided in various formats: briefing papers, audiotapes, and ten-minute overview presentations at regular board meetings.

To accommodate the different learning styles of various board members, continuing education should be presented in a variety of approaches and formats, such as lectures, discussions, and briefings. In addition, if appropriate, stakeholders other than board members might be invited to attend certain sessions. Naturally, outsiders should not be invited to sessions that are relevant only to board members or during which in-depth board discussion will take place. However, for those topics pertinent to other stakeholder groups, it may be appropriate to conduct joint sessions. These sessions are particularly useful when board members must understand the perspectives of other stakeholder groups, such as physicians or network partners.

The benefits to be derived from expanding the education and learning opportunities for board members can be significant. At Borgess Health Alliance, the impact of board members' level of knowledge and understanding has resulted in increased active support and advocacy for the organization's change efforts. These, in turn, have facilitated the smooth and efficient implementation of strategies.

EDUCATIONAL OPPORTUNITIES FOR MANAGEMENT

Other key stakeholder groups to consider when planning programs of education are the executive (senior) and administrative (upper) management group and the departmental (middle) management group. Because these management groups serve different roles within the organization, programs of education should be tailored to meet each group's needs.

Executive and Administrative Management Programs

The educational programming for executive and administrative management must prepare these individuals for two functions: (1) the direction of the strategy implementation process and (2) the facilitation of the education and learning of other stakeholder groups. It is most effective for the organization if the executive and administrative management group can be positioned to support the education of the board, other levels of management, physicians, and network partners. The dual roles of the executive and administrative management group require that the educational programs created for them be far more extensive and more in-depth than the education for other stakeholder groups.

At Borgess Health Alliance, the commitment to executive and administrative management education is broad ranging and strongly supported by the CEO. Education and learning opportunities for executive and administrative management at Borgess include participation in national and regional meetings, publication and speaking engagements, as well as quarterly retreats.

Participation in National and Regional Meetings Members of executive and administrative management at Borgess are encouraged to attend national and regional educational sessions related to the organization's key strategies. Sessions regarding the impact of managed care, network development, and systems integration are emphasized. Depending on the topic, attendance can be on an individual basis, as part of a team of Borgess executives, or as a combined group of Borgess stakeholders (for example, management, board, and physicians). In any case, participants are expected to network with counterparts from outside the local area so that the perspective of different marketplaces can be incorporated into Borgess's strategic thinking. In addition, participants are expected to share information gathered at these meetings with the appropriate people at Borgess.

Publication and Speaking Engagements Because Borgess's CEO believes strongly in "learning by teaching," members of executive and administrative management are encouraged to expand their own learning by giving presentations and writing journal articles. The topics of these presentations and articles are typically related to Borgess's experience in the application of specific management practices or in the implementation of particular strategic objectives, such as the formulation of clinical practice redesign, work reengineering, and the management of strategic change.

Quarterly Management Retreat Borgess also holds quarterly one- to two-day retreats at off-site locations that provide a comfortable, relaxed setting away from the distractions of the office. The agendas include items that require action as well as educational activities. So that the educational sessions facilitate the discussion of action items, attempts are made to coordinate action items and educational topics. This technique has been used for such diverse topics as the impact of managed care and the implementation of values-based leadership.

Facilitation of Education for Other Stakeholders   Executive and administrative management's role in facilitating the education of other stakeholder groups is another example of learning by teaching. At Borgess, senior management generally receives education on a particular topic, such as managed care or work reengineering, before other stakeholder groups do. In this way, the management group can play an active part in future education sessions with other stakeholder groups. The management group's responsibilities for these sessions include such activities as role-playing and leading small group discussions.

Departmental Management Programs

The educational and learning opportunities for departmental management must support the dual roles also held by this management group. First, departmental management must be prepared to perform specific tasks in the strategy implementation process. Therefore, their education must increase their understanding of the implications of the organization's strategies as well as the specific implementation requirements of these strategies. Second—and similar to the executive and administrative management group—the departmental management group also plays a key role in facilitating the education of other stakeholder groups, particularly employees.

To assist the departmental management group in meeting their dual roles, Borgess provides an educational series on topics of specific concern to the organization. Custom development of these sessions enables Borgess to tailor the information to the organization's specific needs and to provide this information to the entire departmental management group.

To determine the group's interests and needs, Borgess held focus group sessions with both senior management and departmental managers before the sessions were developed. The series, which is mandatory for departmental managers, covers specific technical issues, such as managed care and work reengineering, as well as such management skills–related topics as values-based leadership and team development.

Managed Care Educational Program   The managed care educational program was developed when managed care was relatively new in the local environment and departmental managers were, therefore, unfamiliar with both the concept and its implications for the organization.

Following input from both senior management and departmental managers, the program was designed as two half-day sessions covering a broad range of managed care information. The information included managed care concepts; the perspectives of employers, hospitals, and nonhospital providers; local trends compared to national trends; Borgess's specific managed care strategies; and the assistance to be provided by departmental managers.

"Work Redesign University" Sessions   When the work reengineering project was in its initial planning and design phases at Borgess, specific sessions for departmental management were developed under the title "Work Redesign University." Four different sessions were held during a six-month period, each session being two to three hours in length. They served both communication and educational purposes with regard to work reengineering generally and the specific work redesign process at Borgess.

Ten-Week Management Development Series   As a follow-up to the Work Redesign University sessions, Borgess initiated an extensive management development program designed to provide participants with the new management skills required in a work-redesigned environment. The program was led by in-house staff (with initial development and support by the external work redesign consultant) and included weekly half-day sessions over a ten-week period. Both technical skills and leadership skills were covered. The technical information included such topics as fact-based decision making and outcomes measurement. The leadership information included such topics as understanding individual style differences, delegation and empowerment, and coaching and mentoring.

EDUCATIONAL OPPORTUNITIES FOR EMPLOYEES

Because of the magnitude of changes in the current health care environment, it is more important than ever that educational opportunities also be provided for employees. Traditionally, education programs for health care employees have been designed to support their ongoing clinical and technical work. But if the organization's change efforts are to be successful, other types of education must be provided.

Two Types of Education

Employee education should include information that will help employees better understand the strategic issues facing the organization and develop the personal skills needed to deal with organizational changes. For example, work reengineering is an important initiative being undertaken by many health care organizations that has significant and difficult operational implications. For employees, it is easy to see and understand the operational implications of work reengineering. However, unless additional education is provided, employees may miss the strategic rationale for this initiative. The implementation of work reengineering will be hampered unless the rationale for pursuing this path is discussed with employees. Additionally, employees need to be provided with educational opportunities that can help them develop the personal skills needed to succeed in a work-redesigned environment, such as working in teams and effective conflict resolution.

For employees to understand the complex issues health care organizations face today, information must be provided on an ongoing basis. Initial educational efforts should build a base of knowledge; then subsequent efforts can enhance and augment this information. In short, educational sessions for employees should start small and then build on one another.

Approaches to Employee Education

At Borgess Health Alliance, the most extensive educational experiences for employees have been developed to support the organization's work reengineering or redesign efforts. This education was specifically focused to create awareness and support for the need to undertake this strategic initiative. The learning opportunities include a brown bag lunch series, sessions with union representatives, a video, and publications.

Brown Bag Lunch Series   Prior to the formal initiation of work redesign, an informal series of brown bag lunch educational sessions were held for employees. These voluntary sessions were led by in-house staff and provided an overview of major health care trends. Specific topics included health care reform, managed care, and healthier communities. The purpose was simply to acquaint employees with issues facing the organization.

Sessions with Union Representatives   Prior to the introduction of the work redesign project, special education sessions were held with representatives from each of the unions at Borgess Medical Center. The purpose of these sessions was to describe the environmental and organizational contexts that were creating the need for work redesign at Borgess. The meetings focused on providing an overview of the changes occurring in the health care environment and the actions that were required as a result of these changes. They created a positive, informed starting point for continuing discussions with the unions.

Video on Industry Changes   As part of the initial introduction of the work redesign initiative, all employees were required to attend employee discussion and educational sessions about the work redesign project. The educational component of these sessions was presented through a video prepared in-house. In a TV news magazine–style format, the video described the changes in the health care environment and why they created the need for Borgess to pursue work redesign.

Publications   As part of ongoing communications and education related to the work redesign initiative, a special section of the employee newsletter, "Work Redesign at Borgess Medical Center," was developed. On a routine basis, information was provided regarding the status of work redesign efforts. Most important, information was also provided that reiterated the expected outcomes of the work redesign initiative and its importance to the overall success of the organization.

Additional Industry Trend and Personal Development Information
A significant portion of the work redesign–related training/retraining required of all employees dealt with topics other than the clinical and technical aspects of new roles. The training time for the majority of employees was between 80 and 120 consecutive work hours. More than 10 percent of this time was devoted to presenting industry trend and personal development information. The industry trend topics included managed care trends and implications and the principles of patient-focused care, while the personal development topics included values-based decision making and team development. After the formal training sessions, there were additional meetings held to follow up on the topics covered, particularly those related to personal development skills.

Benefits of Employee Education

Borgess, like other health care organizations, has found it beneficial to provide employees with increased and ongoing educational and learning opportunities related to both strategic issues and personal development skills. Initiatives such as work reengineering are implemented with far less organizational stress if employees are given the opportunity to understand the strategies being pursued and to develop the personal skills needed to effectively cope with their implications.

EDUCATIONAL OPPORTUNITIES FOR PHYSICIANS

Along with the board, the physicians who are associated with the organization are a key group to target early in the education process. It is best to address their education and learning needs early on for two reasons: first, the physician stakeholder group generally includes a large number of individuals, and, second, physicians have a significant ability to influence the organization in both the short and the long term.

Health care organizations typically provide ongoing clinically oriented education to physicians associated with their organization. However, the organization's strategy implementation efforts will be improved if physicians are also provided with education and learning opportunities related to the key strategies being pursued by the organization, such as managed care contracting and physician-hospital integration.

Information about Organizational Strategy

Physicians need to understand the organization's key strategies, the rationale for pursuing the strategies, and the organizational implications of implementation. If their understanding of organizational strategies is increased, they can provide valuable assistance in strategy implementation. Conversely, if education and learning opportunities regarding the organization's strategies and their implications are not provided, physicians can become powerful barriers to strategy implementation.

The Challenge of Providing Education

Health care organizations are closely linked with the physicians who utilize them. However, because this affiliation is generally voluntary rather than through an employment or contractual agreement, the development of effective education programs can be challenging. To obtain and maintain the attention of this important stakeholder group, educational programs must target their interests and concerns as well as the interests and concerns of the organization. If the information is relevant and appropriately presented, physicians will be motivated to attend without added inducements, such as continuing medical education credits.

The Need to Segment the Group

Because the number of physicians associated with health care organizations can be large, it is recommended that this stakeholder group be segmented for the purposes of development of education and learning opportunities. Although there are no hard-and-fast rules for segmenting the physician audience, the definition of audience segments should consider at least two factors: (1) the level of actual and potential involvement of particular physician specialties and specific individual physicians in the organization's strategies and (2) the level of commitment of individual physicians to the organization. Through audience segmentation, the organization can narrow the individuals targeted for a specific type of education to those physicians who are most directly associated with or in a position to significantly influence particular organizational strategies.

At Borgess Health Alliance, for example, the segmentation of the physicians' stakeholder group included seven targeted groups. An individual physician could be in one or a number of these groups. The intent of the segmentation was to create more homogenous groups of physicians for the purposes of communication, education, strategy development, and strategy implementation. Table 8-2 provides a description of the seven physician audience segments used by Borgess.

TABLE 8-2. Description of Physician Audience Segmentation Used by Borgess Health Alliance

Audience Segment	Estimated Number of Physicians	Description
Entire Medical Staff	500	All members of the medical staff
Medical Staff Officers and Service Chiefs	20	Elected and appointed leaders of the medical staff
Employed Physicians	35	Individuals employed directly by the organization
Medical Foundation Physicians	40	Members of the physician group who have a contractual agreement with the organization's medical foundation
"Pacesetters and Innovators"	50	Informal physician leaders as identified by the organization's senior management
Specialist Subgroup of the "Pacesetters and Innovators"	30	Key physician specialists in the Pacesetter and Innovators group
"Medical Leadership Group"	100	Systemwide, formal and informal physician leaders, as identified by senior management from across the network

The types and amount of educational programming developed for each segment of the physician stakeholder group will vary. At Borgess, the type of education available to each physician audience segment was determined by the level of organizational involvement and commitment that physicians had demonstrated. The criteria used to evaluate the involvement and commitment included such characteristics as whether or not the physician was employed by or had a contractual arrangement with the organization, as well as the proportion of the physician's inpatient and outpatient activity at the organization.

Approaches to Providing Education

Borgess developed different types of educational experiences for each of the physician audience segments. The educational tools and techniques included approaches typically used by health care organizations as well as selected approaches less frequently used by other institutions. Table 8-3 summarizes the types of educational approaches available to each of Borgess's physician audience segments.

The more unique educational approaches used by Borgess were generally targeted at the smaller, more selective segments of the physician stakeholder group. Three specific, less typical approaches were emphasized.

Participation in a "Managed Care University"   This program was developed using the resources of a national research and think tank. It was designed to address both the clinical and organizational implications of managed care. Because the topics are relevant, timely, and practical, physicians are very interested in attending. The "university" is provided on an ongoing basis and uses a variety of educational formats. The formats include off-site presentations, on-site presentations, written reports, audiotapes, and videotapes.

Participation in a "Physician Leadership Institute"   This three-day off-site program is provided in conjunction with a leading graduate school of business. It is designed to provide physicians with an introduction to business management concepts and techniques. The intent is to give physicians a business framework in which to understand and discuss organizational strategies.

Specific Sessions on Integration Strategies   For selected groups of physicians, special sessions on the topic of physician-hospital integration have been developed. The sessions combine education with strategy clarification and action planning.

TABLE 8-3.   Summary of Educational Approaches Used by Borgess Health Alliance with Physicians

Educational Approaches	Entire Medical Staff	Medical Staff Officers & Department Chiefs	Employed Physicians	Medical Foundation Physicians	"Pacesetters & Innovators"	Specialist Subgroup of "Pacesetters & Innovators"	"Medical Leadership Group"
Strategy-Focused Topics in Medical Staff Newsletter (written and audio versions)	X	X	X	X	X	X	X
Specialized Newsletters Focused on Industry Trends and Organizational Strategic Issues					X	X	
On-site Speakers	X	X	X	X	X	X	X
Off-site In-depth Education and Training		X					
Participation in National Meetings Focused on Trends and Strategic Topics					X	X	
Participation in the Organization's Annual Board Education Retreat					X	X	
Participation in "Managed Care University"			X				X
Participation in "Physician Leadership Institute"					X		X
Specific Sessions on Integration				X	X	X	

Evaluation of Program Effectiveness

The benefits resulting from the development of physician education and learning opportunities can be significant for the organization and its strategic change efforts. However, the cost of developing and maintaining multiple forms of physician education can also be quite high. Therefore, it is important for organizations to develop mechanisms to evaluate the impact of their physician education efforts.

Such mechanisms may include surveys of the physician participants as well as the organization's management. Survey questions can be developed that address whether the education is increasing the physicians' understanding and support of the organization's strategies and is, thereby, enabling the strategy implementation process. In addition to quantitative surveys, it is also important to collect anecdotal information from both the physician participants and the management within the organization to evaluate whether there has been a positive impact from the educational efforts. Based on both the quantitative and qualitative feedback, the physician education efforts can be adjusted so that they continue to be aligned with the organization's changes processes.

EDUCATIONAL OPPORTUNITIES FOR NETWORK PARTNERS

Many health care organizations are currently involved with the development of integrated delivery systems or networks. However, the partner organizations involved in these networks are frequently not included in a sponsoring organization's educational efforts. If strategy implementation efforts are to be most effective, it is important to obtain the understanding, support, and advocacy of network partners. If network partners are knowledgeable about a sponsoring organization's strategic initiatives, they can make important contributions to their implementation. Conversely, these network partners can become significant barriers to strategy implementation if the sponsoring organization's strategies are not fully understood.

The Challenge of Providing Education

Similar to the situation with physicians, network partners are frequently not under the direct "control" of the sponsoring organization. Although some type of contractual agreements may be in place, the ability of the sponsoring organization to direct the activities of the network partners may be limited. The form of association is essentially one of voluntary affiliation. The challenge in the development of education and learning opportunities for network partners, then, becomes the need to target the interests and concerns of these partners, as well as to promote the needs and concerns of the sponsoring organization.

Types of Education

Educational efforts with network partners should be developed with a focus on the needs of the partner organizations' key stakeholder groups: the board, physicians, and senior management. For some types of education and learning opportunities, it will be most effective to combine the sponsoring organization's targeted stakeholder group with the corresponding stakeholder groups of the network partners.

For example, for some types of educational programming, it may be beneficial to combine board members from the sponsoring organization with those from the network partners. However, separate educational sessions exclusively for stakeholder groups from the network partners should also be developed. For example, the board, physicians, and senior management from all of the network partners may be combined in education and learning sessions separate from those of the sponsoring organization.

At Borgess Health Alliance, educational efforts with network partners have included both on- and off-site sessions. On-site sessions frequently combine education with organizational updates and the discussion of specific action items. Borgess has also invited key stakeholder representatives from the network partners to participate with Borgess representatives at off-site national meetings. The topics of these meetings have focused on managed care trends, network development, and systems integration. The joint attendance at meetings permits networking among Borgess and network partner representatives, as well as networking with other meeting participants.

From these network partner educational efforts, an organization may find that more formalized opportunities for ongoing education, communication, and action are developed. At Borgess, the informal educational and update sessions with its affiliated hospitals resulted in the formation of a regional hospital council that was developed as a standing committee of the Borgess board. It now functions as a more formal means of communication, education, and action planning with these particular network partners.

The development of education and learning opportunities for network partners serves to draw these partners closer to the sponsoring organization. The experience of Borgess has been that network partners' increased familiarity with the sponsoring organization's strategies has led to their increased support for the organization's implementation efforts.

EDUCATIONAL OPPORTUNITIES FOR THE COMMUNITY

In recent years, health care has become a frequent subject of general media attention. Health care organizations can use this increased level of public interest to their benefit if they enhance their educational efforts with community stakeholders. Specifically, education and learning opportunities should be developed that enable various groups in the community to better understand the strategic and business issues faced by health care organizations. Educational approaches, such as those used by Borgess, can build a base for ensuring that the understanding and support of community stakeholders for the organization and its strategies are maintained and increase.

Traditionally, health care organizations have provided education for their communities on topics of health and wellness. The current societal focus on health care is related to issues of cost, quality, and access. This focus makes it more difficult for health care organizations to rely on the continued support of members of their community. To maintain continued community support, it may be beneficial for organizations to develop community education and learning opportunities related to the strategic and business issues faced by health care organizations.

Information about Strategic and Business Issues

The intent of the community education and learning opportunities is to go beyond traditional health education and community relations activities. The purpose is to create an awareness and understanding among community members of the complexity of issues to which health care organizations must respond. In this way, they are in a position to be more supportive of the organization when they see or hear about specific change efforts.

Borgess Health Alliance has begun to develop specific educational sessions related to health care strategic and business issues for the community stakeholder group. In the coming years, it is expected that this will be an increasing area of focus for senior management, particularly for the chief executive officer. The topics for these sessions have included such issues as health care reform, managed care, the quality and cost of health care services, health care integration, and healthier communities. The educational presentations typically provide a description of the issue, a discussion of the implications, and an explanation of Borgess's response to the issue.

Approaches to Providing Education

Borgess has used various approaches to providing education to the community stakeholder group, including an informal speakers' bureau and presentations targeted to key segments of the community.

Informal Community-Wide Speakers' Bureau   Members of senior management make themselves available to various groups in the community who may desire a speaker. These sessions are conducted in response to requests from various community groups. Their format is generally informal and more conversational.

Targeted Presentations   Groups within the community are also targeted by Borgess for specific educational sessions. These groups include such individuals as business leaders and employee benefits managers. These sessions are generally longer in length, involve more formal presentations, and frequently include guest speakers from outside the immediate local area.

LESSONS LEARNED AND RECOMMENDATIONS

If health care organizations are to be successful in the implementation of their strategies, they need to secure the understanding, support, and advocacy of all their stakeholders. Developing stakeholder support requires an organization to undertake efforts in two areas: (1) leadership development activities for management in order to ensure that the organizational culture will be supportive of the strategic changes being implemented, and (2) widespread stakeholder education in order to ensure that all stakeholders receive the information needed to understand the nature of the strategic changes being pursued, the reasons for these changes, and their expected impact.

The cost to the organization of implementing enhanced leadership development activities and widespread stakeholder education can be high, in terms of both time and dollars. Therefore, it is important to make sure that these efforts are positioned correctly within the organization and remain focused on critical activities. Based on the experiences of Borgess Health Alliance, recommendations for ensuring the effectiveness of leadership development and stakeholder education efforts are offered from both a conceptual perspective and a practical perspective.

The Conceptual Side

In establishing the position and priority of both leadership development and stakeholder education efforts within the organization, four concepts should be kept in mind:

1. *Leadership development and stakeholder education need to be high organizational priorities.* In order to be effective, these efforts must be both recognized and treated as high priorities

within the organization. It is important for the organization to understand that the benefits from these efforts will come gradually over time and will be fully achieved only in the long term. Additionally, benefits will only be achieved if these efforts are consistently pursued. Therefore, the organizational investment in these leadership development and stakeholder education efforts must be consistent and continue over time.

2. *Leadership development and stakeholder education can be used as a competitive advantage for the organization.* Organizations that can more effectively and efficiently implement their strategies have an advantage over their competitors. Leadership development and stakeholder education can ensure that this competitive advantage is achieved and maintained. An organization must carefully monitor and evaluate its leadership development and stakeholder education efforts to ensure that they are continuing to assist the organization in better implementing its strategies.

3. *There will never be enough leadership development and stakeholder education.* An organization can always do more in the areas of leadership development and stakeholder education. Since the cost associated with these efforts can be high, it is important for the organization to establish expected outcomes. These should be determined for each educational effort, as well as for the overall educational program. Periodic evaluations should then be conducted to ascertain the degree to which these expected outcomes are being achieved. In this way, the payback from the organization's investment in leadership development and stakeholder education can be maximized.

4. *Leadership development and stakeholder education are not the total answer.* As critical as these efforts can be to an organization's success, they are not the only areas on which the organization needs to focus. It is sometimes tempting for an organization that is encountering difficulties with strategy implementation to look at more leadership development or stakeholder education as the sole solutions. The paradox that organizations need to recognize is that as a result of these efforts, fundamental differences of opinion may surface even sooner. That, however, should not be viewed negatively. The sooner these fundamental differences are identified, the sooner they can be resolved or alternative approaches found.

The Practical Side

In organizing and developing leadership development and stakeholder education efforts, five practical considerations should be remembered:

1. *The educational efforts must be in response to needs identified by the stakeholders.* The key to effective leadership development

and stakeholder education is to match the timing and content of the efforts to the stakeholders' readiness to learn. This will also ensure that the cost benefit of the efforts is maximized.

2. *Education must be accessible.* The various learning styles and needs of individual stakeholders should be considered. Therefore, the organization must offer educational programming in various formats at a variety of times, using different techniques.

3. *Education and action planning should be combined whenever possible.* Educational efforts are most effective if they can be linked to specific actions that the organization must take. If both elements can occur in a single session, the effectiveness of each one will be enhanced.

4. *Attention to the details of each and every session is required.* Participants are better able to learn in settings in which the details of the educational materials, the environmental setting, and other personal amenities have been considered. Participants should perceive all programs to be "professional," even though they may have been developed and presented by in-house personnel.

5. *The power of fun should never be underestimated.* In both leadership development and stakeholder education, adding elements of fun increases both retention and learning. Fun can be added through a variety of ways, including educational techniques, room decorations, refreshments, and break-time activities. Fun educational approaches include adapting television game show formats, modifying well-known board games, creating role-play/case-example situations, and using computer-assisted decision-making technology.

CONCLUSION

Leadership development and stakeholder education require a large investment by an organization. This investment includes expenditures on staff, materials, and outside resources. However, perhaps the greatest investment is in the time devoted to these efforts by the organization's stakeholders. Continuous monitoring and evaluation is required to ensure that the organization's investment is achieving the expected outcomes.

The benefits of effectively designed leadership development and stakeholder education efforts can be significant. Organizations like Borgess Health Alliance have found that these efforts can lead to significantly enhanced stakeholder understanding, support, and advocacy for the organization's strategies. With this increased stakeholder support and advocacy, strategy implementation is not only more efficient and effective, but it is also more sustainable. As a result, the organization's strategy implementation efforts are ultimately more successful.

9

Moving from Events-Based Management to Systems Thinking

Carolyn J. C. Thompson, M.Ed.

Even under the most stable economic conditions, organizations face cultural change driven by evolving technologies, customer demand, and leadership fluctuation. Add to that an entire industry facing dramatic shifts in the way it delivers good and services, and the conditions become ripe for chaos that results in poor decision making, duplication of work, and questionable odds for survival. Health care in the United States is facing just this kind of situation, as traditional hospital-based organizations seek to shift their business practices and create new cultures that will help them meet increasing demands for cost-effective quality care. Thinking clearly and coherently takes on added importance as organizations tackle daunting systemwide change issues while continuing to manage the day-to-day business of providing care to patients.

This chapter explores ways to approach the day-to-day crises that come with change not as isolated incidents, but as opportunities to tackle issues and make decisions that benefit the larger systems we are learning we must influence.[1] The chapter analyzes the roots of events-based management, examines the shortcomings of this approach, and presents a model for systems thinking in times of change.

THE NEED FOR SYSTEMS THINKING

Given the uncertain future and dwindling financial resources in health care today, we must explore new, more sustainable solutions to the problems we face. We must begin by understanding that most events are not isolated, disconnected occurrences. Rather, almost all events are part of a larger, more complex, interconnected system. And when we identify these interconnections, we begin to see events in the context of the patterns and deeper structures of which they are part.

Figure 9-1 illustrates the importance of systems thinking. The upper portion of the iceberg represents the emergent situation—the in-the-moment event to which we must respond. Often, we tend to focus on the event as the whole problem, without attention to the larger system. We strive to resolve the immediate issue, and when the crisis subsides, we consider our work done. The problem is that this approach often creates a solution that is not sustainable, and we find ourselves cycling back to the same issue in the future. However, if we dive below the water line, we will likely find that this event is connected to a series of similar events that have formed a pattern over time. Dive a little deeper, and we begin to understand the structure of the system from which these patterns emerge. It is only when we dive deeply that we begin to recognize that influencing or changing the structure of this system is critical to our ability to more effectively manage the events that are so draining of energy, creativity, and resources.

Many challenging examples of the need to take a more structural approach to solutions can be found as we move into managed care environments. For example, advances in medicine reported in the media have helped to create more savvy health care consumers who want to live longer, healthier lives and who expect the best and latest "fix-em-up" technologies. The events-based approach would be to meet consumer demands by using the technology. However, under managed care capitation, the more these high-tech innovations are applied, the fewer dollars remain for other health care purposes. The structure of managed care links financial viability with keeping people healthy. Our new challenge—and the way we leverage the structures that influence our success—is to find ways to redirect patients to focus on disease prevention and wellness.

A Lesson from Emergency and Preventive Medicine

Our own industry can give us insight into how we can effectively manage events without sacrificing attention to structure. Let us look briefly at how the practice of emergency medicine, paired with preventive medicine, can produce the most effective medical outcomes. In emergency medicine, practitioners are well aware of the need to act quickly and decisively but with attention to the entire system. In a medical emergency, such as the trauma associated with an automobile accident, skill in emergency medicine is critical to the survival of the patient. At times, drastic measures must be taken to save a patient, and sometimes

FIGURE 9-1. Events, Patterns, and Structures

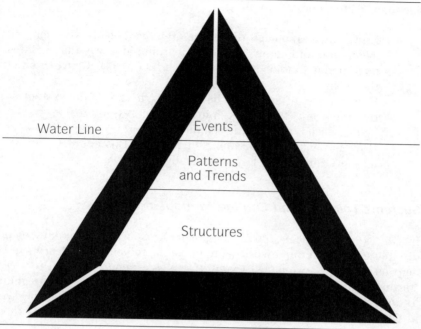

Water Line

Events

Patterns
and Trends

Structures

Note: This figure appeared in *The Art and Practice of the Learning Organization* (December 1994), a workbook distributed by Innovation Associates, Inc., to participants in their Leading Learning Organization course.

those measures result in severe scarring or even the loss of a limb. We know that our skill in dealing with emergencies is critical. We also know that promoting the wearing of seat belts, a preventive medicine tactic, is critical to reducing the need for such drastic interventions in the future.

Sometimes the same type of heroic measures called for in emergency medicine must be taken within an institution. Unexpected budget overruns move us into action to "stop the blood flow." A sudden decrease in satisfaction ratings rallies us to "increase the flow of oxygen," or services, to our customers. We find, just as in medicine, that skill in emergency intervention is often critical to the organization's survival. And, just as in medical emergencies, our adrenaline kicks in, spurring us into action. Yet if we practice only "emergency medicine," "lost limbs" and "scarring" in the form of such drastic, reactionary interventions as downsizing often result, leaving our organizations and the people in them alive but frequently the worse for wear. So we must carefully consider what types of "preventive medicine" measures we must take to avert, or at least to manage more effectively, the same situation in the future.

As we deepen our awareness of this events-based management dilemma, critical questions emerge:

- How can we manage the event effectively, learn through the event, and, ultimately, apply our learning in a way that enables us to understand and influence the structures that have created the event?
- How can we influence or change the structure of the system so that the events that are draining us of energy and resources can be decreased or altogether eliminated?
- How, in health care organizations around this country, can we learn to think and act systematically?

Systems Thinking and Change Management

In *The Fifth Discipline*, Peter Senge speaks of systems thinking as a discipline that "is a framework . . . to make the full patterns clearer, and help us see how to manage them effectively." Senge goes on to say, "through learning we become able to do something we never were able to do. Through learning we perceive the world and our relationship to it. Through learning, we extend our capacity to create, to be part of the generative process of life."[2]

Perhaps we can discover ways to become more creative and generative with our solutions to health care dilemmas if we approach systems thinking as a tri-level process involving events, patterns, and structures. In our day-to-day experience, this process is most often initiated by an event. We might choose to approach the situation as an isolated incident, taking action that only addresses the immediate, visible circumstances. This is a reactive mode. Or we may choose to take a step back, looking at the broader system for patterns that may include other similar events that have occurred in the past. This much more responsive approach allows us to identify patterns over time and become curious about what is causing the patterns. It is this curiosity that opens the door to our understanding the structure of the system. And when we understand the structure that has been supporting the event all along, we find the best opportunity to modify or change that structure, which in turn can enhance our ability to influence future events.

At this point, systems thinking moves out of the realm of theory and into the domain of action. That is the generative "real-time" process that occurs when we make space for our thinking to become clear and coherent and we stop behaving as if each crisis were an isolated incident. Given the constantly changing environment in health care, our future success depends on our ability to maximize the use of our energy, using every crisis as a new opportunity to learn about our system to enhance its effectiveness.

THE ROOTS OF EVENTS-BASED MANAGEMENT

To move toward a systemic approach to managing our organizations, it is helpful to understand the forces that have created our propensity for the events-based approach that is so common.[3] We can explore these dynamics by using the loop of events-based management and examine how the "fight or flight" syndrome impels us into this cycle.

The Loop of Events-Based Management

Although our ability to manage isolated events effectively is critical, we seldom recognize the cost to our organizations when this type of management becomes the dominant behavior. People are pulled away from their customers, patients, and strategic work to focus on addressing the crisis, forsaking the long view to deal with the short-term need. Energy and awareness are diverted away from the system as a whole toward the specific part in need of attention. Just as in medical emergencies, sometimes this course of action is the only possible one. But when crisis mode follows crisis mode, a type of chain reaction can result. Our actions become nothing more than a series of reactions. We lose sight of where one crisis ends and another begins. Most of all, we lose our ability to see patterns in the events that can help us to understand and influence the structures that may be key contributors to the crisis. And as our vision becomes clouded, so does our ability to align the energy required to work toward the vision.

That we, as a society, love and reward heroic acts only reinforces the loop. This is a classic "fixes that fail" dynamic that is reinforced by societal structures. Figure 9-2 illustrates the events-based management dilemma.

Balancing Loop 1   The first loop in the figure—Balancing Loop 1 (B1)—is the loop that illustrates our discussion so far. An emergent situation occurs, causing us to go into adrenaline-driven activity. Our brains demand that we take action, and we respond by focusing our energy and activity on the event. The event is managed. The crisis abates, albeit sometimes just long enough for us to catch our collective breath until the whole pattern repeats itself with another crisis.

Reinforcing Loop 1   Reinforcing Loop 1 (R1) begins to explain the forces that reinforce our propensity for events-based management. It turns out that the more we engage in events-driven management, the greater our tendency to fall into "structural complacency." Our energy is consumed in the moment, leaving us with little energy and time to address the more fundamental questions about whether the structures we have created continue to serve our needs and the needs of our patients and customers. This complacency can contribute to our being "blindsided" by similar emergent situations in the future, since we have not focused on understanding their underlying causes.

Reinforcing Loop 2   Reinforcing Loop 2 (R2) illustrates a series of emergent situation and events management cycles that tend to result in "vision alignment entropy" when the organization's energy, previously

FIGURE 9-2.   The Events-Based Management Dilemma

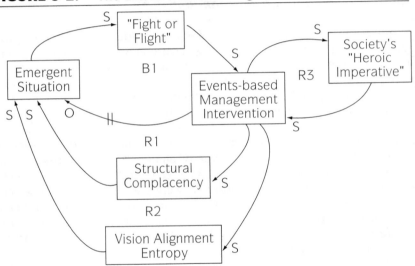

Understanding Causal Loop Diagrams

Arrow: Indicates a link between two variables in which one thing "causes" another

B: A *balancing* feedback loop that seeks equilibrium

R: A *reinforcing* feedback loop that creates a snowball effect in which events become amplified

S: Indicates a change in the *same* direction, for example, increasing pressure on a car's accelerator results in an increase in speed

O: Indicates a change in the *opposite* direction, for example, increasing the amount of food consumed decreases hunger focused on attaining the vision, becomes distracted. As entropy increases, the vision that served as the organizing idea for the system fades, resulting in a general disintegration of alignment of people, purpose, and activity toward the longer-term goals of the organization.

Reinforcing Loop 3 Reinforcing Loop 3 (R3) suggests that our tendency to engage in events-based management is reinforced by society's love and rewarding of heroics. We honor and reward our "superheroes," who step in just in time to save the day. This dynamic plays out in health care organizations just as it does in other areas of business and industry: Many who reach upper levels of formal leadership in their organizations are recognized and promoted for their action orientation and ability to react swiftly in a crisis.

The dynamics described above may be disheartening for all those who devote their lives to making decisions that will lead to the highest possible quality of care and service. However, our willingness to understand how our physiology can work either for or against us, depending on the choices we make, should give us cause for celebration.

The Physiology of the Brain

To better understand our natural tendencies to engage in fight-or-flight reactions, it is helpful to know something about the physiology that is governing our behavior. As discussed below, P. D. MacLean has identified three major layers of the brain that have been developed to respond to changing evolutionary needs of human beings.[4]

R-Complex, the Reptilian System The R-complex part of the brain is made up mostly of the brain stem. The main purpose of the R-complex brain is survival. Circulation, breathing, and fight-or-flight responses are all located in this, our "reptilian brain." According to Geoffrey and Renate Caine, the overriding characteristics of the R-complex behaviors are that they are automatic, have a ritualistic quality, and are highly resistant to change.[5] When we are facing significant cultural changes in our organizations, this is the part of our brain that encourages us to say, "No thank you. I'd rather have things stay just as they are." It is also this part of the brain that becomes dominant when we are hit with a crisis. We joke about our engaging in "brain-stem storming," which results in reactive, self-protective, and, sometimes in hindsight, illogical solutions.

The Limbic System The limbic system, the part of the brain that controls emotion, was the second part of the brain to evolve. R. L. Isaacson calls this part of the brain "nature's tentative first step towards providing self-awareness, especially awareness of the internal conditions of the body and how we feel."[6] Because the limbic system can combine messages from both inner and outer experiences, it can balance or inhibit the R-complex reactions and habitual ways of responding to events.[7]

The Neocortex   The neocortex has been referred to as our "thinking brain." The neocortex is responsible for language, speech, writing, and processing much of the sensory data we receive. It is the neocortex that allows us to think logically, see ahead, and plan for the future. It is rich and complex and is "at the heart of science and art."[8]

The Promise of Brain Integration

We know from our own experiences that these functions of our brains are interconnected, and that even while we are thinking logically (neocortex function), our emotions are present (limbic function). We know that when we are in the midst of taking action to avoid danger (R-complex), we may be feeling emotions about our loved ones (limbic) or planning our next course of action (neocortex).

Caine and Caine tell us that the three parts of our brains, appropriately integrated and operating together, can enable us to learn to redirect old brain propensities and develop new approaches and solutions to survival problems.

SYSTEMS THINKING IN HEALTH CARE MANAGEMENT

The question remains: How, in health care, can we approach an emergency in a way that appeals to our logic, our emotions, and our natural propensity for action? Senge provides us with insight into the answer by introducing the laws of the fifth discipline. More specifically, Senge tells us that as we strive to think and act more systemically, we must remember that "faster is slower" and "the easy way out usually leads back in."[9] The message here for all of us who desire to make decisions that will lead to the best outcomes for patients and customers is to slow down, look around, become curious about what else is happening, and not allow our actions to be driven solely by our initial reaction to an event. As we invite ourselves to become reflective, we are actually creating space for questions to emerge that can produce decisions resulting in more fundamental and sustainable solutions.

An effective metaphorical framework for creating just such conditions can be found, once again, in the practice of emergency medicine.

The ABC's of Emergency Medicine

Among the first protocols committed to memory by anyone receiving training to become an emergency medical technician (EMT) are the emergency medicine ABC's. Upon finding a victim at an accident scene, this mnemonic device helps the EMT to remember the critical steps he or she must take to assess the condition of the patient:

- Airway: Does the patient have a viable airway? Are there any conditions that threaten the airway, such as a decreasing level of consciousness?
- Breathing: Is the patient moving air in and out of his or her body? Are the respirations adequate to sustain life?
- Circulation: Is the patient's heart beating? Is there profuse bleeding that threatens the patient's life?
- Disability: What is the patient's level of consciousness? Has the patient sustained a spinal cord injury?
- Expose: Is there anything that must be looked at more closely and exposed to greater scrutiny for the sake of providing the best outcome for the patient?

This initial assessment insures that the EMT finds threats to life and treats them as they are discovered. It is a routine and reliable approach that provides the EMT with a framework for focusing on events without compromising attention to the system. The ABC's provide reminders to the EMT to attend to the body's critical systems: those that sustain life.

Borrowing from the common medical practice of using mnemonic devices and acronyms to trigger thought processes, we can apply this same type of routine approach to address critical situations in our organizations.

The ABC's of Organizational Emergent Management

A formulaic approach similar to the one that can save a patient's life has been adapted to assess and address organizational emergencies. This system may be called the ABC's of organizational emergent management.

This mnemonic device and the questions it elicits form a framework for both managing an event and exploring underlying structures. It addresses our desire for action by setting us on the path of "doing something" to deal with the emergent situation. It also frees us to explore and understand our emotional responses to what's going on. And it insists that we use our logic to explore the event in terms of the larger system of which it is a part. The resulting effect is a sort of synaptic synergy, an integration of our brain's parts, producing solutions that would at first appear paradoxically impossible as we manage events and the structures that cause them at the same time.

Researchers are becoming increasingly aware that the mind is really a brain/body system. Fluctuations in body chemistry, for instance, play upon our emotions, which in turn affect our reasoning. Especially pertinent to this discussion is that the body secretes adrenaline and other chemicals that prepare us to fight or flee when facing what we perceive to be a dangerous situation. These secretions increase heart and breathing rates, send blood rushing to our large muscle groups, and induce a state of guardedness or anxiety. This response is very helpful when we suddenly need to leap out of the way of an oncoming car, but not terribly useful in managing a complex system.

The ABC's present a logical framework for understanding an event, which can begin to stabilize our thinking as we face the stress of the situation. They provide space for active reflection, which will allow us to explore the deeper questions related to the system. They insist that we become aware of our own responses and use of energy. And they encourage the discovery and implementation of solutions that solve the short-term crisis while optimizing our chances for long-term sustainability.

In short, the ABC's of organizational emergent management provide a framework for systemic thinking during times of crisis and change. During each step, we are reminded to draw into our awareness the particular laws of the fifth discipline identified by Senge that are most critical at that point. We are also reminded of questions that will help us to focus our attention, develop our awareness, and expand our understanding of the current events, patterns, and underlying structures.

Step 1: _Awareness_   The first step in addressing any crisis is to become aware of what is actually going on. Often we are aware only of our immediate reaction to the event. That can result in our "shooting from the hip" to create solutions without understanding the nature of the system of which the event is a part. Actions taken without awareness may very well lead to additional problems in the future. Asking ourselves the following questions will lead to increased awareness:

- What is the "emergent situation"?
- What events have immediately preceded this emergency?
- What is happening right now? What is capturing my attention?
- How am I feeling right now?
- How are my emotions affecting my perceptions?
- Who else is affected?
- How are others behaving?
- If I were to take action right now, what would I do?
- What are the likely consequences of that action? Of inaction?
- What is likely to happen next?

*Step 2: **B**reathing*   In this context, "breathing" refers to our understanding of our current physical state, as well as stepping back to assess our reactions and the reactions of the organization as a whole to the situation. Without taking time for this reflection step, we may take actions too quickly, with little understanding of the readiness of ourselves and our organization to accept the "solution." Such miscalculated interventions often result in rework, thereby slowing down our ability to reach a solution that is both satisfactory and sustainable. The following questions help to create a reflective space in which to "breathe":

- Am I taking in enough oxygen to enable me to think clearly?
- Am I remembering to breathe in and out fully and completely?
- Is my respiration rate rapid?
- How about the respiration rate of our organization?
- Can we slow our collective breathing down?

*Step 3: **C**uriosity*   When we become curious about the events surrounding an emergent situation, we begin to access the "thinking brain" powers of our neocortex. As our curiosity leads us toward awareness of patterns and structures, we get the first glimpse of the event as a part of a complex system. This newfound understanding helps us to see that interventions that might appear to be quick and easy solutions may have adverse effects over the long term. The following questions fuel our curiosity as we begin to look at the event in a larger context:

- Is this the first time this event has occurred?
- Is there a pattern to the occurrences?
- What are our mental models about the potential causes and solutions?
- Are our mental models shared with others?
- Who might hold key knowledge about this situation?
- How will we tap into that knowledge?
- How can we create an environment conducive to inquiry, dialogue, and action?

*Step 4: **D**ialogue*   Mature curiosity insists that questions and potential solutions be explored in dialogue with others who have insight, knowledge, and vested interest. The outcome of a sincere attempt at collective exploration is a reduction in the tendency to focus energy on placing blame. We also discover how some of the least obvious changes may actually produce the greatest results. Most importantly, from the exploration of these questions will emerge the wisdom to act deliberately and systemically:

- What structures have contributed to creating this situation?
- Where is the leverage that will produce the best results?

- How can we influence these structures?
- Do we have the information and wisdom to create sustainable solutions?
- How will we know if we are successful? How might future events be different?

Step 5: Engagement   As we take the final step of engagement, we integrate all we have explored and learned to this point to select and implement solutions. We assess the need for immediate action, and we measure that need against the impact today's solutions may have on the future. We recognize that there are very few "once and for all" solutions and that we must be willing to continually monitor our progress and change course if necessary. We also increase our patience for the long view, knowing that some of our interventions may not immediately produce the results we desire, but that actions focusing on the long term may ultimately be more sustainable. These questions help us to articulate accountabilities and, within our plan of action, allow for those adjustments that will, ultimately, lead us toward success:

- What is our course of action? Who is accountable for which aspects of our plan?
- What is our plan for communicating our actions with others in the system?
- How will we deal with any delays we might encounter between the time we initiate action and get results?
- When we implement a solution, what are the likely effects of that solution on other components of the system?
- Under what conditions will we adjust our course of action?
- How will we measure and monitor our success?
- How will we maintain our awareness of the new emerging conditions?

THE ABC'S IN ACTION: CASE EXAMPLE

An opportunity to apply the ABC's within a health care organization arose within days of the tool's development. Presbyterian Healthcare Services in Albuquerque, New Mexico, was in the midst of reengineering its entire billing process. An in-house team made up of those whose work would be affected contributed to the redesign. Communications with managers and staff had been constant throughout the design phase, with plenty of opportunity for individuals to learn how the changes would affect their work. Everyone involved had been trained to perform new jobs required within the redesigned process. After

18 months of planning, implementation was finally occurring. Then the change crisis hit.

The Change Crisis

Employees became change averse almost overnight. People previously known for their flexibility and can-do attitudes were sobbing in the corridors. Some seemed to freeze, forgetting everything they had learned about how to do their new jobs. Others became verbally abusive to their managers and to one another. Still others threatened to quit. Adrenaline was doing its work.

The reengineering design team was close to panic. Phone calls were made to Presbyterian's Organizational Learning Center (OLC) with requests for change management training to fix the situation. The OLC responded by scheduling an assessment meeting to be held that same week. During that meeting, the design team expressed its own shock and concern at the behaviors being exhibited by employees. Clearly, the team was driven to take immediate action to correct the problem.

Introduction of the ABC's

After listening to the team's concerns, The OLC introduced the idea of events-based management. The OLC asked the team to consider whether the current crisis was perhaps triggered or influenced by patterns or structures in a larger system. Design team members immediately began talking about their frustrations having to do with a perception of lack of organizational support for the reengineering initiative. They were feeling isolated, with full responsibility for the success or failure of the project on their shoulders. As the discussion progressed, the OLC introduced emergency and preventive medicine metaphors as a way of suggesting that the team would need to identify and influence structural aspects of the system in order for any interventions to result in long-term gains.

The OLC then presented an explanation of the ABC's of organizational emergent management as a framework for action through which the group might organize their many thoughts, feelings, and ideas about their dilemma. Almost immediately, the team members spoke up, expressing the opinion that the team had been attempting to move directly to the engagement phase of the model. During a lively discussion, members went on to say that the team had not devoted the time necessary to become aware of the full nature of the issues. Someone suggested that the design team was breathing too fast to be able to think beyond their own emotional reactions to the crisis. Space for curiosity had not been made, so questions that could lead to deeper knowledge of the current problem had not been asked. And, finally, the team had not engaged in dialogue with others to better understand the structure of the system that was influencing the strong reactions to the reengineering changes. By the end of the assessment meeting, the design team agreed to spend a half day identifying the underlying structures that must be addressed in order for a change management intervention to be effective.

Application of the ABC's

During the resulting meeting, team members used the ABC's to identify missing or incomplete structural components that they believed contributed to the change crisis. For example, they found that the organization had not established policies for addressing workforce issues related to major changes in the nature of work due to reengineering. Without written protocols, employees were left guessing what the policies really were concerning the organization's commitment to supporting them during the changes. The lack of a defined policy contributed significantly to creating a climate ripe for strong emotional reaction. The team then understood that an organizational policy guiding workforce change was a critical component of the structure necessary to support essential just-in-time change management interventions, such as transition training or individual counseling. Understanding the systemic nature of this powerfully emotional crisis helped the team to design a plan that addressed the immediate needs of the workers while influencing organization-wide structures for the future.

Partially as a result of the experience of this team, Presbyterian identified a need to develop an organization-wide change management strategy and established the creation of such an approach as one of its major strategic objectives.

CONCLUSION

As we continue to experiment with new ways to think and act systemically in a volatile health care environment, these key principles can help to guide us:

1.   We can learn to use to our advantage the natural human tendency to become action oriented during a crisis. The very part of the brain that served to save us from predators at the dawn of human existence can, today, continue to alert us to dangers and impending crises in our organizational lives.

2. When we consciously connect the parts of our brain and engage in a reflective act, we avoid falling into the trap of becoming reaction oriented. We can choose to integrate our brain more fully in order to save ourselves from the folly of modern organizational decision making made solely in a reactive mode. And we can choose to apply lessons learned from our past experiences to positively influence future outcomes.
3. Systems thinking enables us to better understand the structures underlying current events and therefore to influence the forces governing future events. When we are willing to explore beneath the level of events to understand the structures that may be causing them, we can devise more fundamental interventions that acknowledge interrelationships within the system.
4. We can choose to define our mental model of "crisis" as a potentially positive turning point for our organizations. Instead of fearing emergent situations, we can learn to anticipate them as opportunities to understand and recreate our structures so that our systems truly provide the highest quality of care and service for our patients and customers.
5. We must always remember that we, alone, have the power to make choices about our own behavior during times of crisis. When we choose to think and act systemically rather than reactively, we focus our energy on producing intelligent decisions and sustainable results.

There is no evidence that the turbulent times our industry is facing will end anytime soon. Regardless of whether we are the instigators of change or implementers of change mandated by others, the ability to think reflectively and act systemically are core competencies for health care leaders today.

References and Notes

1. "System" can be defined as a whole with component parts that continuously affect each other over time and operate toward a common purpose. Examples of systems include biological organisms, the human body, ecological niches, families, industries, organizations, and communities. The word comes from the Greek verb *synistanai*, which means "to cause to stand together."

2. Peter Senge, *The Fifth Discipline* (New York: Currency Doubleday, 1990), p. 7.

3. Systemic structure is the pattern of interrelationships among components of a system. In an organization, these may include hierarchy,

decision-making bodies, policies, procedures, processes, attitudes of employees, employee-employer relationships, the products or services manufactured, and the ways in which resources are allocated. The word *structure* originates from the Latin *struere*, which means "to build."

4. Renate Nummela Caine and Geoffrey Caine, *Making Connections* (Alexandria, Va.: Association for Supervision and Curriculum Development, 1994), p. 57.

5. Ibid., p. 59.

6. Ibid., p. 62.

7. Ibid., p. 63.

8. Ibid., p. 63.

9. Senge, *The Fifth Discipline*, pp. 60-62.

Bibliography

Caine, Renate Nummela, and Geoffrey Caine. *Making Connections*. Alexandria, Va.: Association for Supervision and Curriculum Development, 1994.

Damasi, Antonio. *Descartes' Error.* New York: Avon Books, 1994.

Senge, Peter. *The Fifth Discipline.* New York: Currency, 1990.

10

Using 360° Feedback®
in Leadership Development

Lawrence A. Pfaff, M.A., Ed.D.

I n today's environment, health care professionals and administrative staff are expected to adapt rapidly to change. This requires leaders who are change agents, or role models for dealing with change. To help leaders successfully take on this new role, many organizations provide leadership development programs.

This chapter focuses on the use of one-on-one feedback in the leadership development process. More specifically, it looks at the uses of the 360° or multirater feedback tool, a means through which a leader receives information about his or her behaviors from employees, peers, boss, customers, and patients. (See figure 10-1.) With the 360°, feedback is usually gathered through the use of a survey with objective questions. Alternatively, open-ended questionnaires or face-to-face interviews may be used.

Although the 360° has proven to be an effective tool for helping people to understand their behavior, many organizations overlook it when designing their leadership development programs. This chapter explains how to integrate the 360° into the leadership development process and effectively use 360° feedback. For readers who are unfamiliar with the 360° feedback process, figure 10-2 shows sample 360° questions from the Management-Leadership Practices Inventory.

THE NEED FOR EFFECTIVE LEADERSHIP DEVELOPMENT

Because organizational change is inevitable and constant, health care organizations must approach leadership development as a continuous improvement process. An effective development process empowers

---

360° feedback® is a registered trademark of TEAMS, Inc.

FIGURE 10-1.   360° Feedback

Boss

Peers

Practices

Self

Employees

leaders to strengthen and shape their own direction and that of the organization. Continuous development is a positive way to challenge leaders to live and work with change.

Unfortunately, many leadership programs fail to take into account the nature of the learning process and individuals' varying degrees of readiness to learn. As a result, true learning, which is evidenced by changes in behavior, does not occur.

For example, suppose that the CEO of a health care organization reads a series of reports asserting that healthy employees are more productive. Inspired by the reports, the CEO decides to increase staff productivity by having every employee train to compete in a 10K run. The organization buys everyone running clothes, a good pair of running shoes, and a videotape on running techniques. In addition, employees are given work time to watch the videotape and practice for a week with a personal trainer. After the one-week training period, employees are given the date of the next local 10K run and encouraged to train on their own time. The company has spent thousands of dollars on videos, running equipment, and the trainer, and the CEO feels confident that he has done everything he can to improve the health and productivity of his employees. After all, he has invested a large amount of money in employee development.

You are probably thinking, "That's ridiculous! A one-week training program won't produce healthier, more productive employees." And you're right. Yet the example depicts the path that most organizations follow when providing management and leadership development. They provide a one-day leadership training program and then expect participants to become accomplished leaders overnight. When the leaders show little or no change in their behavior, top management is disappointed. What is wrong with this approach?

Traditional employee development programs are based on the unsophisticated notion that change is a dichotomous event, a dramatic shift from one stable state (inappropriate or unproductive behavior) to another (appropriate or productive behavior).[1] In reality, human development is a complex process that takes time. Lifelong behaviors cannot be changed quickly.

The Change Readiness Model

A more accurate model of how people change has been developed by several researchers.[2] At the heart of this model are four stages of readiness to

FIGURE 10-2. Sample 360° Questions from the Management-Leadership Practices Inventory

This leader:	Never		Sometimes			Always	
1. Makes sure people know what they are expected to do before they begin	1	2	3	4	5	6	7
2. Allows individuals to direct their own activities	1	2	3	4	5	6	7
3. Understands the technical aspects of the work	1	2	3	4	5	6	7
4. Asks for employee input	1	2	3	4	5	6	7
5. Clearly communicates the strategy and direction of the unit	1	2	3	4	5	6	7
6. Makes sure people are properly trained for their jobs	1	2	3	4	5	6	7
7. Supervises workers closely	1	2	3	4	5	6	7
8. Organizes and coordinates the work of the unit	1	2	3	4	5	6	7
9. Tells people when plans change to meet changing demands	1	2	3	4	5	6	7
10. Encourages people to perform at high levels	1	2	3	4	5	6	7

change: precontemplation, contemplation, action, and maintenance. (See figure 10-3.) These stages were first identified in a 1982 study comparing the processes of change used by smokers quitting on their own and smokers participating in two commercial treatment programs. Subsequent research has established that the amount of progress people make in changing behavior depends on their stage of change readiness.

Precontemplation Stage   Individuals in the precontemplation stage have no intention of changing their behavior in the near future (that is, the next six months). Many precontemplators deny they need to change or do not feel their situation is serious enough to merit changing. They are resistant to acknowledging that a problem exists. It isn't that they cannot see the solution but that they cannot see the problem. For them, the cost of changing behavior clearly outweighs the benefits.

Precontemplators may feel that others are pressuring them to change without due cause. Thus, when the pressure is off, they revert to old behavior patterns. The precontemplator is the leader who, during training, says, "I don't understand why I'm here. I don't need any of this."

Contemplation Stage   Individuals in the contemplation stage acknowledge that they need to change and are seriously considering change. Movement from stage 1 to stage 2 is critical if change is to occur. An individual must acknowledge that he or she has a problem and know specifically what the problem is in order for productive change to take place. Con-

FIGURE 10-3.   Stages of Change

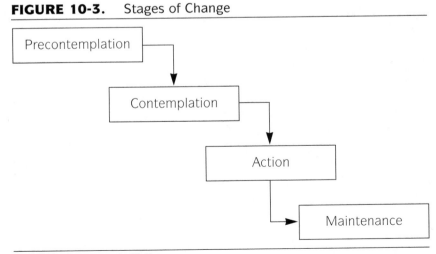

templators weigh the pros and cons of the problem and examine possible solutions. An individual who is at this stage has somehow gained a new awareness of his or her current behavior.

Action Stage   The action stage is a period of genuine effort to change behavior. Action involves overt changes and requires considerable commitment of time and energy. Training programs are action oriented and designed to help people at this stage. Unfortunately, action does not always result in permanent change.

Maintenance Stage   The maintenance stage is the period during which people work to consolidate gains and prevent relapses. Traditionally, the maintenance stage is viewed as static. However, maintenance can be a continuation, rather than an absence, of change. In an organization, maintenance occurs when coworkers and management support the changes the individual is making.

Implications for Training Programs

The four-stage model is helpful in explaining why some people fail to change their behavior as a result of training programs. Training is intended for people in the action stage of the change cycle. Although training can help move an individual from contemplation to action, the vast majority of training programs are designed for the minority who are ready to take action. Leaders who are in the precontemplation stage probably do not understand why they are in the training program and therefore are unreceptive to learning. To move ahead in the cycle of change, precontemplators must acknowledge the need for personal change.

What causes people to begin to think seriously about changing? J. O. Prochaska found that people can be motivated through "consciousness-raising"; that is, systematically confronting people with observations about their behavior. [3] The implications for training are clear: to benefit from employee development programs, people must be helped to see their behavior from others' perspectives. The 360° provides the feedback that people need to benefit from training.

A reliable, valid 360° can be the impetus a person needs to move from the precontemplation to the contemplation stage. It also can encourage contemplators to take action. For those at the action stage, it provides a clear road map to help accelerate the change process. Follow-up assessments can be used to measure continued change from action through maintenance. And when the feedback is delivered by competent trainers or consultants, its impact is even greater.

PREPARATION FOR THE 360°

Unfortunately, some health care organizations have been led to believe that the 360°, by itself, will solve all their leadership problems. This is not the case. Although the 360° can play an important role in a leadership development program, it should not be viewed as a development program in and of itself. The 360° feedback process must be thoughtfully integrated into an overall development program.

A number of issues must be considered before and during introduction of 360° feedback. These issues include the degree to which the organization is ready for change, the type of tool best suited to the organization, and the manner in which the 360° is to be administered.

Organizational Readiness

The 360° can provide powerful personal information about the individuals being assessed. But before it can be successfully used, the organization must assess its readiness for the 360° feedback process. That involves answering two questions:

1. *What is the level of trust in the organization?* There is no simple way to measure the degree to which people trust their organization, but there are some indicators. If the organization has higher than normal levels of employee grievances or turnover, trust in the organization may be lacking. On the other hand, if employees are regularly involved in critical decisions that affect their work, their trust level is probably high. A more detailed assessment of the level of organizational trust can be obtained through the use of industrial psychologists or management consultants.

2. *What is the organization's history with using survey data of all kinds?* If surveys have been used primarily for negative purposes, such as to eliminate positions, then the accuracy of 360° survey data may be compromised. Once an organization has used survey results in ways perceived as negative, people are reluctant to be honest. Past history will determine the speed with which 360° feedback can be introduced. Unfortunately, organizations with the lowest trust levels typically want to implement the 360° the most quickly. Premature implementation is bound to fail. Organizations with low trust levels will first need to conduct voluntary pilot 360° feedback programs to build trust in how the information collected will be used. After a pattern of positive use has been established, 360° feedback can be expanded to include all managers.

Selection of the Survey Instrument

Several issues should be considered when choosing an inventory. (See figure 10-4.) First, the organization should consider whether the instrument measures the skills critical to effective functioning in the organization. To answer this question, the organization must understand what is critical to the success of leaders within its culture so that the inventory can be chosen or designed around those characteristics. The inventory should be designed to measure behavior or practices, not attitudes or traits. For example, one health care organization began by examining the overall expectations of its leaders before looking at any instrumentation. This allowed for a more logical choice of inventory.

Second, the organization should check to ensure that psychometric procedures were used to develop the instrument and that the instrument has been validated in work settings against outcome criteria. In this way,

---

FIGURE 10-4.   Preparing for the 360°

Step 1:   Conduct a thorough analysis of the leadership skills critical to manager success in your organization. This can be done quickly and simply by conducting interviews and focus groups with key management personnel. You may want to receive help from a consultant experienced in 360° feedback.

Step 2:   Survey the available 360° feedback inventories to determine if there are any that adequately measure the critical leadership skills for your organization. You should be able to find one or more inventories that provide a close match to your needs.

Step 3:   Evaluate the inventories that match your needs. You will want to be sure that the one you choose is designed to measure behaviors and skills, not traits. The inventory should have adequate reliability and validity data to support its use in your organization. Validity and reliability are terms that are used inappropriately by many developers. Check to see if the instrument you choose has been used in numerous organizations, especially ones that are similar to yours. Try not to be overly influenced by the appearance of the inventories. Focus on their content.

Step 4:   Once you have decided on a 360° feedback inventory, you will need to follow the steps outlined under the "Feedback Phase."

---

the organization can be confident that the inventory accurately measures what it purports to measure. If the instrument is purchased from a publisher, the organization should check to see that the publisher has done the appropriate validation work. If the organization is designing its own instrument, it should be able to show that leaders who have more productive work groups also score better on the instrument. However, it is strongly recommended that most organizations *not* attempt to design their own 360° inventory. Inventory design is a complex task that requires specialized personnel. Most organizations do not have the proper personnel on staff to design a valid instrument.

Finally, the organization should consider who will administer the tool. Feedback must be conducted by highly skilled individuals. They must understand the sensitive nature of feedback and its potential emotional impact on participants. They must be prepared for and able to deal with a wide range of reactions from enthusiastic acceptance to aggressive denial. And they must be able to recognize possible unethical or illegal use of feedback data and know how to avoid it. In one health care organization, these individuals were called "feedback coaches." Feedback coaches are typically *not* the superiors of the people being assessed. Feedback coaches need to be people who have outstanding interpersonal skills, understand 360° feedback, and are respected in the organization. The title "feedback coach" indicates a person who has many of the characteristics needed to help other individuals change.

Administrative Issues

How the 360° process is administered will depend on the trust levels discussed earlier. In any organization, anonymity of responses must be guaranteed. If employees have any reason to believe that anonymity of responses will not be maintained, they will fear giving honest responses and will deliberately give false information. In organizations with low levels of trust, it may be necessary to have an external organization collect and process all data. High trust organizations will be able to do in-house collection and storage of the data.

In addition, the organization must consider who will see the feedback results. Will results be given only to participants, or will results be given to superiors? Again, these are highly dependent on the trust levels of the organization. Low trust organizations will need to guarantee that only participants will see their own 360° feedback. As trust builds, access to the data can expand.

All confidentiality issues must be decided in advance and openly described to participants and those completing the instruments. They must be formally stated in terms of the organization's policy concerning 360° feedback.

OVERVIEW OF THE 360° PROCESS

Once the organization has selected an appropriate instrument and decided who will administer the process, it is ready to move on to the feedback process itself. This process typically consists of three phases: the prefeedback phase, the feedback phase, and the postfeedback phase.

Prefeedback Phase

The prefeedback phase is a time of preparation. Before beginning, the 360° process must be clear to all participants in advance. They must know and understand all the steps, procedures, policies, and requirements for participating in the process. Participants should be aware of the reasons the organization is pursuing a formal management development program. Reasons can include:

- Continuing professional growth to maintain functional expertise
- Improved leadership performance through more effective leadership strategies
- New skill development
- Ability to tackle new challenges and look at old problems in new ways
- Greater sense of control through clearer direction and plans
- Better goal setting (for self and work team)
- Feeling more successful as a manager

Prefeedback begins with the organization's announcement of the desire to use 360° feedback and a statement of how it will be used. This includes the administrative issues mentioned previously. Individual participants attend an orientation session prior to participating in the 360°. At the orientation participants will

- Receive detailed information on the process
- Meet their assigned feedback coaches
- See sample 360° results
- Obtain 360° inventories for distribution
- Be told what they will be required to do as a participant
- Obtain sample development plans

Typically, participants will distribute surveys to peers and staff. Completed surveys will be returned directly to a neutral party, either inside or outside the organization. At this point in the process, it would also be useful to describe a development plan and the developmental planning process. 360° feedback helps the manager decide *what* he or she wants or needs to change. The development plan is a written document that defines *how* the manager is going to go about making those changes. It can be thought of as the manager's road map to change. The development plan contains the criteria against which success will be measured. It is the document that the organization can use to evaluate the manager's ability to change and the cumulative success of the 360° program. The development plan should require approval of the participant's superior and be included with his or her performance review. Figure 10-3 is a sample development plan.

Feedback Phase

During this phase, participants receive their 360° feedback results. This is done at group or individual feedback sessions. The feedback coaches help participants understand the data contained in their 360° feedback reports. At this time participants are also given additional examples of the development planning process discussed above. In keeping with the change readiness model discussed earlier, participants should not be pressured to create a professional development plan too quickly. To do so would result in a plan that the participant will be unable to complete. Remember, the development plan is the manager's road map for change. It cannot be developed in a hasty manner.

Highly skilled feedback coaches are critical from this point forward. It is at this meeting that participants who were at the precontemplation stage may be thrust into contemplation. This can manifest itself in the form of shock, denial, anger, or other emotional reactions. The coach will need to assist these people in understanding the data and dealing with their reactions. These participants will not be ready to begin formulating a development plan until the postfeedback phase.

Participants who were at the contemplation stage prior to 360° feedback will be ready to move more quickly. For those participants, the feedback coach will help in early formulation of a development plan, perhaps even during the feedback session. It is important that the feedback coach *not* be the direct superior of the participant. Superiors should be involved in the 360° process, but not at the point of receipt of feedback.

Postfeedback Phase

Real change takes place well after the manager receives feedback. Again, feedback coaches can be critical in making individual change occur. Typically, participants will be capable of developing a meaningful development plan one to three months after receiving feedback. During that time participants may use the coaches for advice and counsel.

During this phase, superiors become critical. Participants will discuss their plans with their superior and obtain formal approval of the development plan. Participants also may present their completed plans to their employees as a public declaration of their intent to change. This phase is the time for commitment to change.

WAYS TO INCREASE THE EFFECTIVENESS OF THE 360°

Although the 360° is an effective tool in and of itself, there are several other ways to increase the impact of 360° feedback. These include pilot-testing, integrating results into performance reviews, and development planning.

Pilot-Testing

Before imposing the process on all managers, it is valuable to pilot-test the process on a select group of managers. That allows the organization to test the 360° feedback process. Organizational resistance can be determined during the pilot. The pilot can also be used as a way to build support for the process. Participants in a pilot should be respected managers who have volunteered for the pilot. They should know in advance that they are a unique group being called on to test a new approach to management development.

Integration with Performance Reviews

There is much disagreement about whether 360° feedback should be made an integral part of the performance review process. Some experts claim that the 360° should never be connected in any way to reviews. Although this gives the 360° a completely developmental focus, it may also remove any motivation for managers to actually change their behavior. Others claim that the 360° should replace the traditional performance review. That sounds like a good idea, but in truth, most organizations are not immediately ready for that big a step. Employees and peers are not ready to formally evaluate others. Evidence has shown that when the 360° is integrated into performance reviews too quickly, most managers simply receive uniformly high ratings.[4] Probably the best approach is to keep the 360° feedback a confidential process but require managers to create a development plan and require that the development plan be made an integral part of the performance review. As the organization gains more experience, the 360° can become an integral part of performance reviews. But the 360° should never be substituted for the performance review.

Development Planning

The formal development plan is critical to the success of the 360°. (See figure 10-5.) As mentioned above, the 360° should be directly linked to the performance review through the development plan. Development plans should include areas of improvement, actions to be taken, results, and timelines. Developmental actions can include

- Career planning and counseling
- Training
- Cross-functional job rotations
- Special assignments
- Daily coaching and feedback
- Mentoring

Management Support

Unfortunately, management support is often lacking in management development strategies. Managers develop plans for change only to find their management is not supportive of their new behavior. So leaders quickly abandon new ways and revert to old methods of management.

CASE EXAMPLE OF A SUCCESSFUL 360°

Bronson Healthcare Group in Kalamazoo, Michigan, is a health care group that includes a 400-plus-bed regional medical center, outreach facilities, and a health insurance provider, all located in southwestern Michigan. Like many health care institutions, they have recently undergone a comprehensive work redesign process. They determined that for work redesign to succeed, they would need management that would initiate and lead change.

Bronson first established expectations and accountabilities for all management personnel. Included was a list of overall and specific expectations, such as fiscal, human resources, organizational, customer service, and performance improvement. Then a leadership development

FIGURE 10-5. Individual Development Plan

Name:

Development Area (define as completely as necessary): Feedback—explore and improve upon the qualitative and quantitative exchange of information with staff.

What are the steps you will take to change in this area?	What will your activity produce? What is the result of each step?	Completion dates for each step?	Date actually completed.	How will you know if the desired changes have occurred? Check (N) when each occurs. Note differences.
1. Establish needs and wants of staff with regard to management, direction, and interdepartment information. Use individual and group meetings.	1. A better-informed and more involved staff. I will also be better informed.	April '98		Fewer complaints
2. Establish needs and wants of management with regard to information staff should be aware of. Meet with manager (several times if necessary) to clarify.	2. Clearer line of communication between self and manager. I will be better informed.	April '98		Enhanced sense of community among all levels of staff (can be measured through 360° follow-up)
3. Establish a plan of action based on steps 1 and 2. Share plan with staff.	3. An elevated sense of trust between and among staff and management.	May '98		Agreement and understanding among all department levels of corporate and division goals
4. Implement that plan.		June '98		
5. Evaluate that plan.		July '98		

Agreed to take the above actions:

_____ _____ _____ _____
Signature   Date   Superior   Date

advisory group composed of respected managers from throughout the organization identified a leadership "core curriculum" that would be offered to support Bronson's management accountability standards. Their research led to the conclusion that for leadership development to be successful, it had to be a *self-directed* process. A core curriculum must still be available, but leadership development could no longer simply be a series of prescribed courses that all managers attended. Leadership development will occur when the development process is individualized and the manager takes self-directed actions and accountability to change.

A five-step self-directed leadership development process model was created:

Step 1: Assess development opportunities (360° feedback)
Step 2: Create a personalized development plan (identify learning needs, set goals, establish time frames)
Step 3: Initiate supervisory support of development plan (formal support of the development plan by superior)
Step 4: Access development strategies (select delivery options, including training, mentoring, readings, experiences, and so on)
Step 5: Evaluate effectiveness (achievement of plan, supervisor feedback, 360° follow-up)

This process model was seen as providing the structure to plan, access, and evaluate individualized development opportunities according to the educational values and performance expectations of Bronson.

For this self-directed model to work, it required that each manager have (1) a clear idea of the organization's expectations and accountabilities for management personnel and (2) a clear picture of his or her current practices relative to these expectations.

To complete step 1 (asssess development opportunities), numerous 360° feedback inventories were examined. What each measured was compared to the management expectations and accountabilities. The Management-Leadership Practices Inventory (MLPI) was chosen for use at Bronson, and a Bronson trainer was certified in its use. The MLPI was chosen because of its validity and the close match between what it measured and the Bronson accountabilities. An external consultant was employed to establish an implementation process. Bronson determined that the 360° process would first be pilot-tested.

The pilot group was primarily composed of the leadership development advisory group. Each member of the pilot group was assessed on the MLPI. Each participant then received feedback and created a development plan. In addition, participants in the pilot were surveyed about their reaction to the 360° process and asked for suggestions on its implementation process. Specific suggestions that were incorporated in the implementation plan involved timing, inventory modifications, and accountability of managers in carrying out their development plans. The 360° process was then formally added to the leadership core curriculum outline as created by the leadership development advisory group. The MLPI was also licensed for unlimited in-house use at Bronson.

An implementation schedule was established. To show the importance of leadership development, Bronson decided that the process would be implemented first with upper management. The first group to participate in the 360° process would be senior management. All senior management would complete the 360° process within six months of implementation. Participation included completion of individual development plans by all senior managers. All managers would be participating in the 360° process within 12 months of implementation.

Support systems were put into place. The data collection and scoring were housed in the organizational development and training department. A group of feedback coaches was chosen from the initial pilot group of participants. The coaches were given training in the feedback process. At this time, Bronson has completed the pilot, customized the 360° inventory, designed the process, and is conducting the 360° process on all senior management. The elapsed time from design of accountabilities through pilot-testing to formal implementation was approximately 18 months. Modifications will continue to be made to the 360° process as implementation progresses.

CONCLUSION

Discussing the difficulty of modifying problem behavior, Mark Twain commented: "Habit is habit, and not to be thrown out the window but coaxed downstairs a step at a time." Thus, improved manager and employee performance does not occur with one bold training effort. Change requires movement through discrete stages. Proper design of the total training and development effort, including 360° feedback, training activities, and follow-up, can greatly enhance training effectiveness. Otherwise, we are delivering training that is likely to fail.

References

1. J. O. Prochaska, "Assessing How People Change," *Cancer* 67 (1991): 805–7.

2. J. O. Prochaska, C. C. DiClemente, and J. C. Norcross, "In Search of How People Change," *American Psychologist* 47 (1992): 1102–14;

J. O. Prochaska and C. C. DiClemente, "Stages of Change in the Modification of Problem Behaviors," in *Progress in Behavior Modification*, ed. M. Hersen, R. M. Eisler, and P. M. Miller (Sycamore, Ill.: Sycamore Press, 1992), pp. 184–214; Prochaska, "Assessing How People Change," pp. 805–7; and E. A. McConnaughy and others, "Stages of Change in Psychotherapy: A Follow-up Report," *Psychotherapy* 26 (1980): 494–501.

3. J. O. Prochaska, "Assessing How People Change."

4. S. Shellenbarger, "Reviews from Peers Instruct—Sting," *Wall Street Journal* 75, no. 248 (1994): B-1.

Bibliography

Conger, J. A. *Learning to Lead: The Art of Transforming Managers into Leaders.* San Francisco: Jossey-Bass, 1992.

DiClemente, C. C., and others. "The Process of Smoking Cessation: An Analysis of Precontemplation, Contemplation and Preparation Stages of Change." *Journal of Consulting and Clinical Psychology* 59, no. 2 (1991): 295–304.

Lublin, J. "Turning the Tables: Underlings Evaluate Bosses." *Wall Street Journal* 75, no. 248 (1994): B-1.

McConnaughy, E. A., and others, "Stages of Change in Psychotherapy: A Follow-up Report." *Psychotherapy* 26 (1989): 494–501.

Myers-Briggs Type Indicator. Palo Alto, Cal.: Consulting Psychologists Press, 1987.

Pfaff, L. *Analysis of the Decision-Making Process Used by Chief Student Personnel Administrators.* Western Michigan University Doctoral Dissertation, 1980.

Prochaska, J. O. "What Causes People to Change from Unhealthy to Health-Enhancing Behavior?" In *Human Behavior and Cancer Risk Reduction: Overview and Report of a Conference on Unmet Research Needs*, ed. C. C. Cummings and J. D. Floyd. Atlanta, Ga.: American Cancer Society, pp. 30–34.

Prochaska, J. O., and C. C. DiClemente. "Stages of Change in the Modification of Problem Behaviors." In *Progress in Behavior Modification*, ed. M. Hersen, R. M. Eisler, and P. M. Miller. Sycamore, Ill.: Sycamore Press, 1992, pp. 184–214.

Prochaska, J. O., C. C. DiClemente, and J. C. Norcross. "In Search of How People Change." *American Psychologist* 47 (1992): 1102–14.

Wilson, C. L. *Survey of Management Practices.* New Canaan, Conn.: Clark Wilson Publishing, 1973.

11

Strengthening the Executive's Leadership Skills through Coaching

Patricia Chehy Pilette, Ed.D., C.N.S.

Ellen Wingard, M.Ed.

During this chaotic period of transition in health care, more and more health care leaders are turning to executive coaches to learn new skills and secure a sense of grounding. Over the next several years, health care leaders will face many Herculean tasks, none more urgent or compelling than the growing need to reinvent their own role. To orchestrate career and organizational success, leaders need to drive a wedge into the leadership treadmill and find time to reflect on what they do and how they do it. The central premise of this chapter is that the major benefit of coaching is its ability to create a "reflective space" in which leaders can contemplate their new roles and craft better personal and organizational futures. In short, coaching affords a unique conduit for thinking and acting "outside the leadership box."

Unlike prepackaged leadership training and "remedial" coaching that focus on problem behaviors, the coaching model described in this chapter affords an opportunity for individualized leader development. Operating on the most profound level of change—the self—coaching in this up close and personal approach provides a powerful vehicle for deep and lasting change. As one leader stated during a coaching conversation, "change happens by design with a coach instead of by chance, which is the best—if not the only—way to guarantee success."[1]

The model proposed in this chapter provides the reader with a reference point for understanding what coaching is, how it works, how to select a coach, and what outcomes may be derived from this transformational process. The chapter begins with a brief overview of some of the consequences of the shifting health care paradigm that are creating a need for coaching and driving executive role reinvention.

THE DIFFICULTY OF LEADING IN TODAY'S ENVIRONMENT

The expectation in today's high-stakes, high-risk, precarious environment is for leaders to perform flawlessly under the watchful eyes of empowered boards, stakeholders, and regulatory and public scrutiny. Figure 11-1 contrasts the traditional system of health care delivery with the system that is currently evolving, and highlights the changing roles of executives within this process. These seismic shifts in role expectations are enough to keep any leader awake at night.

With roles and rules in flux and no blueprint or immediate feedback to go by, today's leaders wonder how to lead their organizations successfully. As one coaching client astutely observed, "It's close to impossible to manage a career when success is a shifting target."[2]

Leader Isolation

Organizational psychologist Harry Levinson warns that our age of reorganization and self-reliance makes it difficult for leaders to find an objective sounding board for ideas and career direction. All too often, leaders find themselves isolated and lacking support.[3] The following comments of a CEO of an integrated health network in an initial coaching session echo this stark reality:

> While it is perfectly acceptable to discuss operations, it is quite another story to discuss one's career goals, fears, and concerns. Turning to another executive can easily prove disadvantageous. Today's environment is volatile and highly political, with everyone jockeying for a place and piece of the action in the new order. It would be great to comfortably toss down a current hot topic on the table and to talk about how it impacts your career without appearing too self-serving. But right now, that's not possible. Trust and loyalty are significant casualties of organizational change.[4]

Leaders' Need for Support

Support is a critical success factor during times of turbulence. It keeps leaders grounded amidst the shifting sands of a changing environment. Indeed, trying to manage a career without it is analogous to E. L. Doctorow's description of how it feels to write a book: "It's like driving at night in the fog. You can only see as far as your headlights, but you make the whole trip that way."[5] Fewer supportive relationships means fewer benchmarks, fewer standard-bearers, and fewer road maps for career development, which lead to shortsighted decisions and wayward directions.

FIGURE 11-1.   Consequences of Paradigm Shift

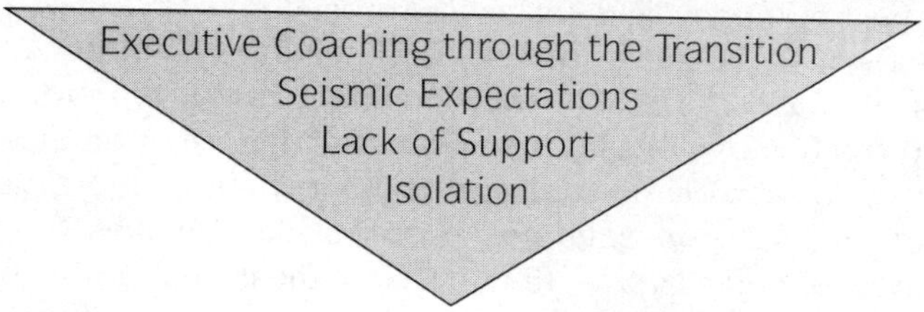

Executive Coaching through the Transition
Seismic Expectations
Lack of Support
Isolation

1900–1990s	*Late 1990s and Beyond*
Executives as adversaries	Executives as collaborators
Hospital-based disease management	Healthy communities
Organization as machine	Organization as living system
Fragmented departments	Networks
Provider focus	Service driven
Autonomy of discipline	Communities of practice
Fee for service	Capitation
Command/control hierarchy	Participative governance
Narrow span	Systems thinking
Solo achievement	Team competencies
Win/lose	Ability to negotiate results
Reactive communication	Authentic dialogue
Expert imposes solution "outside in"	Learner transforms "inside out"

The fabric of coaching is woven around a supportive, guiding relationship that helps a leader find a focus so as to see beyond the horizon.

Coaching and Strategic Spielraum

The most meaningful emergent theme challenging today's leaders is the need to step back before moving forward, to create a reflective pause. In the words of Daniel Kim, "For leaders in health care . . . when in a crisis, or coming out of a crisis, you are still deeply focused on not being what you used to be. You have to be able to step back from that mode to a creative, generative place, and deeply question underlying assumptions."[6] Or, as a coaching client accurately noted, "You can't welcome anything new into your life unless you have the space for it."[7] Yet all too frequently many leaders think in highly reactive, nonreflective ways in response to crises and key events. Being coached creates the space to slow down, to see the possibilities and consequences of actions. Indeed, the simplest definition of an executive coach is that of an artful designer of this needed "space," one who pulls together work and relationship themes, best practices, and strategies for leadership success.

The German language has a word that more fully captures the nuances of "space." Loosely translated, the word *Spielraum* means "room to freely move or play—elbowroom." It is the rich diversity and imagery of *Spielraum* that allows us to penetrate more deeply the notion of "space." For example, "room to play" evokes the image of being fun-filled and carefree. Illustrative of these qualities is the *play* of sports, with its mindfulness of the need to focus on the moment.

In their book *A Simpler Way*, Wheatley and Kellner-Rogers describe play as serious business: "It requires great focus and concentration. If we are not mindful, if our attention slips, then we can't notice what's available or discover what's possible. Staying present is the discipline of play"[8]—and of coaching.

Both play and coaching can also be understood as preparation or rehearsal for potential later action. Learning organizations *and* individuals need rehearsal, or what Senge calls "practice fields," for experimentation and exploration as part of the quest for personal and role mastery.[9] Often caught up in a crisis frenzy, leaders have little rehearsal time. Most have to act on strategies that have not been tested, at a time when the fear of personal failure is great and there is no way to develop new skills or replay an important decision.

Continuous growth in any leadership role requires an openness to opportunity and feedback for learning at both a personal and organizational level. Continuous growth requires elbowroom for reflection, rehearsal, and the ability to see one's choices from different angles.

THE EXECUTIVE COACHING MODEL

Conversation is the powerful medium within which the coaching process occurs. It is through the art of conversation that a shift in viewpoint begins. And it is the simple conceptual framework of reflection, reframing, and rehearsal that builds structure around an otherwise ordinary conversation to produce compelling results. (See figure 11-2.)

The framework of reflection, reframing, and rehearsal have their underpinnings in the heuristic method. In the context of coaching, *heuristic* conveys the notion of "existing to discover." Through the three coaching elements, a client is supported through a change in perspective, thought, and action. Rather than the coach advising or imposing answers, through a collaborative process a client discovers his or her own intellectual and emotional capabilities and solutions, thereby fostering autonomy and self-governance and avoiding dependency on the coach.

FIGURE 11-2. Executive Coaching Model: A Transformational Vantage Point

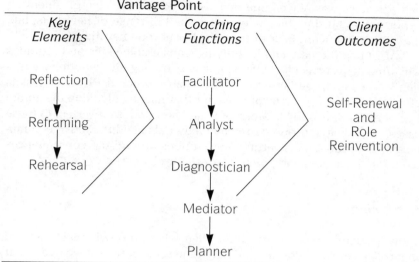

The transformational outcomes of the coaching process that result in role reinvention and renewal are

- Clarifying and deepening personal vision
- Realistically seeing one's strengths and needed areas of improvement
- Focusing on personal renewal and enrichment impacting the health care environment from the "inside out"

Reflection

Because of the isolation inherent in the leadership role, assuring executives that their reactions are indeed normal is an important first step in the coaching process. Appraisal and assessment by the coach provide useful informative feedback upon which behavior can be maintained or relearned.

For example, in a recent coaching session with a senior vice president of patient care services, making an accurate client evaluation proved to be an important ingredient in reestablishing the client's self-confidence and energy level. The incident was one in which the vice president had been asked by the CEO to "give up" a piece of her territory to a new executive on the block. After pondering the request, the vice president began, within the confidential confines of the coaching session, to surface feelings of anger, fear, and diminished confidence around her image and competence—thought patterns that were leading to a negative energy level. Reflecting on past experiences of how previous obstacles were faced and managed allowed the vice president an opportunity and the objectivity to see the full range of her skills, and this was a significant factor in moving her beyond negativity.

Affirming the past and identifying transferable skills and attitudes will often help correct and put in perspective a negative emotional experience—an important ingredient in the change process. However, just as often, established patterns of behavior that may be blocking the ability to reach goals need to be interrupted and new actions inserted. In these cases, providing appropriate reading materials and interactive communications facilitates insightful conversations around the consequences of certain behaviors and potential areas for change.

Reframing

Many leaders unnecessarily limit themselves through their view of themselves or the labor market. Oftentimes, executives have lived their entire leadership career within the walls of one system. A coach coming from outside the system can lend a new broad-based perspective. Information sharing of trends and practices within health care and from other organizations as well as exploration of proven strategies that have been helpful to other leaders in similar situations can help widen the client's horizon and encourage benchmarking "outside the box."

A case in point is a CEO who was concerned that one of his vice presidents had become newly challenging in executive meetings. His worry was that this vice president, whom he had mentored, was now sabotaging some vital projects. Upon analyzing the relationship dynamics, the CEO expressed his disappointment in the executive, a person he had "developed" and whom he felt "owed him." Reframing some of the behavior and interaction options between the two executives proved to be powerful leverage in changing the dynamics. In particular, a recasting of the vice president out of the protégé role was the key domino in a succession of complex relationship changes.

Reframing perceptions and moving fixed thought processes are often challenges in the coaching process. Assessment tools such as 360° Feedback®, the Myers-Briggs Type Indicator (MBTI), Personal Style Inventory, and Symlog can be used to leverage change. Such tools help leaders clarify and articulate their role, leadership, and decision-making style by objectively sorting information and identifying key issues that may be impeding their effective action.

Testing as part of reframing becomes a form of empowerment by which leaders come to see a more realistic picture of themselves and in which a path can be cut through relationship and political entanglements between individuals and teams.

Rehearsal

New behaviors need to be learned, and for that leaders need to have the opportunity to rehearse or practice various actions. The coaching element of rehearsal not only helps with action planning, but moves one beyond perceptual impasses.

Rehearsal takes place at two different levels. The first level is to mentally rehearse and imagine the specific details and behaviors prior to direct action. By imagining each of the various actions, leaders can become better prepared for actual situations and may also attain new insights. A classic example of this first level is mentally rehearsing a request for a raise.

The second level of rehearsal is direct behavior practice and role-playing. The effect is crystallized through the use of constructive positive feedback, building of self-confidence, and correct problem solving.

An example of the second level of rehearsal is the case of a chief financial officer (CFO) who needed to make a critical presentation to the executive committee on some painful financial imperatives. His rehearsal began by working backward, visualizing the meeting's ending and the critical factors that had contributed to a successful outcome. The verbal exchange between the coach and the CFO was a beneficial troubleshooting effort identifying many potential pitfalls that were later avoided.

OVERVIEW OF COACHING

Coaches can help leaders navigate through difficult problems and relationships. Through their ability to facilitate discussion and reflection, analyze leaders' behavior, diagnose leaders' typical thought patterns, and offer leaders alternative ways of looking at situations, coaches are an invaluable part of the leadership development process.

Five Functions of a Coach

There are five essential functions a coach brings to the table that catalyze change and trigger new ways of thinking and working by expanding and shifting viewpoints:

1. *Facilitating:* Making the process of drawing out the client's own vision, values, and solutions easier—thus lending clarity to desired outcomes.
2. *Analyzing:* Detecting and unraveling patterns, hidden organizational and relationship dynamics, themes, and trends.

3. *Diagnosing:* Identifying the client's mental models—the internal pictures or critical and hidden assumptions about the way the world works. This particular function can be assisted by the use of the various assessment tools cited earlier to accelerate self-awareness.

4. *Mediating:* Creating a strategy or option where there doesn't seem to be one. Helping to negotiate a treaty directly or designing a plan between parties. Strategizing before a meeting to allow greater maneuverability and swifter movement through any issue or relationship maze.

5. *Strategic Planning:* Formulating and forecasting plans that will be effective in getting from where one is now to where one wishes to go within the larger system and political playing field. That is done by creating scenarios, building alliances, and networking.

Learning Outcomes

Relationships, strategic decision making, organizational and self-explorations, operational issues, and performance feedback are key areas of learning in the coaching process.

Relationships   "The organizational road is paved with bodies of people who have become entangled in political webs," warns one seasoned chief operating officer following a coaching session.[10] That explains why such a large percentage of the coaching process revolves around such relationship issues as:

- Navigating sensitive political and territorial issues
- Avoiding communication and relationship blunders
- Handling and neutralizing relationship crises
- Facilitating and building alliances

For example, the CFO of a community hospital had begun to hear from in-house staff and community members that the CEO had come under fire from the board. The CFO, even though new to his role within the last year, had on more than one occasion felt that the CEO's decisions were not financially advantageous for the organization. Recently, the CFO had begun to publicly fault his superior for having made short-sighted, flawed decisions.

The frustration of the CFO culminated at a board meeting when he outlined the financial inadequacies of a new initiative the CEO was presently negotiating. He had, however, underestimated the political ties of significant members of the board and medical staff to the CEO. As a result, the CFO found himself with a diminished number of supporters and great difficulty in "being heard" within the organization.

Coaching sessions revolved around identifying the CFO's lack of political skill as an Achilles' heel and discussing various reparative actions that would assist him in reversing his precarious position.

Strategic Decision Making   The opportunity to strategize and plan individual and organizational actions is a prime focus in many coaching conversations. These include

- Influencing or changing the direction of board or other power holders
- Stepping through critical success factors in organizational initiatives, mergers, and buyouts
- Identifying and planning potential career opportunities

For example, in a meeting of the transition team of an integrated system, the discussion focused on the need to replace the administrative level of a newly acquired midsize facility. The CEO quickly made a unilateral decision declaring his intent to appoint an individual from within the integrated network to the position of vice president of clinical services. The team members were aware that even though the individual's performance as nursing director had been outstanding, she had only held the position for the past year, had never held a leadership role outside the organization, and was still in the process of fine-tuning her political skills.

The chairperson of the team, who was also vice president of human resources, met with a coach to develop a plan that would address the CEO's hasty appointment decision by identifying the consequences of such action and proposing alternative plans.

Explorations and Discoveries   The intent in coaching is to help leaders trigger new ways of being by calling these traits forth from within, as opposed to trying to force them upon leaders from without.[11]

There are many explorations and discoveries that evolve from the coaching process, such as the following:

- Cultivating the leadership capabilities of self-awareness, authenticity, and life/work integration
- Introducing innovative methods for accelerated organizational change and alignment of diverse constituents
- Providing a client with "best practices" or cutting-edge resources

For example, a CEO whose organization was facing a financial shortfall enlisted a coach to share information on what other leaders were doing with regard to fluctuating census, role redesign, and resource allocation. His goal was to walk through practices that were working and to develop an exploratory proposal for the board.

Operational Issues   Every day is grist for the coaching mill when it comes to such operational issues as

- Orchestrating and facilitating work redesign and process improvement
- Handling an employee town meeting or other potentially volatile meeting
- Negotiating in a unionized environment
- Constructing presentations and formulating business plans

For example, in a recent coaching session with a vice president of clinical services, the topic on the table was how to move forward with the organization's plan for product line services, knowing that it would result in the loss of some union positions. The coaching dialogue centered on identifying union concerns and avoiding political minefields. A plan was formulated as to how he might ensure labor union participation and commitment.

Performance Feedback   In Japan, the word is *kaizen*. In America, the term is *continuous improvement*. Both mean the relentless quest for better quality performance through a continuous feedback loop.

No one can afford to rest on a reputation anymore. Leaders have to passionately practice *kaizen*. Coaching centers on

- Offering behaviorally specific observations and recommendations
- Responding to 360° feedback with an action plan
- Suggesting additional training, education, or development

SELECTION OF A COACH

Most often the opportunity to procure an executive coach occurs through collegial networking and referral or through the use of consultants whom the organization has secured for other services.

Given the erosion of trust, relationships, and loyalty in the present health care climate, the trend of securing a coach from outside one's organization will continue. Employing an external coach provides guarantees that cannot be assured with an internal coach. Not being a part of the organizational landscape means not being encumbered by political and emotional ties—an important quality for a noncompetitive, confidential forum.

In addition to demonstrated ability in the previously discussed five functions, it is helpful for a coach to possess an extensive knowledge in organizational dynamics and the current health care industry; and a background in behavioral science that includes excellent listening skills, a strong understanding or sense of when to express an opinion and when to remain neutral, the ability to offer constructive feedback, and facility in analyzing individual and group dynamics. Such a background affords one the expertise to differentiate between true coaching needs and psychological counseling, thereby avoiding a potential minefield in the relationship. In their article titled "Executive as Coach," Waldroop and Butler cite the importance of being able to identify and distinguish the difficult-to-ameliorate, characterologically based traits of a client from leadership traits that are amenable to change.[12]

Formalization of the Coaching Process

To ensure success, the coaching relationship needs to receive as high a priority as any other important organizational challenge and commitment. Even though pressed for time, leaders have to be willing to set aside other business obligations temporarily and schedule regular and frequent meeting times—guarding that time from interruptions. The coaching relationship relies on a consistent interaction over time to achieve results. Formalizing the sessions helps establish an effective working alliance and sets parameters for a professional relationship. Questions to ask a potential coach in making a selection include the following:

- What references can you provide from your prior coaching engagements?
- How would you describe your approach or philosophy?
- What is our agreement for confidentiality?
- How will we determine the scope of our work together in terms of timelines and fees?
- What, if any, assessment tools do you use?
- Will I have a written development plan?
- Do you include follow-up as part of your contract?

The Contract

As the client expresses his or her issues, it's essential that the coach help translate this information into both specific goal statements and steps for realizing those goals. Usually the coaching agreement consists of a written or verbal contract through which ownership and use of space *(Spielraum)* is established; focus is created and the danger of meaningless communication and conversation is reduced; a common language is established; and boundaries are agreed upon.

Timelines are determined by the nature and extent of the agreed-upon outcomes. Common practice is to meet one to two hours every one to two weeks for a set number of months. Follow-up and periodic check-in times are important to measure improvements.

The decision to meet on site or off site requires thoughtful consideration. On-site coaching is the most convenient, while off-site coaching allows for confidentiality. The site plays a part in determining the fee structure. Additionally, fees depend on the coach's level of credentialing, experience, and expertise and range from an hourly rate to an overall project fee.

On occasion the coaching agreement may include a provision for observing the client by attending various key meetings within the organization, thereby allowing a more comprehensive, balanced view of organizational and interpersonal dynamics and issues.

While the focus of this chapter is the one-on-one coaching relationship, the model is extremely effective in achieving sustainable results with organizational teams as well. Indeed, the contract may include components for both individual and team coaching.

THE COACHING PROCESS IN ACTION: CASE EXAMPLE

An integrated health care network enlisted the skills of an executive coach to work with a physician leader who had been appointed as the executive director of ambulatory services following his facility's merger within the network. He was charged with the task of integrating clinical operations of the merged systems for a combined service population of 300 patients per day. The following case study illustrates the catalytic role of the coach in the personal transformation of one physician leader. (See figure 11-3.)

Precoaching Session: A Reluctant Skeptic

Dr. John Taylor, a highly respected 45-year-old clinician of national prominence, had reluctantly agreed to assume leadership responsibilities of a facility he had practiced in for 15 years. Because of his lack of administrative experience, Dr. Taylor was encouraged to meet with a coach to accelerate his knowledge and gain support for his transition.

Dr. Taylor's comments during the first one-on-one session expressed an immediate resistance to the coaching process:

> "I entered medicine to treat and cure illness, not to sit in meetings and waste my time on all this minutiae." Dr. Taylor looked

impatiently at his watch and said, "How long will this take?" He sat with his arms crossed and stated, "I don't really know what the value would be of talking to you. I don't have time for 'touchy-feely' endeavors; it's hard enough to think about what we have to do on the units to turn this place around."

Dr. Taylor proceeded to embark upon an hour and a half monologue about his concerns in assuming the mantle of leadership. He outlined the following demands: "I have to work with an interdisciplinary team that never spoke to each other before, implement process improvements to reduce patient waits, and somehow slash the budget without compromising our patients." Underlying his brusqueness, he conveyed an anxiety about his lack of experience. At the end of the meeting he said, "I was trained as a physician, not as a manager. I don't want our clinic to lose sight of what we are here for. I have a responsibility to pull all of us together. So, if other physicians have used this method, I'll have to talk to them and get back to you."

FIGURE 11-3.   The Coaching Process in Action

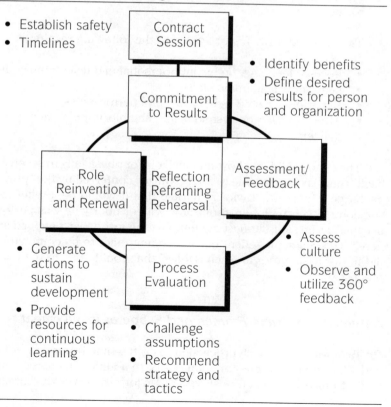

Contracting Session: Creating Safety and Establishing Desired Results

Dr. Taylor agreed to meet to discuss the benefits of the coaching process. The contracting session is critical to establish operating agreements of confidentiality and to commit to future results. Building rapport creates a sense of safety to discuss sensitive issues about leadership style as well as to deliver feedback that may be difficult to hear. By encouraging Dr. Taylor to take ownership of the coaching process results, control and safety were placed firmly in his hands. To establish this sense of safety, the coach asked Dr. Taylor, "What are the results that would make this worthwhile to you?" Dr. Taylor replied:

> We need to get beyond these petty wars and remember why we are here. As for myself, I would want to come out of this being smarter about how to do the job. Stress can make people feel stupid. I want to know how I come across to others and I want time to think through decisions. Ultimately, as much as I'd rather just be seeing patients and writing papers, I have to take responsibility for this group coming together or we won't have any patients left to see.

The coach and Dr. Taylor agreed to the following results:

- Receive feedback on his interpersonal and leadership style
- Learn new leadership skills
- Experience a shift in behavior and performance
- Affect the larger system with tangible improvements in care delivery

The coach validated how unusual it is for physicians to receive feedback from "laypeople" due to the privileges conferred by the "physician-in-charge" status. Dr. Taylor remarked that it would be a relief to have someone "level" with him about how well or poorly he was performing because, as he said, "honest communication just doesn't happen around here." The coach and client made a commitment to be completely candid in discussing the "undiscussables" that could arise in the coaching process.

Agreement on Time Frames and Scope of Involvement

Dr. Taylor and the coach proceeded to craft a time frame of weekly one and a half hour sessions for six months. In addition, an agreement was made to have the coach observe Dr. Taylor at his weekly "integrated" executive team meetings and to complete a cultural assessment of the outpatient facilities. The latter two contractual elements were seen as necessary in order to discover the impact of Dr. Taylor's behavior on the environment and to determine the cultural factors facing him on a daily basis.

Cultural Context

Cultural analysis defines the context for interpersonal dynamics within the health care setting. In the merger climate of Dr. Taylor's network, one unit came from a "warm and casual family-oriented team" where the values of patient-centered care and teamwork were openly promoted. Dr. Taylor's facility, the "host" environment, was described as impersonal, "high tech, low touch" with a hierarchical and divisive atmosphere. Members from both groups described an adversarial climate of 40 years of rivalry and competition. Staff members at both facilities expressed skepticism about the team's ability to work together.

Staff Feedback

Dr. Taylor was described by the staff as a highly principled, dedicated, and intelligent physician who had an intimidating manner with his quick pace and clipped speech. He was labeled "hostile" by the finance administrators interviewed. They interpreted his dislike of meetings, poor eye contact, and finger tapping during their sessions as evidence of his disregard for their input in critical operational decisions and resource allocation. Nursing leadership attempted to mediate between the physician and finance group. Tensions were high among the newly formed governance team, where important resources requested by Dr. Taylor were being held up by the finance administrator as "retaliation" for poor treatment.

Reflection, Reframing, Rehearsal

The coach intended to create a shift in Dr. Taylor's awareness from being reactive to reflective and to challenge discrepancies between how he acted and what he wanted. Observation, inquiry, and validation were crucial underpinnings in the following sequences.

The coach asked, "What unintended results are getting in the way of the team's progress?" and the client responded: "I hate meetings, and as for the team, they're hostile! If only they would formulate their thoughts a little faster. They just use all that business jargon and don't seem to care at all about the patients. And to make it worse, they are competing with me!" Hearing this, the coach questioned Dr. Taylor's sarcastic tone at meetings and challenged his assumptions regarding the competence of nonmedical colleagues. The coach pointed out how Dr. Taylor contributed to a climate of hostility through his condescending manner, gestures, and choice of words.

The coach reframed Dr. Taylor's perception of the finance administrators by pointing out that neither he nor the administrators had expertise or experience leading change of this magnitude. Dr. Taylor was then able to disclose that he did not want to appear foolish because of his lack of business training. He was able to agree that their common ground was fiscal health and that it was in their mutual interest to find a way to invite their joint participation in seeking solutions. The coach encouraged Dr. Taylor to begin relationship repair and alliance building by meeting individual team members for lunch.

Dr. Taylor began to expand his mental model of effective leadership through the observation of his deeply ingrained habits and assumptions. The coach challenged him to see and think "outside the box" by continuing to reframe his assumptions through the power of asking the right questions. Learning was also accelerated by the introduction of executive leadership materials on finance, negotiation skills, and team development, all of which the physician absorbed quickly.

Dr. Taylor rehearsed various scenarios to lead the changes underway on the unit. He strategized ways to gain the support of his physician group in cooperation with nursing, pharmacy, and adjunct staff on patient-flow issues. He demonstrated his intention to build a strong alliance with the nurse leader by taking supportive stands on traditionally polarizing issues.

Dr. Taylor began to show up at meetings as a willing participant rather than a "hostage." He started to pace himself by listening, refraining from interrupting others, and asking questions rather than simply advocating a position. As members of the team became more humanized in Dr. Taylor's view, he became more human to them as well. He began to poke fun at his "dictatorial" style in team meetings. "It's clearly out of vogue in all the management literature I've been reading," he joked.

Results: Organizational Impact in Care Delivery and Collaboration

In the sixth month of the engagement, Dr. Taylor organized a highly productive team retreat to address shared purpose and barriers within the merged group. Thirty participants representing all disciplines came together for a day to develop operating principles, identify expectations, clarify roles, and establish the critical priorities facing the unit. The governance team rotated facilitation while the group tackled difficult issues on cost-containment initiatives and interpersonal conflict. The cultural differences of the two groups were recognized with candid disclosures about differences and strengths. Nurses, physicians, and support staff shared their values as well as struggles in maintaining morale in the midst of unprecedented changes. The executive team, including Dr. Taylor, acknowledged the specific contributions of members. The session was profound in lifting morale and creating a shift of perspective. A monthly all-staff meeting was instituted as a forum to sustain progress in building a "community of practice."

Case Summary: Role Reinvention and Self-Renewal

Four years later, the unit is a seamless provider of patient care with reduced patient waits and low staff turnover. The interdisciplinary leadership team continues to meet weekly, while staff and faculty have maintained their monthly meetings. Patient surveys report high satisfaction with the expanded facility.

Dr. Taylor has emerged in the network as a talented leader who is sought after to address networkwide integration efforts. In a follow-up visit, he recently stated,

> The coaching sessions taught me that there were many things I never learned in medical school. Foremost was the need to get off the treadmill and take time to think through my actions. It's now a habit to ask myself and the team, "Where are we going? How do we want to get there?" I also learned that by starting to appreciate the people around me, we get much more accomplished. I know I am a better physician because of this process. But more importantly, what I have learned through being coached has helped me to coach others in the organization more effectively in managing the change process.

In the case of this "command and control" leader, coaching afforded a wake-up call to help him understand the consequences of his behavior both in himself and the organization he was attempting to change. Most importantly, Dr. Taylor began to turn his attention toward his colleagues with respect for their contributions. By fostering their development and acknowledging their strengths, he recognized that leadership in a time of great change is not a solo activity.

COACHING PITFALLS TO AVOID

Over the course of a coaching process, there are four critical distinctions and pitfalls that need to be recognized and avoided:

1. Executive coaching is not psychotherapy. The coaching emphasis is focused on present-centered performance, not on issues from a person's past, family of origin, or character issues. If the client is experiencing a personal crisis or is exhibiting destructive or emotionally dysfunctional behaviors, the coach will refer the client to an appropriate mental health professional.
2. Coaching is designed to promote a sense of personal self-governance, not dependency. If the client becomes reliant on the coach for advice and answers, the coach must address the underlying performance issues and redirect the focus back to the client.
3. Coaching is not a substitute for disciplinary action, nor should it be used to "rehabilitate" a poor performer. Occasionally, the coaching relationship will be offered as part of a performance management intervention and should only be undertaken if the client is receptive to the request.
4. Coaching can be viewed as an organizational intervention because of the new behaviors being required of the client for strategic direction, operational issues, and relationship dynamics. Therefore, it is important that the coach understand the broader systemic environment and maintain appropriate boundaries as a "facilitator" rather than as a "fixer" of current issues.

CONCLUSION

In spite of the industry's challenge to accelerate, leaders need to create a space for dialogue and conversation. If they want to keep up with the pace and develop winning strategies, they have to slow down. Coaching allows the needed elbowroom to freely move from the boardroom to the patient room.

A coach can help make the necessary breakthroughs in any leader's efforts to create an innovative paradigm. Evolutionary leadership requires the reflection, reframing, and rehearsal to produce the results that coaching brings.

References

1. Personal communication within a coaching session, 1996.

2. Personal communication within a coaching session, 1996.

3. H. Levinson, "When Executives Burn Out," *Harvard Business Review* 74, no. 4 (July–Aug. 1996): 152–63.

4. Personal communication within a coaching session, 1996.

5. P. Pritchett, *New Work Habits for a Radically Changing World* (Dallas: Pritchett and Associates, 1996), p. 15.

6. J. Flower, "We Are What We Can Learn: A Conversation on Learning Organizations with Daniel Kim," *Healthcare Forum Journal* 39, no. 4 (July 1996): 36–41.

7. R. Hargrove, *Masterful Coaching* (San Francisco: Pfeiffer and Co., 1995), p. 134.

8. M. Wheatley and M. Kellner-Rogers, *A Simpler Way* (San Francisco: Berrett-Koehler, 1996), pp. 20–21.

9. P. Senge and others, "Creating a Learning Lab—and Making It Work," *The Fifth Discipline Fieldbook* (New York: Doubleday, 1994), p. 558.

10. Personal communication within a coaching session, 1996.

11. Hargrove, *Masterful Coaching*, p. 42.

12. J. Waldroop and T. Butler, "Executive as Coach," *Harvard Business Review* 74, no. 6 (Nov.–Dec. 1996): 111–17.

12

Establishing Reward Systems That Support Change

Thomas B. Wilson, M.B.A., Ph.D.

rofound change is reshaping the health care industry. Organizations are implementing changes to their strategy, structure, and systems. For these change initiatives to succeed, organizations must also undergo an equally dramatic change in culture. As described in chapter 1, the culture of an organization both reflects and influences behaviors. Thus, organizations that are attempting to create cultural change must address systems and processes that influence what people do and how they do it. One of the most primary is organizational reward systems.[1]

When people are asked to undertake the difficult task of changing their behavior, the question they most often have is "What's in it for me?" This chapter helps leaders provide a satisfactory answer to that question by describing how organizations can establish reward systems that support change. The chapter explores the relationship between behavior and rewards and analyzes the basic elements of reward systems, with particular emphasis on compensation and recognition programs. To help leaders see an effective reward system "in action," the chapter includes a case example of the process one health care organization followed to overhaul its reward system.

THE RELATIONSHIP OF REWARDS TO BEHAVIOR

Every initiative must include strategies for helping people change how they do their work. Whether the change is being more responsive to patients or other customers, managing costs so that unproductive activities are eliminated, or introducing new services, people must be motivated to implement change initiatives successfully.

Causes of Resistance to Change

Although change is often met by resistance, change itself does not necessarily cause resistance. As explained in chapter 3, people generally resist change when they fear losing something of value without commensurate rewards. In addition, people often resist new initiatives when they have seen other initiatives come and go without effecting real improvements. When people see their leaders become excited about an initiative, promote it, then fail to follow through until improvements are made, they tend to develop a cynical attitude toward change. Such has been the case in many organizations after failed attempts to institute total quality management (TQM) initiatives.

On the other hand, people usually welcome changes that bring genuine organizational growth and personal rewards. It therefore follows that to successfully implement change, leaders must consider the role, design, and effectiveness of their organization's reward systems. When these systems are built around the forces that drive human behavior, they are powerful motivators to change.

Forces That Drive Human Behavior

When people are asked to change their behavior, they usually want answers to these basic questions:

1. What do I need to do differently?
2. Can I do what is needed?
3. Am I meeting expectations?
4. What's in it for me? Do I *want* to do this?

These questions center around four primary forces of behavior. (See figure 12-1.) The greater the extent to which these forces are used to support the organization's change objectives, the greater the likelihood of success.

Work Focus   Work focus answers the question "What do I need to do differently?" Focus may be provided by guidelines as specific and straightforward as procedures and practices on how to perform a function or as general and profound as mission, strategy, and values statements. Whatever the mechanisms used, people must have a clear sense of focus to make decisions and take action in a manner that supports the organization's strategic plans. The clearer the focus, the greater the likelihood that people will adopt behaviors that bring personal and organizational success.

FIGURE 12-1. Forces That Drive Behavior

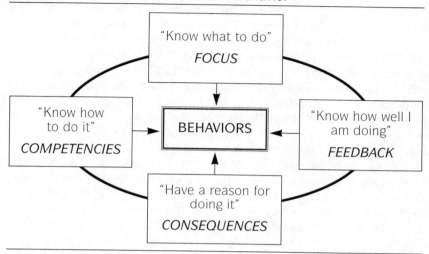

Work Competencies   Once people have a clear sense of focus, they are likely to ponder the question "Can I do what is needed?" This question touches on work competencies—the knowledge, skills, and abilities people need to perform desired tasks. Competencies may be "made" by training current employees or "bought" by recruiting new talent. Many organizations spend considerable time and money on training and recruitment to ensure that staff competencies match organizational requirements. However, if "good" people are placed into a "bad" system, the system will likely prevail over time. For this reason, leaders must create reward systems that support desired competencies.

Feedback on Work Behavior   To sustain changes in behavior, people need feedback that is specific, data based, and timely. People may know what to do and how to do it, but if they do not receive information about their progress, they are left to wonder, "Am I meeting expectations?" Every serious change initiative must include a system by which to measure progress toward meeting desired goals.

Consequences of Work Behavior   Consequences are the punishments or rewards that people receive for their behavior—the results that answer the question "What's in it for me?" Behavior is based on expectations of what is likely to occur. A historical pattern of consequences creates expectations. Thus, people are likely to repeat behaviors that are rewarded and avoid repeating behaviors that are punished or that go unrewarded.

Take, for example, the case of a large health care organization that was implementing a new set of care management protocols. The change involved integrating certain medical records with test results so that clinicians would have thoroughly documented information readily available. The purpose of the change in protocols was to increase the quality of patient care, reduce costs, and optimize the time of physicians and other clinical specialists. On Fridays at the end of each month, when the medical records department had to eliminate all backlogs of pending records, the process broke down. Because transport people were not integrated into the process, information was often late. Equally important, physicians were not held accountable (that is, rewarded or punished) for their lack of attention to the new process. Nursing and clinical departments were the only ones who felt any level of dissatisfaction with the failure of the new protocols. While people knew what to do, no consequences—positive or negative—were in place to support the successful implementation of process changes, and a good idea failed.

If leaders want individuals to institute change, then consequences are essential. Most research indicates that consequences are the primary determinant of behaviors. In fact, the anticipation of consequences often determines the extent of the future behaviors.[2]

Negative consequences: Negative consequences, such as punishment or threats, usually lead to compliance. When leaders need to create a shock or wake-up call, threats can be an appropriate behavioral tool. Leaders must make the negative consequences of resistance or failure to act very clear to all. At the same time, leaders must understand that compliance means people will do just what is expected of them and little more. Negative consequences alone will not instill in people the degree of commitment or discretionary effort organizations need to survive difficult times. Unfortunately, leaders often get rewarded for short-term results that derive from negative consequences.

Positive consequences: Positive consequences, such as verbal expressions of appreciation and monetary rewards, motivate people to adopt desired behaviors. In fact, the combination of intrinsic and extrinsic reinforcement often motivates people to exceed expectations. Providing positive consequences thus leads to a win-win situation in which both the individual and the organization receive something they want. Providing positive consequences is not just a nice thing to do; it is necessary for success.

Thus, we arrive at the fundamental purpose of reward systems. Simply stated, reward systems are a systematic way for organizations to provide positive consequences. Reward systems are important to the change process because they encourage and reinforce needed actions.

When reward systems are designed and managed properly, people feel highly valued for fulfilling organizational objectives. The outcome is improved performance, increased responsiveness, and a workforce that is committed to building a better future.

OVERVIEW OF ELEMENTS OF THE REWARD SYSTEM

To be successful, reward systems must be based on sound, scientific behavioral principles that are applied in an effective manner and utilized in creative and effective ways. Figure 12-2 provides an overview of the primary elements of reward systems. The reward system triangle is a simple conceptual framework for integrating various reward programs into a coherent system.

The Reward Strategy

At the heart of every reward system is a strategy for tailoring rewards to meet the needs of specific groups. The reward strategy should take into account the groups to be targeted, the objectives each group must meet, and the manner in which each group will be rewarded.

Identification of Target Groups   The first task in creating a reward strategy is to identify the unit or units around which reward systems are to be developed. The era of "one strategy fits all" is over. A reward strategy designed to motivate nursing staff is unlikely to motivate marketing specialists; similarly, administrative functions will probably require a different strategy from that used to motivate behavioral changes on the clinical side.

FIGURE 12-2.   Primary Elements of the Reward System

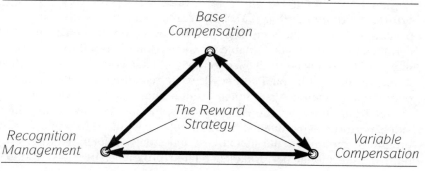

Articulation of Desired Behaviors   The reward strategy must also translate organizational objectives into a set of behaviors or actions for people in the target group. Articulating desired behaviors provides focus and lets people know exactly which behaviors will result in positive consequences. The degree of precision depends on the level of clarity needed to achieve desired results.

Definition of Purpose   Finally, the reward strategy must define the purpose of each major element in the organization's portfolio of rewards, such as base and variable compensation. The definition of purpose should describe how desired behaviors will be encouraged, supported, and reinforced by the organization.

Reward Programs

Once reward strategies have been defined, the organization must implement them through specific reward programs. These programs include base compensation, variable compensation, and special recognition.

Base Compensation   Base compensation, the salary program for the organization, reflects the stable element of rewards (although in the era of managed care, this is changing). There are three basic types of base compensation programs: job evaluation–based, market pricing, and competency-oriented programs. Essentially, base compensation reflects the individual's value to the organization in terms of responsibilities or capabilities, his or her performance track record, and the worth of the function in the marketplace. It is important to retain pay levels that are competitive to the market because this is the primary means by which organizations attract and retain human resources. At the same time, because base pay represents a major cost—frequently as high as 60 percent of the organization's total costs—dollars must be allocated in a manner consistent with the organization's values, requirements, and ability to pay.

Variable Compensation   Variable compensation refers to incentive programs that provide lump sum payouts based on the achievement of certain specified results. Variable compensation often reflects "opportunity pay" (as opposed to the secured pay of base compensation) in that it may or may not be paid and needs to be re-earned each performance period. Organizations can choose from a wide variety of variable programs, from pure discretionary programs and programs based on individual performance or management by objective (MBO) to profit-sharing programs, group or team incentives, and stock options or other long-term organizational performance–related programs. In short, variable compensation rewards achievement of results and should be linked directly to the organization's core strategy.

Recognition Programs   Recognition programs generally provide non-cash formal or informal rewards to a specific individual or team. Because these programs are used to recognize and reinforce contributions as they happen rather than at the end of a performance period, they are sometimes known as "between the paychecks" reward systems. Recognition programs should target different types of specific behaviors that are essential to achieving desired results. In high-performance organizations, recognition is not seen as a "nice thing to do" but as an essential element of the reward management process.

To be successful, reward systems must be meaningful to people. Studies show that what employees want from their workplace is to be recognized for their contributions. Recognition programs are an effective way to reinforce people's efforts.

The Reward System in Action: Case Example

To understand the various elements of a reward system, it is helpful to look at specific examples of each component. For purposes of illustration, imagine that an organization called Concordian Health Care Corporation is pursuing a strategy to renew itself and be more competitive, responsive, and responsible. The organization is composed of a major medical center and several community-based hospitals, plus several subsidiaries for ambulatory care, home health care, and other health care services. Concordian is facing increasing pressure to reduce costs from managed care customers and needs to strengthen its link with physicians. In response to changing market conditions, the senior executive team decides to make a series of major changes in the organization's structure. These initiatives require making a fundamental shift from a functional-based organization to a service-line orientation. Senior executives realize that a culture shift must accompany structural and system changes. Because reward systems have a dramatic impact on the organization's culture, senior executives want to make drastic changes there as well.

In their discussions, it became clear that many areas of the organization would need to change and that the strategy should focus on specific groups. Before they could address the new requirements of each group, however, the senior managers needed to define the new requirements for the entire organization, which then became the target group for changes in the reward system. It was expected that these requirements would be translated down to each unit within the organization through the development of specific reward systems.

Articulation of Desired Behaviors   After an analysis of the organization's strategy, values, and key success factors, the senior executive team determines that the primary desired behaviors are as follows:

- To focus on those the organization serves
- To foster collaboration within and across organizational units
- To encourage people to take personal responsibility for the organization's resources
- To make continuous improvements in process and systems
- To encourage people to take personal initiative to do new things, learn from them, and share this learning with others

From a technical viewpoint, these are not behaviors. However, they set the stage for pinpointing specific behaviors needed by different units within the organization—nursing, marketing, finance, human resources, clinical services, management, and so on.

Within this context, the organization then proceeds to establish the purpose of each reward system. The purpose statements, which are simple, provide a general sense of direction for the development and management of specific base compensation, variable compensation, and recognition programs.

Base Pay Purpose Statement   The organization's purpose statement reads as follows:

> We will associate pay with talent and competencies needed by the organization. Further, pay opportunities should be sufficiently competitive for the organization to attract and retain desired talent. Pay levels need to be fiscally responsible and consistent with the degree that competencies are employed to achieve desired performance.

Variable Pay Purpose Statement   To articulate the organization's variable pay program, the organization creates this statement:

> Variable pay programs will provide the mechanism by which we share the gains realized by the organization with those who made it happen. We will provide an opportunity for all members of the organization to participate in a variable pay program consistent with key success factors of their primary organizational unit (that is, department, division, or overall organization). Measures need to reflect a combination of financial, service, operational, and customer needs. Payout opportunities need to be consistent so that units are not treated unfairly because of their inability to make a financial impact on the organization.

Recognition Programs Purpose Statement   Finally, the organization creates this statement of purpose for its recognition programs:

> Our recognition programs will be how we will recognize contributions of individuals as well as achievements of teams. These programs will provide the everyday process by which we value the effort and results of our employees. We will have several organization-wide programs, as well as ones specifically suited to departments. They will support managers as well as all employees in saying "thank you" for making a difference to our organization.

Summary of Results   The organization's reward strategy establishes a framework for all reward programs within the organization and provides focus as well as basic design principles. It supports the organization's renewal strategy and demonstrates the commitment of management to the change efforts. In this way, the desired changes are likely to be implemented and employees will share in the benefits of improved results.

Now that the basic elements of reward systems have been described, the stage is set for a more detailed analysis of compensation and recognition programs. Organizations can choose from a variety of approaches to these systems. Given the range of approaches and their importance to the reward system as a whole, compensation and recognition programs warrant special attention.

THE DESIGN OF BASE PAY SYSTEMS

As stated earlier, base pay systems determine the salaries individuals receive and provide the process for increasing salaries. To create a base pay system that effectively supports change initiatives, it is necessary to understand the primary elements of these systems as well as basic approaches to base pay.

Primary Elements of Traditional Base Pay Systems

In general, base pay systems are composed of the following elements:

- *Job descriptions:* Written documents that define the primary accountabilities, scope, and requirements of a job
- *Job evaluation:* A system of measurement criteria that establishes an internally based rank order of the jobs

- *Comparative market information:* A set of data that is used to establish relative competitiveness of salaries in relation to other organizations
- *Salary ranges:* Guidelines for managers that relate the grade structure to a marketplace, so that each job has a range of pay associated with it, including a minimum level of pay, a midpoint or control reference point, and a salary maximum
- *Salary administration policies:* Procedures and practices necessary for managers to administer salaries for handling hiring, transfers, promotions, and salary increase decisions

Although most base pay systems are made up of these elements, the format, criteria, structure, and policies differ from organization to organization. In lieu of a job evaluation process, some organizations assign grade levels to jobs based on comparisons to the level of pay awarded to similar positions in other organizations (for example, competitive, market-based pay).

The reward strategy depicted in the Concordian Health Care case example relates pay to the external marketplace, with a particular emphasis on competencies. The organization refocused the base pay system from rewarding the employee for the *responsibilities* he or she carries out to the *competencies* he or she has and employs in the organization.

Competency-Based Pay Programs

There are two directions an organization may take for competency-based pay programs. The organization may tie an individual's base pay to performance and management, emphasizing and reinforcing desired competencies, or it may create a career development program.

The Performance Contribution Approach   In the performance contribution approach, certain competencies are applied to all individuals. For health care organizations, these competencies may include such dimensions as

- Responsiveness to patients/customers
- Teamwork and collaboration
- Personal initiative
- Optimal use of resources
- Innovation and continuous improvement

Each of the competencies is defined, and behavioral statements illustrate what is meant by each competency. The competencies are then integrated into the performance review process in addition to results or goal accomplishments. In this approach, competencies define how achievements were made and may be valued equal to or greater than what was accomplished. When performance evaluations are used to determine merit increases, the process assesses the "what" (results) and "how" (competencies) to determine adjustments to salaries. Thus, competencies provide the focus for assessing of individual performance.

Figure 12-3 depicts an approach to pay increases based on three dimensions. The first is the performance of the individual or team (being judged as an individual department or unit), measured against standardized competencies as noted previously. Once this performance has been determined, the second dimension—the individual's contributions and competencies—is determined. The key is to identify how well the individual fulfilled his or her responsibilities to the team, the contributions made, and utilization in the key competencies. The matrix cell determines the individual's pay increase. If appropriate, a third dimension—the organization's overall performance—may modify the pay increase.

The purpose of the performance contribution approach is to reinforce the principle that when performance of the larger group improves, the individual has greater pay opportunity. If one helps another department, and this enhances the performance of the team or company, the individual will be rewarded. The situation works both

FIGURE 12-3.   Three Dimensions of Competency

Performance of the Individual or Team		Falls Short	Meets	Exceeds	
	Exceeds	4%	6%	8%	
	Meets	2%	4%	6%	Organization Performance
	Falls Short	0%	2%	4%	
		Falls Short	Meets	Exceeds	

Contributions and Competencies of the Individual

ways. If the company's performance is strong, the merit increases may increase; if the performance is weak, the merit increases may decrease.

The Career Development Approach   A second approach is to use competencies as the anchor for a career development pay system. Competencies may be defined within a function or across the entire organization. These competencies define career paths within the organization and are used by managers and individuals alike to target training and development efforts. As competencies increase and are applied to the job, pay is increased as well.

The Concordian Health Care case example illustrates the career development approach. The base pay statement of purpose shows a commitment to career paths and the development of competencies throughout the organization. The basis for the salary program is to provide more pay to individuals who clearly demonstrate increased abilities and utilize them on a regular basis. This framework requires the pay program to identify and define career paths within primary functions and define the levels of competencies associated with these career paths.

Concordian utilized a building-block framework to describe career levels. The levels are as follows:

- *Novice:* One who is in an entry-level role in which the emphasis is on learning the tasks of the function and performing basic level tasks
- *Applier:* One who has the ability to perform basic functions in a fully competent manner
- *Expander:* One who has the ability to perform all functions of the unit in a fully competent manner and the ability to develop process improvements or other critical changes to improve the performance of the overall unit
- *Master:* One who has the ability to define the work process and systems and to provide the leadership necessary for the unit to perform effectively

Requirements for these levels are generally defined through an analysis of tasks and competencies. The key is to ensure that competency criteria accurately reflect current or future requirements. Once levels are determined, the compensation function establishes a relative value of these levels, determined by selecting the career stage that is most comparable to jobs in other organizations and then collecting market pay information. Target pay levels are then selected to balance what is needed to achieve competitive salaries as well as adapt pay level internally.

The outcome of this analysis is a series of pay levels associated with each stage of the competency or career ladder. Figure 12-4 shows these levels. The figure illustrates how career levels may be associated with pay levels. Competency criteria enable the manager and employee to discuss current competencies in relation to requirements and to determine pay opportunities. The compensation function has accountability for establishing pay levels, and the manager assigns individuals to appropriate competency levels based on an objective analysis. In addition, the manager is accountable for applying compensation levels in relation to his or her payroll budget. In this way, the manager assumes responsibility for managing the development and compensation of his or her staff consistent with the guidelines of the competency-based pay structure.

Advantages of the career development approach: The career development approach to base pay has several important advantages. These include

- A focus on learning and applying knowledge to the performance requirements of the department or function
- A means for providing individuals with a sense of opportunity and an investment in their development
- A means of encouraging the application of the competencies either as common values within the organization or as a basis for career levels

Disadvantages of the career development approach: Although the career development program affords important advantages, it also has

FIGURE 12-4. Sample Pay Levels for the Career Approach

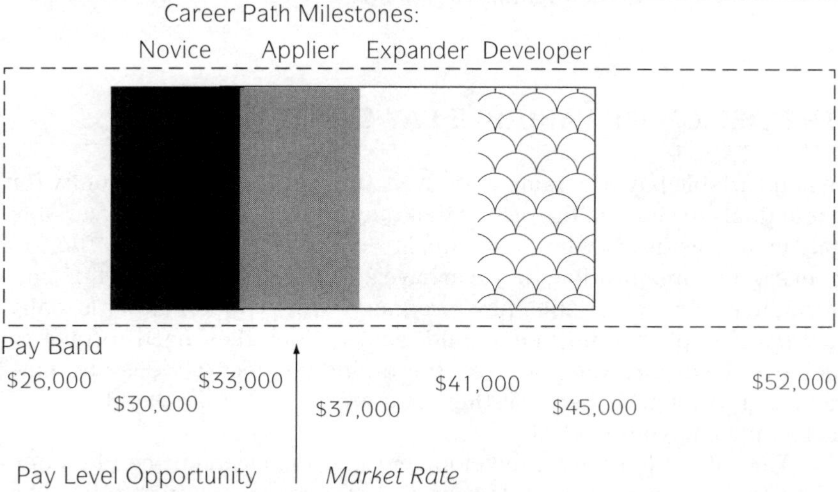

Career Path Milestones:
Novice   Applier   Expander Developer

Pay Band
$26,000 $33,000 $41,000 $52,000
     $30,000 $37,000 $45,000

Pay Level Opportunity | *Market Rate*

certain drawbacks. The organization has to consider the complexity of developing and managing the program so that the desired gain is realized. Primary concerns are as follows:

- The considerable amount of time the program takes to develop and implement. The organization cannot utilize an existing program from another organization and expect it to work. The process requires heavy involvement by human resources and the target group's line managers. To be worth the effort, the approach must have multiple applications; that is, be useful for the purposes of recruitment, selection, placement, and planning for staffing levels.
- The program may establish expectations for training and career opportunities that the organization may be unable to meet. The number of people at each career level needs to be controlled if the organization is to manage its compensation costs. Everyone cannot and should not be expected to move to the highest level. However, if employees feel that opportunities are limited by existing staff and the number of positions or roles open, frustration may ensue.
- The program needs strong, active management. As needs change for the function and as the market changes in pay levels, the program needs to change. It cannot be administered solely by human resources. Line managers need to take full accountability for the program.

Many organizations may be unwilling or unable to invest the resources necessary to develop a program of this nature. The central question the organization must answer is whether the program is likely to yield the results the organization needs.

THE DESIGN OF VARIABLE PAY SYSTEMS

When variable pay programs work well, they provide an opportunity for individuals to share in the results that they help create. Because variable pay programs directly link individuals' economic fortunes with the fortunes of the organization, they can have a very significant impact on performance. When variable pay programs work poorly, it is usually because people do not understand what actions they need to take to achieve desired results, because the timing between actions and payouts is too long, or because the goals are so high that the chance of achieving a payout is small.

Variable pay program development and management can be complex. To develop a successful program, both managers and staff must be committed to making the program work. During the development phase, it is essential that the organization provide opportunities for both groups to have input into the program. When the program has been approved, the components must be clearly communicated to both management and staff so that they understand how the program works. And once the program is implemented, both managers and employees will need frequent feedback on their progress toward meeting desired behaviors.

It also important to note that incentive pay plans can be risky. If there is no payout, individuals may become discouraged and feel the program is a facade. This risk can be minimized by ensuring that measures are challenging but achievable.

Types of Variable Pay Programs

There are two basic types of variable pay programs. The first is based on sharing of a portion of financial gains over a threshold level of performance. This type of program is typically referred to as profit sharing, but the concept also applies to gain sharing, commission-oriented sales compensation plans, and Improshare or Rucker plans.[3] The second type of program provides a payout when certain goals are achieved. In this case, if an individual or a team achieves specific goals or improves performance in specific measurement areas, then a payout is provided. This type of program is typically referred to as goal sharing. A common example of goal sharing is a management incentive plan that uses MBO as the basis for determining awards. Other forms will be described in more detail later in this chapter.

Overview of the Design Process

In designing variable pay programs, a systematic process should be used. The design wheel depicted in figure 12-5 illustrates one such process. The wheel starts with identification of the purpose and overall approach of the program. This is important, because once the program's purpose is determined, the target group is initially identified and the overall approach (that is, gain sharing or goal sharing) to the design process becomes easier. Further, by identifying critical results and behaviors, the program can be directed toward those areas that have a significant impact on the organization. This ensures that the variable pay program will have a meaningful influence on the culture change process.

The improved results should enable the organization to reduce costs, improve the satisfaction and retention of customers, and optimize

FIGURE 12-5.   The Variable Pay Program Design Wheel

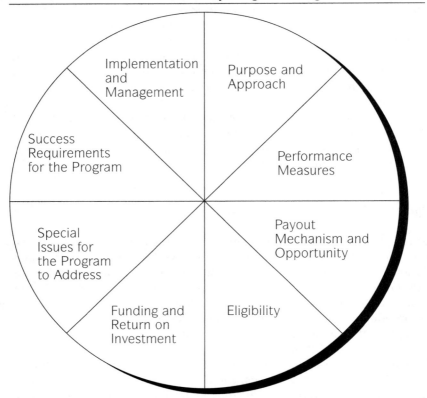

the use of resources. Gains in one area should not be offset by additional costs in another. Further, improvements in one area should enhance the performance of another group. For example, when an admitting office of a hospital was able to devliver 100 percent error-free admitting information to the billing office, the hospital experienced reduced accounts receivable and improved cash flow.

Design of Performance Measures   Perhaps the most important design element is determining performance measures. These measures establish the focus that the organization will provide for people's actions as well as the basis on which additional compensation expenses will be incurred. Measures that organizations may use include

- Financial measures
    —Net surplus or net income
    —Revenues and growth in revenues
    —Contribution or gross margins

- Operational measures
  - —Expenses to budget
  - —Error-free rates
  - —Quality of care or quality of service ratings
  - —Wait times for patients
- Customer satisfaction measures
  - —Customer satisfaction survey scores
  - —Number of patients/customers served
  - —On-time delivery of a service
- Capability measures
  - —Introduction of specific new services
  - —Implementation of special projects or programs
  - —Teamwork or internal employee satisfaction survey scores

To be effective, measures must be clear, objective, and action oriented. People respond more effectively to measures when it is clear to them what actions result in improved performance and when they perceive results to be generally under their control. In short, people must be confident that when desired actions are taken, performance will improve.

Of course, it is difficult to design a measurement system that is perfectly clear, objective, and action oriented. If an individual's total compensation were dependent on measures, they would have to be as finely honed as possible. However, since most variable pay programs provide additional pay, "perfection" is somewhat less important.

Selection of Award Mechanisms   Once the measures have been selected, the next step is to develop a mechanism for determining the award. The gain-sharing approach involves determining the threshold level for performance and the formula "share" of the pool. In addition, the organization needs to determine how money will be allocated to participants. The allocation process can include a common dollar amount to all members, an award based on a percentage of their current salary, or some combination of both.

Mechanisms based on two measures: When the organization uses the goal-sharing approach, it can choose from several award mechanisms. The mechanism to be used depends upon the number and type of measures selected. If one uses two measures, such as net surplus or gain over budget and customer satisfaction, there are two basic approaches. The first is to use a portion of the surplus funds to create an incentive pool and then modify it (for example, plus or minus 25 percent) by scores on a customer satisfaction survey.

The second approach is to use a payout grid such as that depicted in figure 12-6. The payout grid links the two measures together, and the award for individuals is based on the performance of both factors. The figure illustrates someone with a $10,000 payout target, which can range from $5,000 to $15,000 (or 50 percent to 150 percent), depending on performance. If threshold performance is not achieved in both measures, the payout is zero.

A mechanism for three or more measures: If the organization uses three or more measures, the performance scorecard is a useful tool to employ. Figure 12-7 illustrates a five-measure scorecard, with each measure weighted according to its importance, reliability, and controllability. A range of performance levels is determined for each measure. This array, displayed on a scale of 50 to 140, provides an opportunity to demonstrate incremental improvements in performance. Performance levels are established by examining current or baseline performance and desired performance. The performance levels are organized around the following milestones:

- *Threshold* (set at the 50 level): the minimum level of acceptable performance
- *Target* (set at the 100 level): the desired level of performance

FIGURE 12-6.   Sample Payout Grid

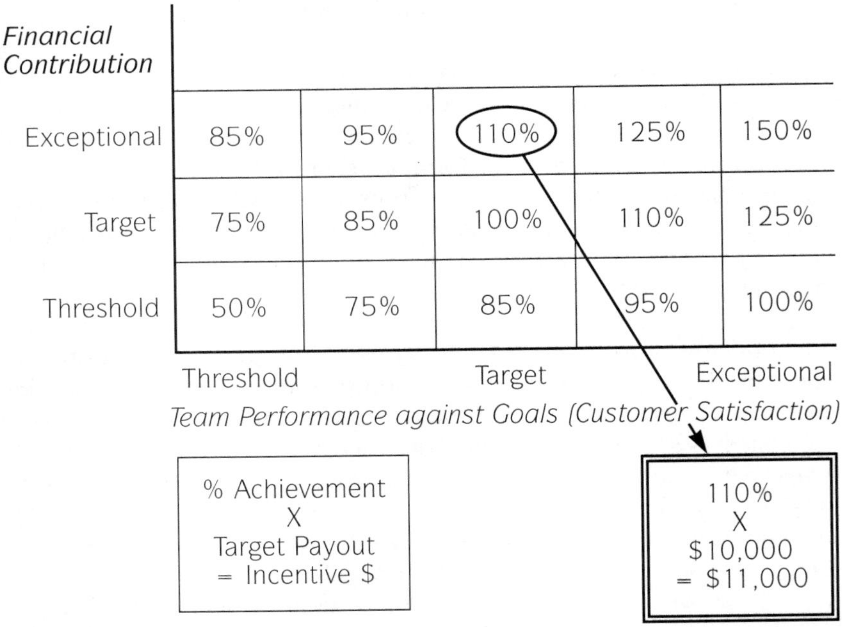

FIGURE 12-7.   The Team Performance Scorecard

MEASURES	X Weight	50	60	70	80	90	100	110	120	130	140	Points
Corporate-wide Performance Score	20%	50	60	70	80	90	100	110	(120)	130	140	24
Department Customer Satisfaction Score	15%	60	65	70	75	80	85	(88)	90	92	95	17
Department On-Time Service Delivery	20%	70	75	80	85	87	(90)	93	96	98	100	20
Quality of Service Index	15%	5 pts.	8 pts.	11 pts.	(14 pts.)	17 pts.	20 pts.	24 pts.	27 pts.	30 pts.	35 pts.	12
Controllable Expense to Budget	30%	110%	105%	100%	98%	95%	(93%)	90%	88%	85%	83%	30

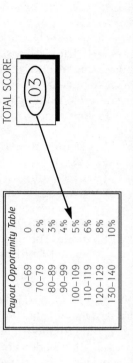

Payout Opportunity Table

0–69	0
70–79	2%
80–89	3%
90–99	4%
100–109	5%
110–119	6%
120–129	8%
130–140	10%

TOTAL SCORE

(103)

- *Exceptional* (set at 140): the performance that would reflect the highest conceivable achievement

The steps in between are determined through a performance planning process. The progression of steps may be incremental or reflect an increasing level of difficulty. The scale does not indicate percentage of performance to a target, but rather is a numeric scale. This scale will be used in determining the total score.

Payout is determined in three steps:

1. Determining the level of performance achieved for each measure (shown in the circles in figure 12-7).
2. Calculating the points earned by multiplying the weight of the measure times the performance level achieved (for example, 90 × 20 percent = 18 points) by the weight.
3. Tallying the points up and referring to the payout opportunity table. The payout in figure 12-7 is shown as a percent of an individual's current salary to determine the amount of the incentive payment.

The scorecard affords the organization two important advantages. First, it can display both individual and team measures and weight them according to importance. Second, it can utilize measures for the overall organization, a division or clinical specialty, and a team. Weighting and performance levels determine the degree of impact the measure will have on the performers' attention and effort.

There are many other approaches, but those illustrated should enable the health care organization to begin designing an effective variable pay program. One of the key principles in the design of any pay program is to keep it relatively simple; people need to understand how it works and be able to determine what their payout will likely be during the performance period. If that cannot be achieved, then the impact of the variable pay program on behavior will likely be limited.

Goal sharing in action—case example: In the Concordian Health Care case example, the focus of the variable pay program was on creating a stake in the success of the department or unit most relevant to the individual. A design team was utilized to design the variable pay program. The team developed the overall framework and policies, then guided each division or department in the development of performance measures relevant to its area. The performance scorecard was used as the program's overall framework.

The design team initially developed a scorecard for the organization as a whole, using the following measures: overall net surplus income for the organization, an index of customer satisfaction scores, and a tally of number of patients served. Space does not permit extensive discussion of how these measures were determined; suffice to say that the organization was able to capture meaningful data with minor modifications to existing management information systems. The overall strategy reflected in these measures related to the need to expand the customer base (both patients and physicians), ensure they receive highly valuable services, and be financially stable.

Initially, these measures were displayed in a matrix similar to that shown in figure 12-5. The matrix served as the basis for an organization-wide incentive program. A major problem, however, was the line of sight between people's actions and these measures. Consequently, the design team encouraged divisions and large departments to develop their own scorecards. They needed to define how they contributed to the three organization-wide measures and to identify the most relevant measures. Once a scorecard was completed, these units could have their own incentive program and would no longer be eligible for the organization-wide program. If a department could not or should not have its own scorecard, then the managers and employees would be eligible for the organization-wide program.

Determination of Payout   The next major step in the reward design process is to determine the amount of money necessary for the program to have an impact on behavior. In research studies[4] and market surveys,[5] the general payout of group rewards for operational and support staff averaged between 3 percent and 5 percent of salaries. In effect, these programs achieved significant increases in performance for a modest amount of money. However, when applied to executives, managers, professionals, and some specialists, the payouts tend to be much higher, ranging from 10 percent to 25 percent, with some as high as 100 percent of salary.[6]

There is no solid research to determine "how much" is necessary. The payout depends on the following variables:

- What do other similar groups receive as payouts? Individuals often compare their payout opportunities to what other people make.
- How well does the program adhere to the design principles discussed above in regard to performance measures, timing, and simplicity of the payout mechanism? If a program is well designed, with timely feedback on meaningful measures, lower payouts may be sufficient to achieve desired performance. In other words, the performance management system, not the payout opportunity, will drive behavioral change. If these factors are less than desired, it may require more money to get and keep the target group's attention. If the measures are too abstract or

require extensive training to understand, then it is best to use conservative payouts until more confidence is established in the measures.

- What is the value of improved performance to the organization? The organization needs to determine the impact of improved performance on the short- and long-term financial health and effectiveness of the organization. This chapter has focused on the most critical elements of the decision process: performance measures, payout mechanisms, and funding. Other factors will need to be addressed in the design process; the reader should seek additional references to assist in this process.

The key principle is that impact is not determined by how much money, but rather by how awards are determined. A key objective for the program designers and managers should be to acheive the maximum gain for the organization and the participants.

Concordian Health Care used the same payout opportunity for the overall organization and with each department or division. This is shown in figure 12-7 under the payout opportunity table. The payouts ranged from 2 percent to 10 percent of the individuals' total base compensation (salary, or wages plus overtime for nonexempt staff).

Analysis of Return on Investment   The final major step in the design of variable pay programs is to determine whether the return on the investment merits the cost. In addition, the organization must decide how the program will be funded.

Calculation of cost and return: In planning a variable pay program, the organization must calculate the potential cost of the program, based on the payout method chosen, and evaluate the cost in terms of the performance achieved. In this way, the organization can determine if the return is worth the payout. Analysis should include input from staff to determine whether the program can offer enough of an incentive to change behavior.

Variable pay programs should be viewed as investments in the organization's future. If performance improvements are important and the pay program is an essential part of achievement, then the return merits the investment in dollars and time. On the other hand, if the organization can achieve desired performance without a variable pay program, it should not implement such a program. Hence, funding should be viewed in the context of performance improvement.

Determination of funding: Funding for variable pay programs may be planned (that is, budgeted) or built into the program measures. With the latter method, the program is "self-funded," meaning that results achieved by the program cover payout costs. In some cases, costs may need to be budgeted in during early stages of the program, then self-funded after some performance level has been achieved.

THE DESIGN OF RECOGNITION PROGRAMS

Although variable pay programs can provide excellent incentive for employees to adopt desired behaviors, they alone may not be enough. In today's environment, most organizational change efforts require employees to effect immediate changes in their behavior. To motivate rapid change, it is helpful to reward desired behavior immediately. With variable pay programs, there is a time gap between changed behavior and reward. Furthermore, organizations whose incentive pay plans are tied to team performance exclusively need a mechanism for rewarding individual contributions. For these reasons, many organizations supplement their base and variable pay programs with special recognition programs. In fact, 83 percent of firms responding to a 1996 Mercer Consulting survey said that they had special recognition programs. Most (59 percent) were service award programs that recognized an individual's length of employment; a slight majority (51 percent) focused on recognizing "above normal job requirements."[7]

Unfortunately, special recognition programs are often poorly managed. As a result, they actually undermine desired cultural values. For example, employee-of-the-month programs tend to discourage teamwork and encourage people to ignore problems in order to look good to their superiors. In addition, rewards such as dinner passes, tickets to movies, or spot cash awards are often distributed in an inconsistent manner.

To develop effective recognition programs, the organization must view recognition as integral to the total reward system and develop these programs with the same rigor as that afforded to the design of compensation programs. In addition, like compensation programs, special recognition programs should reward those behaviors that are critical to the organization's success. For recognition to be truly special, it must focus on core behaviors, be supported with both formal programs and informal practices, and have clear management accountability. In this way, special recognition can be transformed into a strategic process to encourage and reinforce behaviors that lead to desired results.

Seven Key Design Decisions

When planning recognition programs, the organization needs to consider a number of design elements. By answering the following key questions, the organization will address the major elements to be considered.

- *Whom should the program target?* All employees? A specific group of employees, such as clinical, administrative, or operational?
- *What type of group should the program target?* Individuals? Small work groups or teams? Large groups, departments, or organization units?
- *What should the program emphasize?* Results and achievements? Behaviors and special efforts?
- *What awards will be used to recognize excellent performers?* Verbal comments and social events? Tangible items, such as trophies, tickets, and trips? Work-related awards, such as promotions or increased authority?
- *When should rewards be given?* At the end of a performance period? At the time that a desired behavior is performed?
- *Who should determine those who receive the awards?* Anyone? One's immediate supervisor or manager? Senior managers? A special committee of employees and managers?
- *How should the awards be presented?* Privately? Publicly?

Although this list is relatively comprehensive, the organization may wish to adopt other design features based on its experience with other recognition programs or the organizational culture it wishes to effect.

Principles of Effective Programs

Design decisions provide a basic framework for developing a special recognition program. For programs to be fully successful, they should adhere to the following design principles:

- *Awards should relate directly to behavior.* People should know what they did to earn the award, and when appropriate, others should know as well.
- *Awards should be provided as soon after the achievement as possible.* If approval of an award requires a lengthy process, then the purpose of the program becomes unclear. Desired behavior must be quickly rewarded.
- *Awards must be meaningful to recipients.* Many recognition programs fail because managers do not tailor rewards to recipients' needs. For example, being singled out at a public meeting is meaningful to some people but punishing to others, and special parking places are useful only to those who drive to work. For an award to be effective, it must make the recipient want to repeat the behavior that is being rewarded. A simple principle to remember is: "Never give a plaque to someone who doesn't have a wall."

- *Special recognition programs should be fun.* Many programs fail because they are too complicated, involve too many rules, or are too limited. The program must instill a sense of excitement and enthusiasm for the desired culture. The recognition program provides an excellent opportunity to demonstrate the culture's positive attributes. The program should be as enjoyable to observe as it is to manage; it should be as lively to receive as it is to give.

- *Most programs fail because managers are left out.* In many organizations, managers are excluded from receiving awards and receive no positive reinforcement for their efforts to make the program a success. The recognition program is no different from any other initiative; the effectiveness of the program should be measured, and managers should be held accountable for the program's failure or success through positive and negative consequences.

A Recognition Program in Action: Case Example

The Concordian Health Care organization wanted to utilize a recognition process to drive desired behaviors on a more immediate and personalized basis than the compensation programs. It wanted to emphasize individual contributions and team performance and support cultural change in the organization. To meet these goals, Concordian developed a program called STARs—an acronym for Superior Teamwork Achieves Results. With this program, they identified three key actions they seek from employees and managers:

1. Do something special for the customer (internal or external)
2. Do something that is innovative and practical
3. Find ways to increase revenues or decrease costs

If anyone observes another person doing any of these three things, then they complete a simple STARs recognition card, which is sent to the human resources department. Within 24 hours, the individual or team receives the card plus a gold star for each recipient. The awards are given by the unit's manager. Depending on the significance of the action, the award may be given in private or presented at a departmental meeting.

A record of presenters and recipients is kept, and the number of stars given is reported to the CEO and discussed in monthly senior management staff meetings. Every three months, the vice president of each division or large department provides a special luncheon for any individuals who received stars during that period. During these lunches, individuals discuss what they did to receive a star, what stars they gave to others, and how the rewarded actions contributed to the organization and its customers.

On a quarterly basis, a special committee examines all STARs cards, reviewing them to decide which actions, if any, should be given further recognition. Individuals or teams that are selected receive "Super Star" awards, including a framed certificate describing what was done and why it was important. These individuals are then invited to a special dinner held twice a year. Spouses are invited as well. These events, though not extravagant, are important opportunities for building the desired organizational culture.

Once each year, anyone who received a star during the year is invited to a special ceremony. There is usually entertainment at these events, and awards are given to those who received Super Stars in a variety of categories. The purpose is to have fun, recognize a wide variety of contributions, and reinforce the program's three core themes.

This program is very simple, relatively inexpensive to manage, and of great significance to employees and managers. It brings the organization together and creates shared experiences to build the desired culture. In short, it works because management is committed to it and because it is integrated with other reward programs.

CONCLUSION

Reward systems define how new, desired behaviors will be encouraged, developed, and reinforced. Although effective reward systems are no guarantee that strategic and cultural changes will be successful, the organization that has a clear strategy, that lets it members know what behaviors are important, and that uses its reward systems to reinforce desired behavior has a competitive edge.

Organizations that wish to develop new high-impact systems should begin by creating a reward strategy. Once priorities are identified, the change effort needs a clear and committed sponsor, a resourceful and passionate champion, and a willing target group. Change in reward systems should be approached in the same manner as other successful change efforts. The only difference is that these interventions need to support existing efforts and focus on conditions that influence people's actions.

There is no one "right" approach or time frame in which to implement changes in reward systems. In some cases, an overhaul may require three to five years. Organizations should not underestimate the complexity of design tasks or expect results too quickly. The process requires careful thought, involvement by others, and special skills or knowledge. The first year usually includes the design and rollout of a single major initiative, such as a new variable pay program or a new base pay program. During this time, people seek to understand what the new program means and to determine if senior management is committed to the changes. Some level of improvement should be measured and realized by the implementation of the new program, depending on its impact on performance.

The second year involves making improvements to the program or increasing the understanding of it. For example, team incentives may be expanded to other departments beyond a pilot group. Merit increases can relate more to competencies than cost of living. Special recognition programs can become more widespread and meaningful to the organization. Results can and should be tracked, depending on the focus of the intervention.

During the third year, the program becomes integrated into the organization and its new culture. Barring any unforeseen change in structure, ownership, or marketplace, the organization can enjoy the fruits of an effective system. By the fourth or fifth year, the program may need to be reviewed thoroughly, redesigned if necessary, or reinforced with other programs.

This does not mean that the organization should only select one area for change for each five-year period. Instead, the organization should focus on only one major program per year, knowing they will be at different stages of development and life cycle. Managers and employees should view the launch of new programs as further supporting the basic strategy, providing another "leg to the stool," as opposed to yet another program or fad. Programs need to work as a system—integrated and conceptually linked.

Knowledge gained in the development and application of one program should be integrated into the next. This applies to the development of multiple programs or the same basic program applied to different areas of the organization. In this way, the process can be made more effective and the program more effective.

A client of mine once said that the longer his organization waited to make necessary changes to its reward systems, the longer it would take for people to truly believe in the strategy, take necessary actions, and achieve desired gains. Time is not on the side of most health care organizations. Changes in reward systems that are supported by the organization's leadership can provide a way to "touch" each employee. Programs translate what the organization needs to do into what each employee needs to do. It is a valuable chain of commitment whose strength is only realized by each unit working well and working well with other units. Then, the organization will have the strength and flexibility to prosper in a dynamic marketplace.

References and Note

1. T. Wilson, *Innovative Reward Systems for the Changing Workplace* (New York: McGraw-Hill, 1995).

2. T. C. Mawhinney, A. M. Dickinson, and L. A. Taylor, "The Use of Concurrent Schedules to Evaluate the Effects of Extrinsic Rewards on Intrinsic Motivation," *Journal of Organizational Behavior Management,* no. 10 (1989): 109–29.

3. M. Fein, *Improshare: An Alternative to Traditional Managing* (Norcross, Ga.: American Institute of Industrial Engineers, 1981); and J. K. White, "The Scanlon Plan: Causes and Correlates of Success," *The Academy of Management Journal,* no. 22 (1979): 292–312. Improshare and Rucker plans are incentive programs that were developed in manufacturing companies and have been applied to health care organizations. They both focus on establishing a specific threshold level of performance, usually expressed in units, costs, or profitablity; and sharing the gains realized by the organization once the threshold has been achieved. Improshare tends to utilize only labor costs, whereas Rucker uses a combination of labor, material, and other costs. The payout is frequently 50 percent of the gains realized, and requires a sound historical baseline level of performance to set the threshold mark carefully.

4. A. M. Dickinson, "Exploring New Vistas: Performance Management Research Laboratory at Western Michigan University," *Performance Management* 9, no. 1 (1991): 27–31.

5. J. McAdams and E. Hawk, *Organizational Performance and Rewards* (Scottsdale, Ariz.: American Compensation Association, 1994).

6 B. Overton and M. Steere, *Designing Management Incentive Plans* (Scottsdale, Ariz.: American Compensation Association, 1992).

7. 1996 Survey conducted by William M. Mercer, Inc., of 215 midsize to large companies; reported in the August 1996 issue of the ACA News, American Compensation Association, Scottsdale, Arizona.

Bibliography

Belcher, J. G. *Variable Pay.* New York: AMACOM, 1995.

Caldwell, W. *Compensation Guide*. Boston: Warren, Gorham and Lamont, 1994.

Doyle, R., and P. Doyle. *Gain Management*. New York: AMACOM, 1992.

Gross, S. Compensation for Teams. New York: AMACOM, 1995.

Kanter, R. M. "The Attack on Pay." *Harvard Business Review* (Mar.–Apr. 1987): 60.

Lawler, E. *Strategic Pay*. San Francisco: Jossey-Bass, 1990.

McAdams, J. *The Reward Plan Advantage*. San Francisco: Jossey-Bass, 1996.

Milkovich, G., and C. Milkovich. "Strengthening the Pay-Performance Relationship: The Research." *Compensation and Benefits Review* (Nov.–Dec. 1992): 53.

Nelson, R. *1,001 Ways to Reward Employees*. New York: Workman, 1994.

Rock, M., and L. Berger. *The Compensation Handbook: State-of-the-Art Guide to Compensation Strategy and Design*. New York: McGraw-Hill, 1991.

Schuster, J. R., and P. K. Zingheim. *The New Pay*. New York: Lexington Books, 1992.

Tickhy, N. *Managing Strategic Change: Technical, Political, and Cultural Dynamics*. New York: John Wiley and Sons, 1983.

Ulrich, D., and D. Lake. *Organizational Capability*. New York: John Wiley and Sons, 1990.

Wilson, T. "Group Incentives: Are You Ready?" *Journal of Compensation and Benefits* (Nov.–Dec. 1990): 25–29.

13

Using Practice Fields as Tools for Organizational Transformation

Marilyn Paul, Ph.D.

Richard H. Gregg

Cliff Bolster, Ph.D.

Jimmy Carter

Like all who work in health care, leaders are being called upon to assume new responsibilities and take on new roles. They must assess their organization's current culture and ensure that it supports new strategic initiatives, forecast potential business scenarios and envision new and better futures, and build trust and strategic alliances among disparate stakeholders. In an ideal world, leaders would grow proficient at meeting these responsibilities and roles gradually, through practice and experience. But today's competitive and rapidly changing environment leaves organizations with little time for learning and little margin for error. To speed up the learning curve and help leaders quickly build the new skills they need, many organizations are turning to a form of experiential learning known as practice fields.

This chapter describes what practice fields are and how they can be used to build various types of skills. The chapter explains ways to create an organizational climate that is conducive to practice fields and provides case examples demonstrating why this dynamic form of experiential learning has become a powerful way to help health care professionals achieve and maintain a competitive edge in an industry that requires rapid, substantial, and continuous learning.

INTRODUCTION TO PRACTICE FIELDS

A practice field is a training environment in which individuals and groups can practice new tasks, roles, and behaviors without risk. At the core of this type of practice is learning from challenging, yet low-risk experiences. Typically, top organizational players evaluate situations, make decisions, and interact with colleagues without having time to reflect—certainly without much advance practice. Practice field learning dramatically changes this customary way of managing by providing a time and a place to explore options outside the fray of what can often look and feel like organizational chaos. Thus, practice fields can help leaders improve their skills and transform their organizations.

Uses of Practice Fields

Practice fields can be used to develop individual, group, and organizational competence. Ranging in sophistication from low-tech one-on-one role-playing to high-tech computerized simulations, they provide a dynamic way to learn. By creating "virtual reality" types of scenarios, leaders and managers can come to better understand their current behaviors; test out new ones; develop skills; experiment with new assumptions, approaches, and ways of thinking; and envision different avenues of action to test decisions and actions—all without jeopardizing real-life positions, roles, or budgets. By providing a safe forum for modeling new and potentially challenging situations, practice fields help to free up thinking and therefore provide an opportunity to generate better understanding and insight into possible courses of "real-world" action.

Practice fields can be used to develop three kinds of capabilities:

1. *Individual and team skills:* Learning and practicing individual skills and methods of collaboration until people are ready to use them on-line. Examples include role plays, games, and thought experiments.
2. *Organizational capacity for problem exploration:* Exploring the sources of complex problems, often with multiple stakeholders. Dialogue is a good example of this.
3. *Organizational ability to test alternative futures:* Exploring how different decisions might affect or be affected by a range of possible futures. Examples include thought experiments, computer-simulation models, and scenario building.

Types of Practice Fields

Practice fields include "low-tech" verbally based encounters, such as dialogue and role-playing; physically based learning experiences, such as the blind trust walk; and highly sophisticated computer-simulation models that support strategy creation and management development. The sections that follow describe some common practice fields and their uses in developing skills in individuals, groups, and organizations.

VERBALLY BASED STRUCTURED LEARNING EXPERIENCES

As their name implies, verbally based structured learning experiences involve one-on-one or group discussions in which people learn to work collaboratively on analyzing problems, generating potential solutions, and envisioning new ways of doing business. Through techniques such as thought experiments, debriefings, role plays, and dialogue, leaders and staff can practice the skills they need to build a change-friendly culture.

Thought Experiments

The most simple and straightforward practice field is a thought experiment in which an idea is tested by sharing it and imagining how it might develop. Asking the question "What if we did it this way?" is a simple way of framing a thought experiment.

It is surprising how rarely thought experiments are used in a playful or nonjudgmental way to explore different avenues of action. Most organizational cultures place greater emphasis on *knowing* answers than *exploring* questions. To flourish in times of change, the ability to envision different futures is indispensable. Thought experiments can help shift a static culture to a proactive culture by providing a nonjudgmental, creative forum for visioning. In addition, thought experiments support a team-based culture because they enable people to elicit and exchange information, develop shared perspectives, and build trust. Thought experiments can be used effectively in virtually any situation in which people want to generate and explore options and surface opportunities before committing to a particular course of action.

Debriefs or "After-Action Reviews"

A more sophisticated version of thought experiments is the review or "debrief" of an experience, which presents an opportunity for learning. The debrief is designed to produce better decisions, actions, and results in the future. It is best used as a regular practice, employed at key points in any process that is intended to produce a desired and measurable outcome.

The debrief is designed to answer the following questions:

- What results did we seek to accomplish?
- What actions did we take to accomplish the desired results?
- What results did we actually get?
- What might we do differently to accomplish these results?

Supporting questions include:

- What went well?
- What could have gone better?
- Did we communicate effectively?
- Did we involve all the right stakeholders?
- Did we gather sufficient information and interpret it clearly?
- What are we learning about how to create the results we want?

Not every debrief fulfills its intended purpose. A debrief can, for example, become a scapegoating session to find someone to blame for whatever didn't go according to plan. Any debriefing meeting can, however, become a valuable opportunity for people to learn more about what they are doing, what they are thinking, how they interact with each other, and what actions they choose.

Role Plays

Role-playing gives people an opportunity to practice a scene based on actual or hypothetical circumstances, with no negative consequences for "mistakes." Once engaged in role-playing, participants usually see a situation with new eyes and experience it differently. As a result, their range of responses to real-life situations is broadened.

Uses of Role Plays   Role-playing is especially suitable for improving human relations skills, trying out new situations, and heightening self-awareness. Role plays can be used to practice sales and negotiation situations, performance management reviews, and potentially difficult presentations and conversations.

The case study that follows illustrates how role plays helped a group of health care leaders overcome their anxiety about assuming a new role—that of coach. As the case study shows, role plays can lead to a variety of positive outcomes for the "players" as well those who work with them.

Role Play: Case Example   Recently, a large health care organization that reorganized its senior management structure into a web of teams and networks successfully used role plays to help change its management style and culture. A major objective was to shift the leadership approach from traditional "command and control" to "coach and educate."

The planning process: The senior team first engaged in a sweeping assessment and succession planning process for the top 100 managers. Each manager was assigned to a coach whose role it was to communicate feedback from the assessment, formulate a development plan for the manager, and provide periodic coaching sessions over the next two years.

As they thought about their first meetings with the managers, the coaches, anxious about how to deliver some of the feedback, asked for help in preparing for the meetings. In response, the "Coaching Tutorial" was designed to (1) develop each coach's ability to carry on productive conversations and (2) reveal and assess each coach's mental models and skills with regard to the new role of coach. The confidential sessions, which were four hours long, were preceded by some written planning and analysis that was specifically related to an anticipated difficult situation (for example, a situation in which feedback would reveal serious weaknesses that would prevent the manager's further progress in the organization).

Each tutorial session began with a short "getting acquainted" period, followed by a clarification of what the coach wanted to learn and a "contracting" conversation in which mutual expectations were shared and agreed upon. The coach then described the background of the particular difficult case he or she had chosen. Having been briefed, a consultant played the role of the manager.

The taping and analysis of the role play: The meeting was role-played and videotaped for approximately 10 minutes, after which the role play was stopped and the tape played. Consultants paused frequently to ask the coach, "What do you notice about your performance?" After a short conversation, the players returned to the role play. Sometimes the role-play meeting would pick up where it had left off; however, the coach usually went back to the beginning and repeated the performance. During each session, the coach would have a minimum of three, and often as many as five or six, opportunities to try out and refine the conversation with specific videotape and feedback.

Outcomes of the role play: As a result of the tutorials, coaches reported greater confidence going into the session, very productive actual sessions, insight into the role of a coach, and the ability to transfer what was learned to everyday leadership responsibilities. More specifically, the coaches realized

- They had been taking on too much responsibility for the development of the managers and therefore not inviting and inquiring into their thoughts and ideas.

- They had often felt before that if they did not have negative feedback to communicate, the meeting was pointless. But they discovered that if they could engage their manager in a conversation about development in an open and trusting way, the manager would specify areas in need of development that had not surfaced in the formal assessment process.
- They had had a very prescriptive view of the coach's role, instead of helping the manager take responsibility for development and take the initiative to schedule follow-up sessions.
- They had not thought of a much broader role for the coach beyond giving feedback.
- They became aware of a desire to "prove and defend" the assessment in response to questions from the manager. They practiced seeing defensiveness as a natural response and shifted to drawing the manager out through open-ended questions.
- They discovered they could speak candidly and "be themselves," rather than play the role of coach. This shift allowed them to relax and engage the manager in a supportive yet honest way.

A follow-up analysis revealed factors that enhanced the value of the tutorial, such as timing and need, the voluntary nature of the session, and the specificity of the learning. The fact that the tutorial was grounded in leaders' own experiences, rather than an experience created by an instructional designer, made a real difference. Videotaping kept the session focused on the coach's specific actions and allowed for direct feedback without interpretation by an observer or so-called "expert."

Dialogue

Dialogue, as described by Peter Senge in *The Fifth Discipline: The Art and Practice of the Learning Organization,* is a way to practice team learning skills and the quintessential way to practice suspending assumptions.[1] As discussed in chapter 5, when engaging in dialogue, people employ active listening skills to interact in a manner that combines advocacy and inquiry to explore the thoughts, feelings, and perspectives of others in a nonjudgmental manner. Engaging in dialogue enables people to observe both their individual thoughts and the way thought operates in groups.

Much time in meetings is wasted on arguments and people's attempts to influence each other. When people are advocating for their solution to a problem, the emphasis is on persuasion rather than on inquiry into the causes of a problem. Because little real listening takes place, people are often unable to build on each other's thinking. In this advocacy mind-set, they make persistent attempts to solve problems in a way that frequently leads back to familiar clashes and unimaginative approaches. Dialogue is helpful in overcoming this stale rehashing.

The Dialogue Process   Dialogue occurs in a setting of dedicated inquiry. The process is not about problem solving; it is about problem understanding. In dialogues, groups pose a question or topic and learn how to *think together* about this topic. This means probing assumptions, looking for contradictions, and building on each other's ideas. As team members learn to stop persuading each other and to listen for patterns, obstacles, surprises, and incongruities, they can pool their intelligence to develop a much deeper understanding of their situation. Often, this understanding can lead to an unexpected solution or approach.

Dialogue and Change   The practice of dialogue can be particularly useful during times of change. Change upsets people and threatens current ways of thinking. Dialogue creates a context in which they can explore familiar and unfamiliar ways of thinking about problems and issues. Additionally, it provides an opportunity for them to explore their feelings in an empathetic setting. In dialogue, people can create a strong "container," or holding environment; that is, they can create a setting in which they explicitly agree to address difficulties with their full attention. They agree to stay with the process until they understand the "difficulty" well enough to see it in a new way. This commitment to understanding the situation provides a powerful release valve for pressures, confusions, and misunderstandings in times of change.

Dialogue: Case Examples   Dialogue requires patience and persistence. The benefits of this practice don't necessarily show up right away. But with time and discipline, the results can be impressive. For example, a group of health care leaders in a midwestern town were very successful in applying this technique to rethink their entire health network. Leaders of local hospitals and public health services met monthly for a year to consider the competitive pressures that they were experiencing. By participating in noncompetitive dialogue and making a commitment to stay with the profound challenges that emerged, they were able to develop a community-wide strategy for health care that was innovative and effective in allocating limited resources.

In another case, a group of department managers were completely split over the right way to proceed with resource allocation. The group seemed entrenched in their positions until they spent some time in dialogue examining the underpinnings of some of their assumptions. Through dialogue, they were able to perceive a new way of handling an intractable situation.

Managerial teams who become adept at dialogue find that their ability to track discrepancies in their thinking improves. Their ability to make sense out of conflict improves as well. As teams learn how to learn together, they become more adept at moving rapidly through managerial challenges. Culture change presents some of the most difficult managerial challenges. Using dialogue can be a critical factor in addressing those challenges.

PHYSICALLY BASED STRUCTURED LEARNING EXPERIENCES

Physically based learning experiences involve activities through which teams can quickly surface core issues and develop new sensibilities, mind-sets, and behaviors around a particular situation. They can be used by a team, for example, to identify and assess its interpersonal dynamics and behaviors. The team can then consciously change them and practice new, more effective ways of relating.

The Acid River

Many physically based structured learning experiences are used in leader development. One popular activity is the "Acid River," in which a team must cross a "contaminated" area. Success depends on the ability of team members to see things in a new way, to work closely together, to share limited resources, and to be collectively intelligent. Failure to act in these ways leads to contamination and extinction.

Blind Trust Walk

Another popular activity is the "Blind Trust Walk," in which partners take turns as leaders with sight and blindfolded followers, who must go on a cross-country walk together without the aid of verbal communication. The key to success is clear and concise (albeit nonverbal) communication between the sighted and blindfolded partners. Through the course of this experience, participants often develop profound insights into the essential nature of leadership, trust, and following another's lead.

The Maze

At Innovation Associates, we use an experience called "The Maze" in our Leading Learning Organizations program. The maze is an eight-by-ten-foot checkerboard representing a terrain that must be traversed by a team of people as quickly and with the fewest number of missteps as possible. Some of the squares can be occupied and used to cross the terrain. Danger is represented by squares that "beep," signifying territory that cannot be occupied. The game was designed to represent the challenges of meeting a shared goal through teamwork. Like real-life projects, there is a beginning and an end. Certain rules must be followed, individuals have particular responsibilities, and the entire team shares responsibility for getting itself across the maze.

Teams typically move through the maze in many of the same ways they do in real life. Some teams make plans, assign responsibilities, and execute the plans quickly and effectively. Other teams are disorganized and lacking in trust. They find the process difficult and dispiriting. Debriefing the experience provides learning that is easily transferred to work.

Outward Bound

Outward Bound is another example of a physically based structured learning experience. In this program, a team typically exhibits the same habits and patterns of behavior that it exhibits at work. Often, this behavior is dysfunctional and affects performance. The Outward Bound program gives team members an opportunity to recognize their behavior and to change it. Success in the experience depends on their ability to work together as a team.

Outward Bound: Case Example   Take the case of a chief executive officer of an HMO who was an ex-marine colonel hired from outside the organization. He was charged with leading his "troops" into a new era but did not understand the culture of the organization. Increasingly frustrated with the passivity of his top team in relation to his command and control style, he decided to take them on an outdoor exercise to help change the group dynamics. Team members were assigned a task that was structurally similar to projects they faced at work—they were required to retrieve the cure for cancer from a small island in the middle of a lake by suspending someone out on a bridge.

The CEO tried to promote the right solution several times, only to have it regularly rejected by his staff. The team ended up dropping a person into the lake three times. As a result of this experience, the CEO and his team became reflective enough to review what was happening. People were finally able to say, "Half of us don't understand what you want, and the other half are afraid that they don't. And we can never talk about it." Humor and frustration greased the wheels for a new approach. The dynamics did change, and a more consultative approach emerged that produced better results for the organization.

Outward Bound and Team Start-Ups   Physically based structured learning experiences are also useful for new team start-ups. Putting a new team of people in a structured learning situation helps them to quickly discover how they work well together and where their process breaks down. For example, a new team spent its first two weeks together in different types of training, including three days in an outdoor exercise. They reported, "We have learned more about each other in three days than we normally would have in three months."

COMPUTER-SIMULATION MODELS

Perhaps the most sophisticated practice field is a computer-simulation model that incorporates a "microworld." Often called "management flight simulators," these computer models enable users to explore "real-life" situations without "crashing and burning" their organizations. Within the context of a particular microworld, users can develop different environmental scenarios, identify specific results they want to achieve, and then develop and test different strategies to achieve those results. Users get to see the results of their strategies and actions almost immediately on the computer screen. Therefore, they can make immediate changes in their strategies and actions to improve their results.

Computer-simulation models are also valuable tools for developing individual and team competencies that go beyond the specific content of a given model. In particular, team members can learn and practice the skills of dialogue, share their mental models about any and all variables and decisions, and think more systemically about key strategic and operational issues.

Advantages of Computer-Simulation Models

Computer-simulation models offer several advantages as practice fields. They enable participants to

- Engage in shared reflection and experimentation about a particular situation, such as how to make money in a market moving to managed care.
- View and understand a complex system and the key variables within it, such as an integrated delivery system.
- Identify and understand interdependencies among key variables and forces at play, such as the relationship between primary care physicians, specialists, and insurers.

- Identify and track causal factors throughout the system to determine why a particular action may (or may not) produce a particular result, such as the impact on cost and quality of care of introducing better clinical information systems.
- Understand that not all variables and actions have equal impact; for example, understanding that redesigning clinical processes may produce greater economic benefit than large reductions in staff.
- Reveal, explore, and modify mental models, such as the importance of quality to purchasers of care.
- Focus attention on short-term and long-term results; for example, understand that investments made in the near term, which will reduce net income, are essential to strengthen an organization's financial position in the long term.
- Understand the intended and unintended consequences of actions; for example, staff reductions will lower operating costs but may also hurt morale and reduce productivity of the staff members who remain.
- Recognize the influence of structures within the system; for example, the compensation system on performance.

A Computer-Simulation Model for Health Care Leaders

Throughout the health care industry, trustees, executives, managers, and physicians are faced with the critical challenge of developing effective integrated delivery systems and improving the health of people served by those systems. In 1995–'96, Innovation Associates and the New England Healthcare Assembly, along with representatives of thirteen health care organizations and the American Hospital Association, developed a microworld learning experience entitled *Creating Integrated Care and Healthier Communities*.

The computer-simulation program was designed to enable health care leaders to better understand and address the complex factors involved in creating effective integrated care and improving the health of defined populations and communities. With this "management flight simulator," participants play out real-world strategies in a simulated real-world environment—the small urban community of Oakville. They then engage in dynamic discussions with expert facilitators. The microworld allows participants to do a number of things:

- Configure alternative environments and competitive scenarios
- Examine and adjust operational assumptions
- Develop and test different strategies for integrating health care services and improving community health

Creating Integrated Care and Healthier Communities consists of three modules: Module I focuses on the health care delivery system; Module II focuses on improving health; and Module III addresses integrating care and improving health together.

Module I   In Module I, participants are members of the "Acorn HealthNet." They can play multiple roles along the continuum of care—representing primary, specialty, acute, long-term, and home health care, as well as an insurer and the network manager, who presides over the entire system. Participants learn to configure an effective health care delivery system and secure desired market share, net income, cost per capita, and quality of care by effectively managing prices, costs, and quality. They decide upon the number and type of physicians, the number of acute care beds and outpatient procedures, relative compensation for providers, process redesign, demand management, care management, clinical information systems, staff development, and insurance premiums.

Module II   In Module II, participants are members of the "Oakville Health Improvement Authority," which is responsible for improving the health of the community by spending money to manage a range of chronic conditions and health risks. Using health status data from actual communities, participants craft and test strategies and services for improving health. They can choose to expand the medical management of people with chronic conditions; focus on such public health initiatives as screening, environmental protection, and health education; or seek to reduce behavioral and social health risks in adults and children.

Module III   In Module III, participants develop approaches that combine their best strategies for integrating care and improving health to simultaneously create a competitively viable health care delivery system and a healthier community.

As participants design and test strategies in each module, they are guided through debriefs to answer questions such as the following:

- What specific results did you seek to accomplish?
- What strategies did you develop, and what actions did you take to achieve the desired results?
- What results did you actually get?
- What might you do differently to accomplish the desired results?

THE IMPLEMENTATION OF PRACTICE FIELDS

When people are free to take risks with fewer perceived consequences, they seem better able to address issues with substantial consequences.

That is one of the central ironies of practice fields and the reason why their transformational impact is so high. Practice fields provide the freedom to explore new ways of doing things. They also create settings of "safe risk," that is, the simulated risk can be experienced as quite significant, while actual risk is low. Finally, while in "performing" the focus is on success, in "learning" the focus is on improvement. As soon as we say, "This is practice, and we are here just to learn," performance improves.

Development of Organizational Support

Several factors contribute to developing the requisite organizational support for practice fields. These factors include

- Clearly identifying the relevance of practice fields (and particular types of practice fields) for addressing key organizational issues and producing desired business results.
- Developing leadership support for openness, learning, and the use of practice fields.
- Developing participant support and a willingness to explore and learn.
- Developing ground rules for using practice fields (for example, where, when, how, and with whom to ensure that maximum benefit is realized).
- Creating supportive organizational structures and settings, including sufficient time for learning.

Potential Pitfalls

Our experience indicates that efforts to use practice fields can fail for the following reasons:

- The essential foundation—a culture that emphasizes and rewards individual and collective learning—is missing.
- The practice field is viewed as "just a game" and therefore as irrelevant.
- There is no follow-up and no time for reflection.
- People are punished for their "mistakes" on the practice field.

CONCLUSION

We still subscribe to the belief that "practice makes perfect." Executives and managers at all stages of their careers are now in charge of their own development. These days, few mentors are available to guide even the most promising people to the next level of success. That leaves individuals in organizations responsible for taking charge of their own learning. Competence can be developed by "practicing," and this chapter has shown how highly competent professionals have found ways to practice. In creating their own practice fields, they become better learners. As a result, they not only become more effective at work, but in the rest of their lives as well.

Reference

1. Peter Senge in *The Fifth Discipline: The Art and Practice of the Learning Organization* (New York: Currency Doubleday, 1990), p. 10.

Index